YO-ART-763

Baldwin

3-DIMENSIONAL
LEARNING SYSTEM

SISTEMA DE APRENDISAJE
3-DIMENSIONAL

SYSTÈME D'APPRENTISSAGE
EN TROIS DIMENSIONS

DREIDIMENSIONALES
UNTERRICHTS-SYSTEM

LES-SYSTEEM IN
DRIE DIMENSIES

Columbia Pictures Publications
16333 N.W. 54th Ave., Hialeah, Florida 33014

This book is presented in three sections. The first is the instructional material in each language. Following that are the musical examples, exercises, and songs necessary to each lesson. Throughout the instructions you'll see this sign ◆ with a number in it. This tells you to which page number you should turn in order to play the appropriate music, and when to do it.

The third section consists of various familiar songs which are included for your playing enjoyment.

Este libro lo presentamos en tres secciones. La primera sección es del material instruccional, en cada idioma. Luego le siguen, ejemplos musicales, ejercicios y canciones necesarias para cada lección. Vera a través de las instrucciones este signo ◆ con un numero dentro. Este le indicara a que numero de página debera volver con el proposito de tocar la música apropiadamente, y cuando hacerlo.

La tercera sección consiste en varias canciones conocidas que han sido incluidas para que sa divierta tocandolas.

Ce livre est présenté en trois parties. La première est la matière d'apprentissage dans chaque langue. Ensuite il y a les exemples musicaux, les exercices, et les chansons nécessaires àchaque leçon. Dans les instructions, vous verrez ce signe ◆ avec un numéro à l'intérieur. Il vous indique à quelle page vous devez tourner pour jouer de la musique appropriée, et quand le faire.

La troisième partie consiste de chansons familières qui ont été inclues pour votre plaisir.

Dieses Buch ist in drei Abschnitte aufgeteilt. Der erste Teil ist das Unterrichtsmaterial in jeder Sprache. Danach folgen die musikalischem Beispiele, Übungen und Lieder die für jede Aufgabe notending sind. Überall in den Aufgeben sehen Sie dieses Zeichen ◆ in welchem eine Nummer geschrieben steht. Dies zeigt Ihnen welche Seite Sie aufschlagen sollten, um die richtige Musik zu spielen und wann.

Der dritte Teil gibt Ihnen die verschiedenen bekannten Lieder welche beigefügt sind, um Spass am Spielen zu haben.

Dit boek is verdeeld in drie delen. Het eerste deel behandelt muziek instructie. Het tweede deel behandelt muziek oefeningen, in dit gedeelte zal u het teken ◆ zien waarin een nummer wordt aangegeven. Dit nummer geeft u de pagina aan waar u de juiste soort muziek kan vinden die passen by de oefeningen en voorbeelden.

Het derde gedeelt bevat een assortiment van orgel arrangementen.

Baldwin
3-DIMENSIONAL
LEARNING SYSTEM

CONTENTS

WELCOME . . .

to the Baldwin Organ 3-DIMENSIONAL Learning System . . . a new approach to having fun with music. This unique system allows you to choose the approach you want to take in learning all about music and playing the Baldwin organ.

DIMENSION ☐1 Easy

UPPER: Your right hand plays a one-finger melody written in easy-to-read "notes that name themselves."

LOWER: Your left hand plays a one-finger chord accompaniment indicated by small chord symbols above the melody. (☐C)

PEDAL: The Baldwin FunMachine automatically plays the bass for you.

From the Columbia Pictures Release "YOU LIGHT UP MY LIFE"
YOU LIGHT UP MY LIFE

Words and Music by
JOE BROOKS

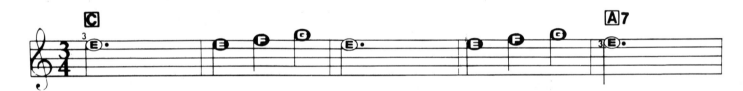

DIMENSION ☐2 Chord

UPPER: Your right hand plays the melody written in standard notation. As this course progresses, the melody will gradually be enhanced by additional notes and rhythmic phrasing.

LOWER: Your left hand plays three- and four-note chords.

PEDAL: Either, a) use Baldwin FunChords to automatically play the bass notes or, b) play the bass notes on the pedals with your left foot.

From the Columbia Pictures Release "YOU LIGHT UP MY LIFE"
YOU LIGHT UP MY LIFE

Words and Music by
JOE BROOKS

DIMENSION [3] Traditional

UPPER: Your right hand plays the same melody line as **DIMENSION** [2].

LOWER
and
PEDAL: You'll read and play the left hand and pedal notes. They're written in easy-to-read "notes that name themselves."

From the Columbia Pictures Release "YOU LIGHT UP MY LIFE"
YOU LIGHT UP MY LIFE

Words and Music by
JOE BROOKS

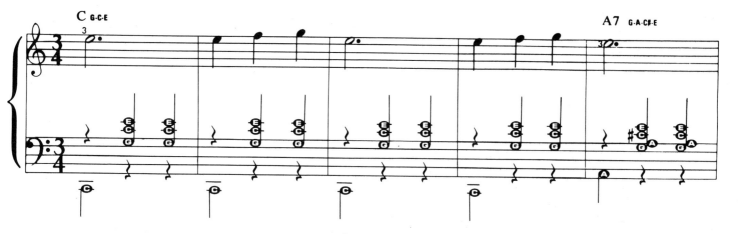

WHICH DIMENSION SHOULD I CHOOSE?

If this is your first musical experience, you'll find **DIMENSION** [1] the easiest to use. You'll quickly learn to play your favorite songs, in addition to learning about music.

If you have some musical experience, you can start this course using **DIMENSION** [2]. You'll read your favorite melodies written in standard notation (no letter names in the notes), and you'll learn to create an accompaniment by forming chords with your left hand.

NOTE: If you own the single keyboard FunMachine, you may use either **DIMENSION** [1] or [2]; disregard **DIMENSION** [3].

If you can read music, or would like to learn, use **DIMENSION** [3]. You'll read two-staff organ arrangements which use organ techniques such as pedal-chord patterns, two-part harmony in the melody, etc.

WHAT IF I'D LIKE TO TRY
A DIFFERENT DIMENSION?

Just because you start with one **DIMENSION** doesn't mean you have to pursue it to the end of this course. Should you decide to try another, just back-track to a point where the instructional material seems familiar and continue forward from there, using the new **DIMENSION**.

YOUR BALDWIN ORGAN

To become familiar with your Baldwin organ, READ your owner's guide. It has detailed information and operating instructions for all the features and controls on your instrument. Keep it handy so you can refer to it often.

KEYBOARD GUIDES

All Baldwin organs have identifying letters placed above the white keys. These are referred to as keyboard guides.

REGISTRATION

THE ARRANGER is an amazing, automatic registration feature on your Baldwin. With THE ARRANGER on, a complete set-up, or registration, is automatically selected for you.

Included are upper and lower keyboard, and pedal voices, plus the appropriate motion controls. THE ARRANGER automatically chooses a different and suitable registration for each rhythm you select. When you turn all rhythms off, THE ARRANGER selects a full organ ensemble. When you turn THE ARRANGER off, you can experiment with your own registrations. Consult the Owner's Guide for a helpful list of suggested registrations.

NOTE: The registrations used for the songs in this book cover many Baldwin organ models. Simply set up the tabs and effects which appear on your organ and disregard the others.

PLAYING MELODIES

In an orchestra, the melody of a song may be played by such instruments as the flute or trumpet. On the organ, it is generally played by the right hand on the upper keyboard. Melodies are made up of specific musical sounds. To represent these sounds, notes are placed on a staff, as shown in Figure A. The staff consists of five lines and four spaces and each is named with one of the letters A through G. Any note that appears on one of the lines or in one of the spaces is called by that letter-name. This course used "notes that name themselves;" just match the letters in the notes with the letters on your keyboard guide.

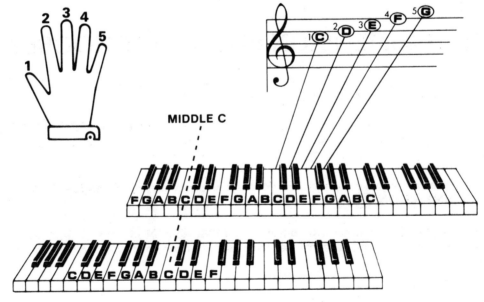

FIGURE A

The S-shaped symbol at the beginning of the staff is called the treble clef and tells you all the notes are to be played with your right hand. Also illustrated are the first five melody notes C, D, E, F, and G and their corresponding keys. To help you play the notes with your right hand, numbers are placed alongside each note telling you which finger to use.

Place your right hand on the keys with your thumb on C above middle Ⓒ as shown in Figure A. Rest your fingers gently on the keys and play the five notes shown.

Note: In this course, middle C appears in a circle Ⓒ .

SONG 1 — WHISTLE WHILE YOU WORK

Step 1 Play the melody on the upper keyboard.

Step 2 Hold the white notes with the black letters a little longer than the black notes with the white letters . . . we'll talk more about this later.

Step 3 Set up the following registration and play WHISTLE WHILE YOU WORK in either DIMENSION $\boxed{1}$ or $\boxed{2}$.

153

PLAYING THE ACCOMPANIMENT

The accompaniment on an organ generally consists of chords played with your left hand and their corresponding bass notes. Chords are represented by chord symbols, which are small boxes containing letters appearing above the melody in each song. To start, you'll learn two chords, the $\boxed{C}$ Chord and the $\boxed{G}$7 Chord.

Press THE ARRANGER on.

Playing the accompaniment in . . .

DIMENSION $\boxed{1}$ Press the 1-FINGER ACCOMP button located in the EASY PLAYER section of your Baldwin Organ. With 1-FINGER ACCOMP, all you have to do is press the lower manual key which corresponds to the letter in the chord box. (FIGURE A) The FunMachine automatically plays the bass for you.

NOTE: To cancel automatic accompaniment press the STOP button.

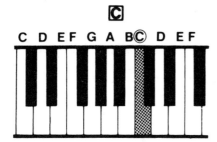 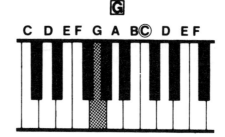

FIGURE A

DIMENSION $\boxed{2}$ Play the chord notes located to the right of the chord symbol. (FIGURE B) There are two ways to obtain the bass notes: 1) play them yourself by pressing the pedal named after the chord (FIGURE C) or, 2) press FUNCHORDS and have these pedal notes automatically played for you.

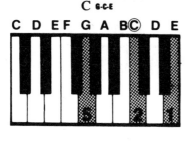 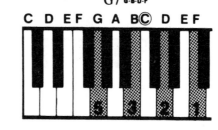

FIGURE B

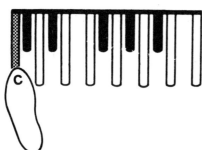 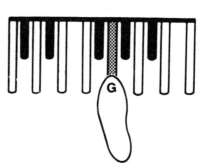

FIGURE C

DIMENSION $\boxed{3}$ Figures D and E on the next page show you how to read bass clef.

THE GRAND STAFF

From this point on, each song is written on a grand staff. The grand staff consists of two single staffs joined by bar lines as shown in Figure D. At the beginning of the upper staff is the treble clef. As you already know, this tells you the notes that follow are played by your right hand on the upper keyboard. At the beginning of the lower staff is a new symbol called the bass clef. This tells you the notes that follow are played by your left hand on the lower keyboard and your left foot on the pedals.

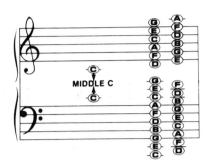

FIGURE D

MIDDLE C

The C note appearing on the first ledger line below the treble staff and on the first ledger line above the bass staff is called middle C. Although middle C may be written in either position, as shown in Figure D, it is the same note. Middle C on the upper keyboard is always directly above middle C on the lower keyboard. It's represented by the circled letter C above the keyboard illustrations.

CHORDS IN THE BASS STAFF

Figure E shows the bass staff location of the C, and G7 chords and pedals you've been playing. Notice the position of notes in relation to middle C. The letter-names within the notes help you locate the correct keys.

Note: The curved lines in **DIMENSION** 3 on the next page are called ties — hold tied notes until a new chord appears. More on ties later.

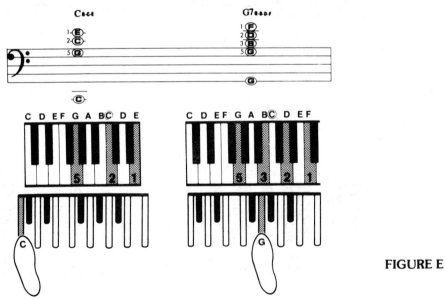

FIGURE E

DIMENSIONS 1 2 3 Set up the registration and practice the accompaniment shown for the dimension you've chosen.

DIMENSION 1	**DIMENSION** 2	**DIMENSION** 3
THE ARRANGER on	THE ARRANGER on	THE ARRANGER on
1-FINGER ACCOMP. on	For auto. bass:	
KEY SELECTOR C on	FUNCHORDS on	
MEMORY off	MEMORY off	

NOTE: Certain features such as KEY SELECTOR are not available on some Baldwin instruments. Whenever you see an instruction to use a feature not found on your instrument, simply ignore that instruction.

PLAYING WITH RHYTHM
DIMENSIONS 1 2 3

Rhythm is the foundation of music. Being able to play with Baldwin's automatic features will be a most rewarding experience.

In addition to telling you which key to play, each type of note has a specific time value which is measured in musical beats. The following illustration shows the four types of notes you'll be playing in the first few songs.

♩ Quarter Note 1 Beat	♩ Half Note 2 Beats
♩. Dotted Half Note 3 Beats	○ Whole Note 4 Beats

FIGURE F

In order to understand rhythm, the **Melody Rhythm Warmup** will help you:

1. Coordinate the rhythm of the melody with the automatic drummer.

2. Coordinate playing the chords with the automatic drummer.

3. Coordinate playing the melody and accompaniment together.

Since you'll repeatedly play only one melody note and one accompaniment chord, you'll be able to use the automatic rhythm feature right away. Turn on the drums and listen . . . notice how it relates to the notes on the top line. If the drums seem too fast or too slow, adjust the rhythm speed to a comfortable tempo. Play the E key with your third finger. Here are a few hints to help you play the songs more easily.

Practice hints:

1. Physically play the music. This involves locating the correct melody and chord keys, observing the suggested fingering, and incorporating any new musical information. Work toward doing it all without taking your eyes off the music.

2. Play the music mentally. This means read the music without playing. Try to "hear" the melody in your mind and imagine how each chord sounds as its symbol appears in the music. Humming the melody may help.

3. Watch the music and mentally play while automatic RealRhythm is playing. As you "hear" the music, notice how it relates to the drum sounds.

4. Physically play the music along with the drum rhythms. By this time, you'll really be familiar with what you're playing.

NOTE: On Baldwin organs with lighted pushbuttons, turning on one feature often causes other features to turn on automatically. On organs with mechanical pushbuttons, it is necessary to select each function individually. All features necessary for each registration are listed; if you have an instrument with lighted pushbuttons, some of them will be automatically turned on for you.

From now on, the word "on" will not be printed; any feature listed should be ON unless noted otherwise.

Use the following registration for the Melody Rhythm Warmup.

DIMENSIONS 1 2 3

1-FINGER ACCOMP., KEY SELECTOR C
(FANCY) FUNBASS
PRO off, MEMORY off
THE ARRANGER
REALRHYTHM

FOX TROT

Set the TEMPO to a comfortable speed such as 3-1/2 or The Conductor = 100 .

To start the drums, press STOP.

155

NOTE: **DIMENSIONS 1 2 3** use the 1-FINGER ACCOMP button to practice the Melody Rhythm Warmups. This will make it easy for you to concentrate on how the rhythm of the melody sounds with the drums.

Play the complete song with rhythm using the appropriate registration:

DIMENSION [1]
1-FINGER ACCOMP.

DIMENSION [2]
For auto. bass:
FUNCHORDS

DIMENSIONS [1] [2] [3]
THE ARRANGER
(FANCY) FUNBASS
MEMORY
PRO
REALRHYTHM

FOX TROT
TEMPO 3-1/2 The Conductor [100]

SONG 2 — CARNIVAL OF VENICE

DIMENSIONS [1] [2] [3]

A NEW NOTE

The note A is introduced in this song and is shown in Figure A. As you continue to learn new right hand melody notes, use the suggested fingering. This will help you move out of the range of the first five notes without "running out of fingers."

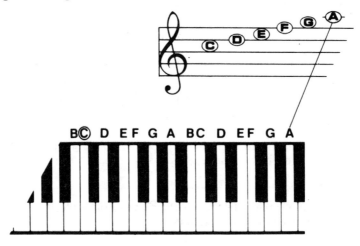

FIGURE A

MEASURES

Figure B illustrates how the staff is divided into equal sections by using vertical lines called bar lines. The sections between the bar lines are called measures.

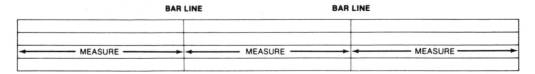

FIGURE B

TIME SIGNATURE

The two numbers at the beginning of a song are known as the time signature. See Figure C. The top number indicates the number of beats in each measure. The bottom number tells you the type of note that receives one beat. In Figure C, the bottom number 4 indicates each quarter note receives one beat. The song CARNIVAL OF VENICE has a 4/4 time signature.

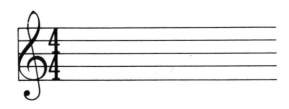

FIGURE C

10

TIES

A curved line connecting two notes on the same line or in the same space is called a tie. A tie indicates the first note should be played and then held for the total time value of both notes. In Figure D, the first group of tied notes is held for a total of four beats and the second group for a total of six. NOTE: Because only the first note in a tied group is struck, the notes following have no letter-names inside.

2   +   2 = 4   4   +   2 = 6

FIGURE D

From now on, registrations are printed at the top of the Warmup or at the top of the song. If the symbol Ø appears before or after a feature name, THAT FEATURE SHOULD BE OFF.

NOTE: No special registrations will be given for Dimensions 1, 2 or 3. From now on, follow these instructions:

DIMENSION [1]

Add these to the given registration:

1-FINGER ACCOMP.
(FANCY) FUNBASS
MEMORY optional
REALRHYTHM

DIMENSION [2]

Add these to the given registration:

(FANCY) FUNBASS
MEMORY optional
REALRHYTHM
For auto bass, also add FUNCHORDS

DIMENSION [3]

Add these to the given registration:

(FANCY) FUNBASS
MEMORY optional
REALRHYTHM

The KEY SELECTOR indicated for each song is for **DIMENSION** [1] only.

Practice the Melody Rhythm Warmup first, then play the song.

◆ 157

SONG 3 — MARIANNE

DIMENSIONS [1] [2] [3]
A NEW NOTE

Song 3 introduces the note B.

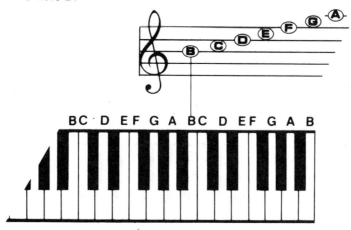

FIGURE A

NOTE: Watch the fingering in measures ⑥ and ⑭.

Practice the melody rhythm warmup for MARIANNE using the automatic drummer.

Play the song using the registration given. Remember the note about Registration (above).

158
159

11

SONG 4 — BORN TO LOSE

DIMENSIONS ☐1 ☐2 ☐3

THE OCTAVE

In Figure A, the new notes C, D, E, F, and G are notes lower than the C, D, E, F, and G you learned before. This span of eight notes is called an *octave*, which comes from the Latin word for "eight."

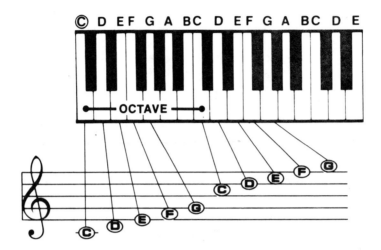

FIGURE A

SUBSTITUTE FINGERING

There are places in this song where you'll see two finger numbers below a single note (3-1), as shown in Figure B. These are called substitute fingerings and merely tell you to press the key with the finger indicated by the first number; then, while holding it down, change to the finger indicated by the second number. This prepares your hand for the notes to follow.

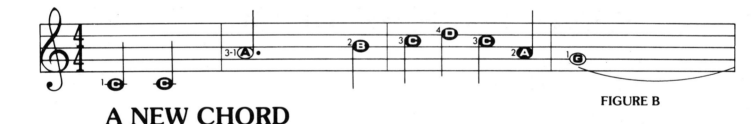

FIGURE B

A NEW CHORD

The F major chord is illustrated in Figures C, D, and E.

DIMENSION ☐1

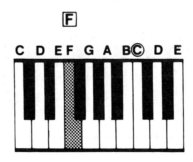

FIGURE C

12

DIMENSION 2

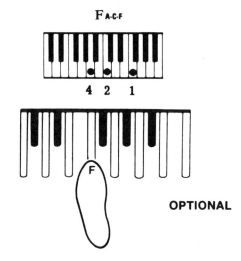

OPTIONAL

FIGURE D

DIMENSION 3

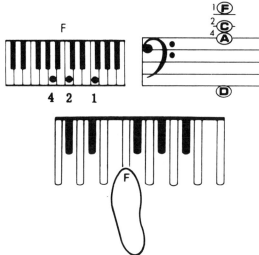

FIGURE E

PICK-UP NOTES

Very often, a song starts with one or more notes whose time values do not equal a complete measure. The notes in this incomplete measure are called pick-up notes. The missing beats are always found in the last measure of the song. In many cases, pick-up notes are played before an accompaniment chord is played.

Practice the Melody Rhythm Warmup for BORN TO LOSE using the automatic drummer.   ◆160 ◆161

SONG 5 — SKATERS WALTZ
DIMENSIONS 1 2 3

A NEW TIME SIGNATURE

Song number 5 uses a new time signature, 3/4. As you learned before, the 4 tells you the quarter note gets one beat. The top number, 3, indicates three beats in each measure. This time signature indicates a rhythm commonly known as a waltz.

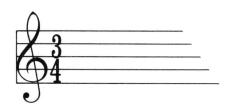

Practice the Melody Rhythm Warmup for SKATERS WALTZ using the automatic drummer.   ◆162

Play the song with the melody an octave higher than written.   ◆163

SONG 6 — CHOPSTICKS

DIMENSIONS ☐1 ☐2 ☐3
RESTS

A rest is a musical symbol that represents a period of silence. Rests have time values equal to their corresponding notes. Three kinds of rests are shown.

A quarter note receives one beat.
A QUARTER REST (1) also receives one beat.
A half note receives two beats.
A HALF REST (2) receives two beats.
A whole note receives four beats.
A WHOLE REST (3) recieves four beats (or one complete measure).

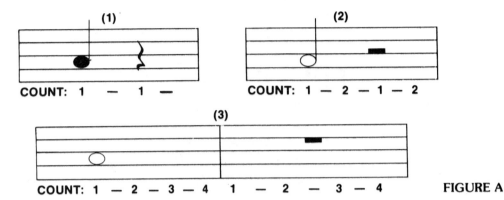

FIGURE A

REPEAT SIGNS

Many musical arrangements require certain sections, or even the entire song, to be played twice. Instead of reprinting these sections, musical symbols called repeat signs are used to indicate the section to be replayed.

Repeat signs appear most often in sets of two . . . one sign at the beginning of the section to be repeated, and one at the end.

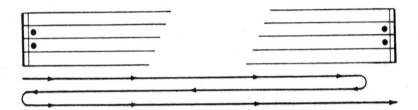

FIGURE B

When you come to the second repeat sign, go back to the first and repeat all of the measures between the two signs.

Occasionally you'll find only one repeat sign at the end of a section or a song. Play to the sign, go back to the beginning of the song and play that section again. If there is more music after the repeat sign, just keep playing.

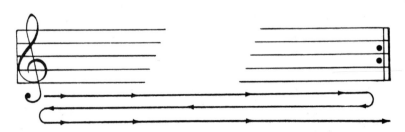

FIGURE C

A song may also contain more than one set of repeat signs. When this occurs, play twice through all of the measures within the first set of repeat signs. Then, all of the measures within the second set should be played twice. In each case, always go back to the closest repeat sign.

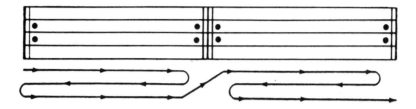

FIGURE D

DOUBLE ENDINGS

CHOPSTICKS contains repeat signs in conjunction with another musical symbol, the double ending.

When you play CHOPSTICKS the first time, play the measure marked by the bracket with the number 1, the first ending. Play up to the repeat sign and return to the repeat sign at the beginning. After playing the song a second time, skip the first ending (1) and play the measures marked by the bracket with the number 2, the second ending.

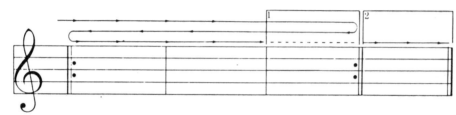

FIGURE E

CROSS FINGERING

In measures ⑫ , ⑬ , ⑰ , and ⑱ , the fingering numbers indicate what is called a finger crossing. As you hold the A note with your right thumb, (measure ⑫), cross over (➤) with your third finger to play the lower G note in measure ⑬ . As you hold the F note with your right index finger (2), (measure ⑰), cross under (➤) with your thumb to play the higher G note in measure ⑱ .

PLAYING DOUBLE NOTES IN THE MELODY

DIMENSIONS ② ③

When you're playing more than one note at a time, different combinations of fingers must be used, depending upon the notes played and the relative movement of your right hand over the keyboard.

For your convenience and ease of playing, follow the suggested finger numbers next to the notes. Should a similar melodic pattern appear more than once in a song, only the first pattern will indicate fingering.

Play the song with the melody an octave higher than written.

REGISTRATION NOTE: Whenever voices are listed for Upper, Lower and Pedals (as they are for CHOPSTICKS), be sure to turn THE ARRANGER off.

SONG 7 — CHAMPAGNE POLKA

DIMENSIONS 1 2 3

CHAMPAGNE POLKA is the first song in which you'll be playing black keys. The black keys are called sharps and/or flats. Before learning about sharps and flats, however, it's very important for you to understand half-steps and whole-steps.

HALF-STEPS

A half-step is the distance between any two keys that are adjacent to one another and have no other key between them. There are three ways of forming half-steps,

1. From a white key to a black key.
2. From a black key to a white key.
3. From a white key to a white key.

WHOLE-STEPS

Two half-steps equal one whole-step. There are four ways of forming whole-steps.

4. From a white key to a white key, skipping a black key.
5. From a black key to a black key, skipping a white key.
6. From a white key to a black key, skipping a white key.
7. From a black key to a white key, skipping a white key.

Figure B shows there is always a middle key in a whole-step formation. ◆ 166

SHARPS AND FLATS

In this song, and future selections, you'll frequently see these signs (♯) (♭) appearing before certain notes on the staff. These signs are called sharps and flats and they're used to indicate tones that are to be raised or lowered one half-step.

♯ **A SHARP tells you a tone should be raised one half-step.**

♭ **A FLAT tells you a tone should be lowered one half-step.**

Figure C shows some sharped and flatted notes and their locations on the keyboard. ◆ 166

When a sharp or flat appears before a note in a given measure, it affects all the identical notes that follow in that measure.

REGISTRATION REMINDER

From this point on, registrations and tempo settings are still shown on the title page of each song. Once you've tried these don't hesitate to try others. ◆ 167

SONG 8 — LAVENDER'S BLUE

DIMENSIONS [1] [2] [3]

EIGHTH NOTES

Up to now, you've been playing four different types of notes: whole, half, dotted half, and quarter notes. Song 8 introduces the eighth note.

When written singly, an eighth note looks like a quarter note with a flag attached to the end of its stem. When eighth notes are written in groups of two or more, the stems are connected by a bar.

The time value of an eighth note is one half that of a quarter note. Therefore, two eighth notes are equal to one quarter note.

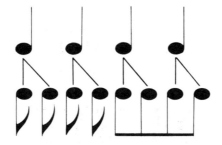

FIGURE A

HALF-BEATS AND COUNTING EIGHTH NOTES

When you count eighth notes, each single beat music be divided into two equal parts, a downbeat and an upbeat. This can be more easily understood if you think about tapping your foot in time to music. Each foot-tap has two parts, a downbeat and an upbeat. For counting purposes, the downbeat is designated by a number, and the upbeat by the word "and" (&).

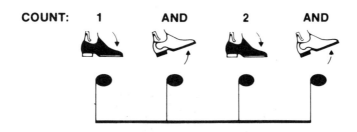

FIGURE B

EXERCISE IN EIGHTH NOTES

Practice Figure C until you can play it smoothly and evenly, without hesitation. To help you play this first exercise, tap your foot and count aloud as you play.

169

A NEW CHORD

The D7 chord is illustrated in Figures D, E, and F.

DIMENSION 1

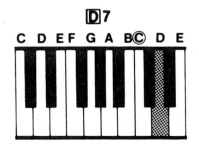

FIGURE D

DIMENSION 2

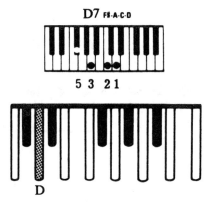

FIGURE E

DIMENSION 3

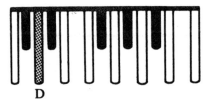

FIGURE F

Play the Melody Rhythm Warmup for LAVENDER'S BLUE.

Play the song. Remember to turn off THE ARRANGER.

SONG 9 — SPANISH EYES

DIMENSIONS 1 2 3
NEW NOTES

The new notes used in Song 12 are A and A♭, and both appear on ledger lines above the staff.

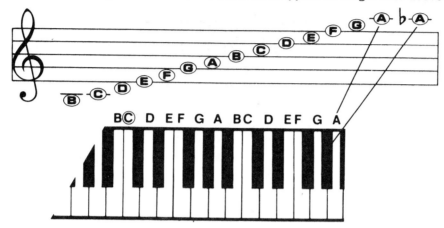

FIGURE A

NEW CHORD

The minor chord is introduced in this song. Minor chords are indicated by an "m" following the letter in the chord symbol.

DIMENSION 1

To play a minor chord, simply touch the MINOR TOUCH strip with your thumb while playing the indicated chord key.

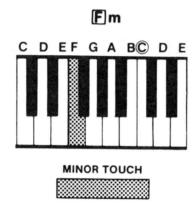

FIGURE B

DIMENSION 2

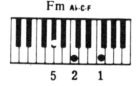

5   2   1

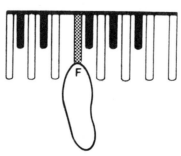

FIGURE C

DIMENSION ③

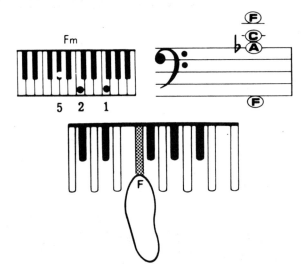

FIGURE D

PRO

This button automatically adds harmony notes to the melody. The harmony notes added are based on the chords you play.

Play the song with the melody an octave higher than written.

◆ 172

SONG 10 — SNOWBIRD

DIMENSION ①

Set up the registration and play SNOWBIRD.

PEDAL-CHORD RHYTHMS (4/4)

DIMENSION ②③

A pedal-chord rhythm can be played in songs written in 4/4 time. A pedal is played on the first and third beats while the chord is sustained.

◆ 174

NOTE: DIMENSION ② — if you are not using automatic bass, play the accompaniment the same as shown in Figure A.

Practice the Accompaniment Rhythm Warmup (B) with the registration given.

◆ 174

When you can play this smoothly and with feeling, practice the melody, accompaniment rhythm warmup (C).

◆ 174

When you can play this smoothly and with feeling, play the complete arrangement of SNOWBIRD.

20

SONG 11 — AMAZING GRACE

DIMENSION 1

Set up the registration and play AMAZING GRACE.

PEDAL-CHORD RHYTHMS (3/4)

DIMENSIONS 2 3

You'll recall that 3/4 time means there are three beats in each measure. In the waltz rhythm pattern, a pedal is played on the first beat and a chord on the second beat, as shown in Figure A.

NOTE: **DIMENSION** 2 — if you are not using automatic bass, play the accompaniment shown in Figure A.

Practice the Accompaniment Rhythm Warmup (FIGURE A). Use the registration given.

When you can play this smoothly and with feeling, practice the Melody, Accompaniment Rhythm Warmup (B).

When you can play this smoothly and with feeling, play AMAZING GRACE.

For a classical organ sound, turn off TREMOLO. Try this song with and without automatic rhythm, with and without PRO.

Play the melody an octave higher than written.

SONG 12 — MAKE THE WORLD GO AWAY

DIMENSIONS 1 2 3

KEY SIGNATURES

In many songs you'll see one or more sharps or flats printed at the beginning of the music between the clef sign and the time signature as shown. This is called a key signature. For example, because a B flat appears in the key signature of "Make The World Go Away", all B notes in the song are played on the B-flat key. In the lower staff, the flat that appears in the key signature after the bass clef applies to the B's in the left-hand and pedal parts. A song having no sharps or flats in the key signature is said to be written in the key of C Major. This song has one flat, B-flat, and is in the key of F Major.

NOTE: **DIMENSION** 1 Key selector buttons are also identified by the number of flats or sharps in the key signature.

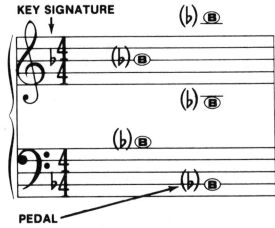

KEY SIGNATURE

PEDAL

FIGURE A

NEW CHORDS

DIMENSION ☐1

Press the F Key Selector and play these chord keys.

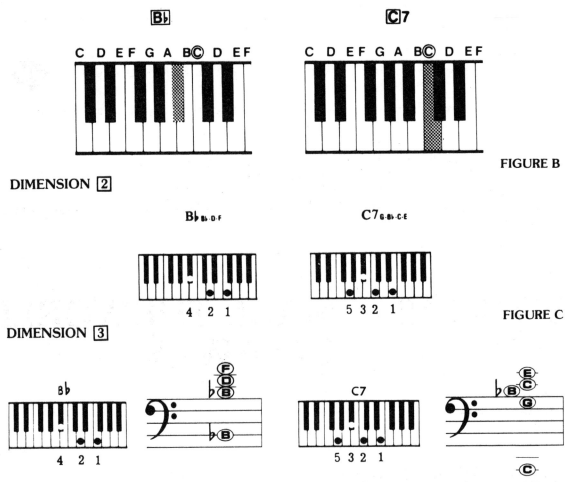

Bb

C7

FIGURE B

DIMENSION ☐2

Bb Bb·D·F

C7 G·Bb·C·E

4 2 1

5 3 2 1

FIGURE C

DIMENSION ☐3

Bb

C7

4 2 1

5 3 2 1

FIGURE D

EIGHTH RESTS

You've already learned about eighth notes. Song 12 uses the silent counterpart of the eighth note, the eighth rest. The eighth rest, like the eighth note, receives one-half beat. The eighth rest is shown in Figure E along with the other rests you've learned.

EIGHTH REST ½ BEAT	QUARTER REST 1 BEAT	HALF REST 2 BEATS	WHOLE REST 4 BEATS

FIGURE E

Play the song with and without PRO.

178

SONG 13 — THE GAMBLER

DIMENSION 1 Set up the registration and play the following song, THE GAMBLER.

PEDAL-CHORD- PEDAL-CHORD RHYTHM (4/4)

DIMENSIONS 2 3

A pedal is played on the first and third beats and the chord is played on the second and fourth beats, as shown in Figure A. Remember to play the B notes as B flat. Practice the pedal-chord rhythms in THE GAMBLER, until you can play them smoothly.

◆ 180

NOTE: **DIMENSION** 2 — if you are not using automatic bass, play the accompaniment as shown in Figure A.

SONG 14 — NADIA'S THEME

DIMENSIONS 1 2 3

NEW CHORDS

DIMENSION 1

To play the minor chords below, simply touch the MINOR TOUCH strip with your thumb while playing the indicated chord key. Be sure to turn off the Key Selector.

Gm   **D**m   **A**m

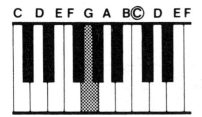  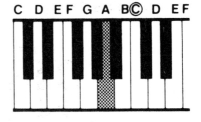

FIGURE A

DIMENSION 2

NOTE: Pedals are optional in **DIMENSION** 2 .

Gm G-B♭-D   Dm A-D-F   Am A-C-E

5 3 1   5 2 1   4 2 1

FIGURE B

DIMENSION ③

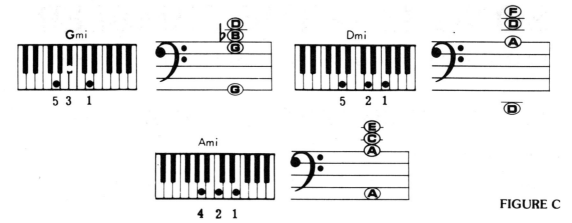

FIGURE C

VARIATION IN 4/4 RHYTHM

DIMENSIONS ② ③

When you listen to a professional organist, you'll find he doesn't always play the same rhythm patterns in his accompaniment. Various patterns are mixed with the basic rhythm to add variety and interest. NADIA'S THEME uses variety in the pedal-chord patterns.

REGISTRATION NOTE: Some of the controls listed in the registration may not be on your instrument. Ignore those controls.

SONG 15 — YOU LIGHT UP MY LIFE

NEW CHORDS

DIMENSION ①.

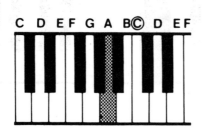

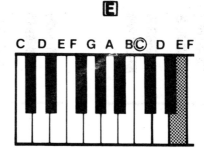

FIGURE A

DIMENSION ②

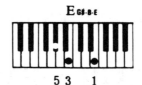

FIGURE B

NOTE: Pedals are optional in **DIMENSION 2**.

DIMENSION ③

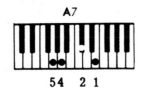

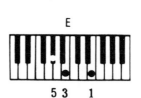

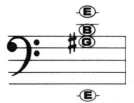

FIGURE C

24

PEDAL-CHORD-CHORD RHYTHM (3/4)

DIMENSION 2 3

A pedal is played on the first beat, and the chord is played on the second and third beats (A).

◆ 184 ▶

NATURAL SIGNS

DIMENSIONS 1 2 3

Natural signs (♮) appear in several measures of Song 15. They are used in two ways to cancel sharps or flats:

1. In measure ⑰ , the naturals cancel the previous key signature of B♭. Play this part of the song in the key of C.

2. In other measures, the naturals temporarily cancel the sharps or flats in the key signature. They are in effect for only the measure in which they appear.

DIMENSION 1

A four-note minor chord, the minor seventh (m7), is used in this song. With the Key Selector set as indicated, FunMachine plays these chords automatically. As with other minor chords, simply touch Minor Touch as you play the chord key.

◆ 184 ▶

SONG 16 — FEELINGS

NEW CHORDS

DIMENSION 1

To play a minor chord, simply touch the MINOR TOUCH strip while playing the indicated chord key.

G   Em7   B7

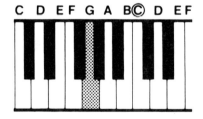 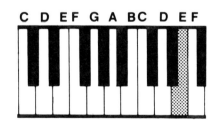 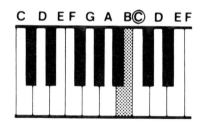

FIGURE A

DIMENSION 2

 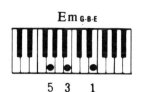 

G G-B-D   Em G-B-E   B7 F♯-A-B-D♯

5 3 1   5 3 1   5 3 2 1

FIGURE B

DIMENSION ③

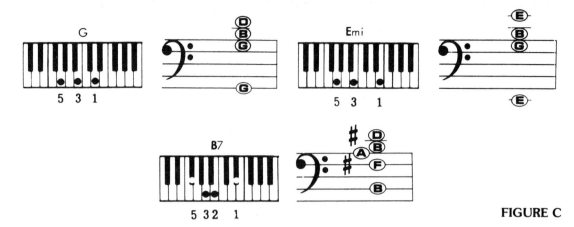

FIGURE C

NOTE: Pedals are optional in DIMENSION ②.

NOTE: **DIMENSION** ③ Sometimes your left hand plays single notes in the accompaniment; this is called a countermelody.
Try playing the melody to this song an octave higher than written.

187

SONG 17 — AFTER THE LOVIN'

NEW CHORD

DIMENSION ①   Ⓐ

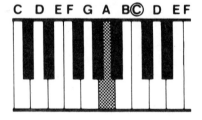

FIGURE A

DIMENSION ②

NOTE: Pedals are optional in **DIMENSION** ② .   FIGURE B

DIMENSION ③

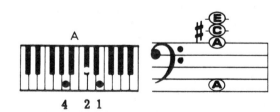

FIGURE C

Play the melody to this song an octave higher than written. ◆190

SONG 18 — BREAKING UP IS HARD TO DO

DIMENSIONS ☐1 ☐2 ☐3

RUBATO (Playing Freely)

An Italian word meaning "robbed", indicates a freedom in matters of tempo and melody rhythm. The performer may "rob" certain notes of their proper length by playing them a little faster or slower.

In Song 18, BREAKING UP IS HARD TO DO, play the first eight (8) measures *rubato*. At measure ⑨, activate the appropriate control so the drums start automatically when you press either a pedal or a key on the lower keyboard.

NEW CHORDS

DIMENSION ☐1

To play a minor chord, simply touch the MINOR TOUCH strip with your thumb while playing the indicated chord key.

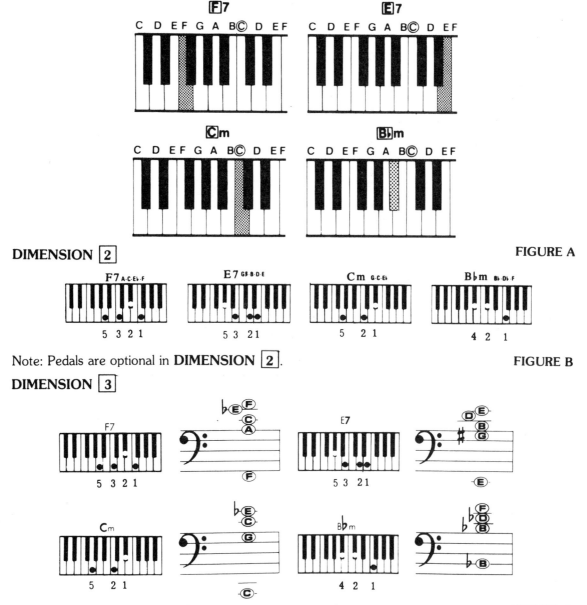

FIGURE A

DIMENSION ☐2

FIGURE B

Note: Pedals are optional in **DIMENSION** ☐2.

DIMENSION ☐3

FIGURE C

Play the melody to this song an octave higher than written.

SONG 19 — YOU ARE THE SUNSHINE OF MY LIFE

DIMENSION 1 Set up the registration and play YOU ARE THE SUNSHINE OF MY LIFE.

DIMENSIONS 2 3

ALTERNATE PEDAL NOTES

In all of the chords you've learned thus far, you've played the note that names each chord in the pedal part; this note is generally known as the root of the chord. The figure illustrates these chords and their roots, which are marked R.

To add interest and variety to your playing, you should know that other notes of a chord may also be played on the pedals. The note most often used is called the "fifth" of the chord; for now, however, these other chord notes are referred to as alternate notes. Alternate notes are also shown in the figure in the column marked A.

CHORD	R	A
C	C	G
F	F	C
G	G	D
D	D	A
A	A	E
E	E	B
B	B	F#
Bb	Bb	F

FIGURE A

196

SONG 20 — COLOUR MY WORLD

DIMENSIONS 1 2 3

EIGHTH NOTE TRIPLETS

A triplet is a group of three notes played in the same amount of time it would take to play two notes of the same type. It's easy to recognize the triplet because the three notes are usually bracketed with the number 3 over the middle note.

In Figure A, each group of two eighth notes (1) and each triplet (2) receives the same time value, one beat or foot tap. Practice (2) until you are able to play the eighth-note triplets, giving each note an equal time value.

198

A hint to help you play (2) evenly: Recite "Hip-pe-ty-Hop-pe-ty-Hip-pe-ty-Hop-pe-ty, etc." playing one note on each syllable.

Figure B used eighth note triplets in combination with other notes. Practice Figure B until you can play it comfortably without hesition. As a help, tap your foot and count aloud with the numbers above the staff.

NEW CHORD

DIMENSION [1]

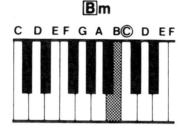

FIGURE C

DIMENSION [2]

FIGURE D

NOTE: Pedals are optional in **DIMENSION** [2] .

DIMENSION [3]

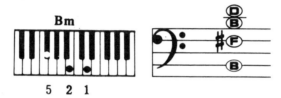

FIGURE E

SONG 21 — GAMES PEOPLE PLAY

REGISTRATION

DIMENSIONS [1] [2] [3]

Registration — the technique of making tonal changes in music — is one of the simplest ways to add considerable interest to your playing. It is easy to learn to make changes in registrations during a song and make your playing more impressive. Keep these points in mind as you create new registrations for your music.

1. Changes should be obvious. The new registration should contrast with the previous sound.

2. Changes should reflect the mood of the music.

3. Keep the rhythm constant. Don't put extra beats in a measure just to make a change in registration.

4. Keep your motions simple. Determine how much time you have, and make no more changes than possible in that time. Fit your motions to the rhythm. Sometimes it is necessary to "rob" beats from a long melody note. Use the "robbed" beats to press the new tabs — as a general rule one tab per beat. See Figure A.

Written like this   **Played like this**

Press   Press
1st Tab   2nd Tab

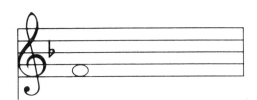
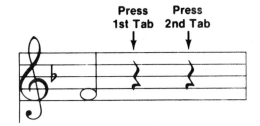

FIGURE A

WHEN TO CHANGE

It is a good idea to use different sounds to play a song but don't make so many changes that the music becomes confusing. Some appropriate places to change your regstration are:

1. Between the introduction and body of the song.

2. Between verses of a song.

3. Any natural break in a song.

NOTE: Rule # 2 is used in Song 21 in measures ⑦ , ⑮ , and ㉓ .

SONG 22 — WONDERLAND BY NIGHT

REGISTRATION: CHANGING RHYTHMS

DIMENSIONS ☐1 ☐2 ☐3

Song 22 shows you how to add variety to your playing by changing rhythms within the song. In measure ⑧ add the BOSSA NOVA, and in measure ⑯ turn the BOSSA NOVA off.

REMEMBER: Sometimes it is necessary to "rob" beats from a melody note in order to press the tabs in time with the rhythm.

SONG 23 — IT WAS ALMOST LIKE A SONG

DIMENSIONS ☐1 ☐2 ☐3

D.S. AL CODA ⊕

In Song 23, you'll see the phrase *D.S. al CODA* ⊕. This tells you to go back to the sign (𝄋) at the beginning of the song, and repeat all the measures up to the coda sign (⊕). Then, without stopping, go directly to the *coda* and finish the song. *Coda* is the Italian term for "tail" and indicates an additional section of a song used as an ending.

SIXTEENTH NOTES

When written alone, a sixteenth note looks like an eighth note with an extra flag added to its stem. When sixteenth notes appear in groups of two or more, their stems are connected by two bars.

FIGURE A

The time value of a sixteenth note is one-half that of an eighth note and one-fourth that of a quarter note. You have already learned that each beat can be divided into two equal parts . . . a number and the word "and" . . . for ease of counting eighth notes.

When you're counting sixteenth notes, each beat may be divided into four equal parts. Each part is indicated by a separate syllable, as shown in Figure B.

Play Figure B at a slow tempo while counting aloud and tapping your foot. Play four sixteenth notes to each foot tap. Make sure you can play them evenly and without hesitation.

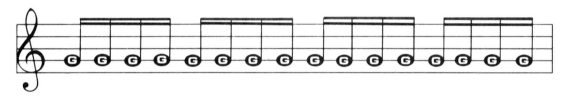

COUNT: 1 — a — & — a   2 — a — & — a   3 — a — & — a   4 — a — & — a

FIGURE B

The rhythm warmup incorporates *D.S. al Coda* and sixteenth notes. Practice until you can play it ◆ 204 smoothly and evenly.

◆ 205

SONG 24 — DISCO or BLUES

DIMENSIONS [1] [2] [3]

Other than the waltz, all the other FunMachine rhythms are based on "four-four" time. Basically, the only musical difference between them is the rhythmic "feel" created by the bass, chords and drums. Many songs can be played with different rhythms; this does not mean the melody is played differently — a whole note still gets four (4) beats, a half note gets two beats, etc.

This next song can be played with any FunMachine rhythm (other than Waltz), however, the Disco, Rock, and Ballad Rock will work well with this song.

When you hear a song that makes you feel like getting up and dancing, go to your organ and set the automatic rhythm at that speed. Listen to the song and ask yourself, "What kind of instrument is featured . . . a trumpet, a sax, a piano? What kind of instruments are in the background?" By listening to your favorite songs and asking yourself these questions, you will become aware of what kind of instruments you want in your own arrangement.

This next song DISCO or Blues is a fun song; use it with different rhythms.

HOW TO FORM CHORDS

A chord is a group of notes formed from certain tones of the major scale.

- Major chords are formed by combining the first, third, and fifth notes of the major scale.

- Minor chords are formed by combining the first, flatted third, and fifth notes of the major scale.

- Seventh chords are formed by combining the first, third, fifth, and flatted seventh notes of a major scale.

- Minor seventh chords are formed by combining the first, flatted third, fifth, flatted seventh notes of a major scale.

Below is a list of all major scales:

	1	2	3	4	5	6	7	8
C	C	D	E	F	G	A	B	C
F	F	G	A	B♭	C	D	E	F
B♭	B♭	C	D	E♭	F	G	A	B♭
E♭	E♭	F	G	A♭	B♭	C	D	E♭
A♭	A♭	B♭	C	D♭	E♭	F	G	A♭
D♭	D♭	E♭	F	G♭	A♭	B♭	C	D♭
G♭	G♭	A♭	B♭	B	D♭	E♭	F	G♭
B	B	C♯	D♯	E	F♯	G♯	A♯	B
E	E	F♯	G♯	A	B	C♯	D♯	E
A	A	B	C♯	D	E	F♯	G♯	A
D	D	E	F♯	G	A	B	C♯	D
G	G	A	B	C	D	E	F♯	G

Example:

C = 1-3-5 of C Scale = C-E-G

Fm = 1-♭3-5 of F Scale = F-A♭-C

G7 = 1-3-5-♭7 of G Scale = G-B-D-F

Dm7 = 1-♭3-♭5-♭7 of D Scale = D-F♮-A-C♮

CHORD INVERSIONS

The notes of a chord may be rearranged and the chord will not lose its identity. This rearrangement is known as an inversion.

Example:

C chord = C-E-G

Inversions of C chord are: E-G-C and G-C-E

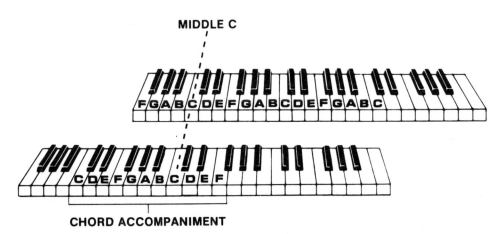

MIDDLE C

CHORD ACCOMPANIMENT

Left hand accompaniment sounds best if chords are played within the range shown above. It also makes it easier to change from one chord to another.

SISTEMA DE APRENDIZAJE 3-DIMENSIONAL

CONTENIDO

BIENVENIDOS . . .

al sistema de aprendizaje del Organo Baldwin 3 DIMENSIONAL . . . una nueva forma de disfrutar la música. Este sistema único le permite escoger la forma que usted desea para aprender música y cómo tocar el órgano Baldwin.

DIMENSION ☐1 Easy (fácil)

SUPERIOR: Su mano derecha toca la melodía de un dedo que está escrita en easy-to-read (fácil de leer), "notas que se nombran ellas mismas".

INFERIOR: Su mano izquierda toca el acompañamiento de un dedo, indicado por medio del símbolo pequeño del acorde arriba de la melodía (☐C).

PEDAL: El Baldwin FunMachine tocará automáticamente el bajo.

From the Columbia Pictures Release "YOU LIGHT UP MY LIFE"
YOU LIGHT UP MY LIFE

Words and Music by
JOE BROOKS

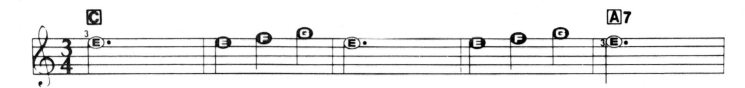

DIMENSION ☐2 Acorde

SUPERIOR: Su mano derecha toca la melodía escrita en la notación estandard. Conforme este curso progrese, la melodía será gradualmente embellecida por medio de notas adicionales y frases rítimicas.

INFERIOR: Su mano izquierda toca acordes de tres y cuatro notas.

PEDAL: Puede ser que usted, a) use Baldwin FunChords para tocar automáticamente las notas de bajo o, b) toque las notas de bajo en el pedal con su pie izquierdo.

From the Columbia Pictures Release "YOU LIGHT UP MY LIFE"
YOU LIGHT UP MY LIFE

Words and Music by
JOE BROOKS

DIMENSION $\boxed{3}$ Tradicional

SUPERIOR: Su mano derecha toca la misma línea de melodía, como **DIMENSION** $\boxed{2}$.

INFERIOR Usted leera y tocara las notas para el pedal, de la mano izquierda. Estas notas están
y PEDAL: escritas en fácil de leer (easy to read) "notas que se nombran ellas mismas".

From the Columbia Pictures Release "YOU LIGHT UP MY LIFE"
YOU LIGHT UP MY LIFE

Words and Music by
JOE BROOKS

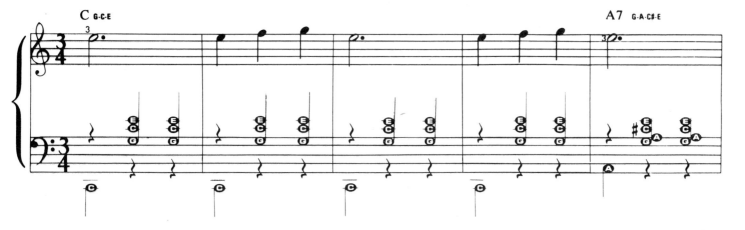

QUE DIMENSION DEBO ESCOGER?

Si esta es su primera experiencia musical, usted encontratá que la **DIMENSION** $\boxed{1}$ es la más fácil de usar. Usted aprenderá a tocar rápidamente sus canciones favoritas, y además aprenderá sobre música.

Si usted tiene alguna experiencia musical, puede comenzar este curso usando **DIMENSION** $\boxed{2}$. Leerá sus melodías preferidas escritas en notación estandar (sin nombres de letras en las notas), y aprenderá a crear un acompañamiento por medio de formar acordes con su mano izquierda.

NOTA: Si usted tiene el FunMachine de un solo teclado, podrá usar la **DIMENSION** $\boxed{1}$ o $\boxed{2}$ ignore la **DIMENSION** $\boxed{3}$.

Si usted puede leer música, o si le gustaría aprender, use la **DIMENSION** $\boxed{3}$. Usted leerá arreglos de órgano de dos pentagramas que usan técnicas de órgano como patrones de acorde-pedal, armonía de dos partes en la melodía, etc.

QUE SUCEDE SI DESEA PROBAR
UNA DIMENSION DIFERENTE?

Simplemente porque comienza con una **DIMENSION**, no quiere decir que debe continuar con la misma hasta el fin de este curso. Si usted desea probar otra, simplemente retroceda a un punto en el cual el material de instrucción le sea familiar y continúe desde ese punto, usando una nueva **DIMENSION**.

SU ORGANO BALDWIN

Para familiarizarse con su órgano Baldwin, LEA su guía de propietario. Contiene información detallada e instrucciones de operación para todas las características y controles de su instrumento. Manténgala a la mano para que se pueda referir a ella con frecuencia.

GUIAS DE TECLADO

Todos los órganos Baldwin tienen letras de identificación arriba de las teclas blancas. Estas son las guías del teclado.

REGISTRACION

THE ARRANGER es una sorprendente registración automática que es característica de su órgano Baldwin. Con THE ARRANGER encendido, un arreglo completo o registración, es automáticamente seleccionado para usted.

Incluidos se encuentran teclados superiores e inferiores, y pedales de voces, además del control de noción apropiados. THE ARRANGER escoge automáticamente un arreglo diferente y apropiado para cada ritmo que usted seleccione. Cuando usted apaga todos los ritmos, THE ARRANGER selecciona un conjunto completo de órgano. Cuando usted apaga THE ARRANGER, podrá experimentar con sus propios arreglos. Consulte la Guía de Propietarios para sugerencias de registraciones.

NOTA: Los arreglos usados para las canciones en este libro, cubren varios de los modelos Baldwin. Sinplemente seleccione las tablillas y efectos que aparecen en su órgano y no haga caso de las otras.

TOCANDO MELODIAS

En una orquesta, la melodía de la canción puede ser tocada por instrumentos como flauta o trompeta. En el órgano, está generalmente tocada por la mano derecha en el teclado superior. Las melodías están compuestas de sonidos musicales específicos. Para representar estos sonidos, se ponen notas en el pentagrama, como mostramos en la Figura A. Estos pentagramas consisten en cinco líneas y cuatro espacios y cada uno está nombrado con las letras de A a G. Cualquier nota que aparezca en una de las líneas o en uno de los espacios, es referida por el nombre de la letra. Este curso usa notas que "se nombran ellas mismas"; simplemente combine las letras de sus notas con las letras en su guía de teclado.

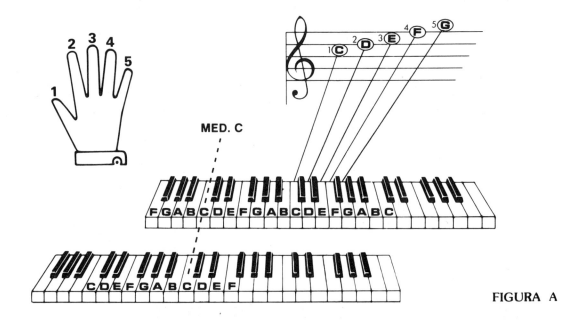

FIGURA A

El símbolo con la forma de S al principio del pentagrama, se llama atiplado, e indica que todas las notas deberán ser tocadas con la mano derecha. También se encuentran ilustradas las primeras cinco notas de la melodía C, D, E, F, y G y sus teclas correspondientes. Para ayudarlo a tocar las notas con la mano derecha, se han usado números al lado de cada nota, indicando qué dedo debe usarse.

Coloque su mano derecha en las teclas con su pulgar en C, arriba de la C de en medio Ⓒ como se muestra en la Figura A. Descanse sus dedos suavemente en las teclas de cinco notas como se indica.

Nota: En este curso, la C de enmedio aparece en un circulo Ⓒ .

CANCION 1 — WHISTLE WHILE YOU WORK

Paso 1 Toque la siguiente melodía en el teclado superior.

Paso 2 Detenga las notas blancas, con letras negras, un poco más de tiempo que las notas negras con las letras blancas . . . hablaremos sobre ésto más adelante.

Paso 3 Arregle la siguiente registración y toque WHISTLE WHILE YOU WORK, en cualquiera de las DIMENSION ☐1 o ☐2 .

■ 153

TOCANDO EL ACOMPAÑAMIENTO

El acompañamiento en un órgano generalmente consiste en acordes tocados con la mano izquierda y con las notas de bajo correspondientes. Los acordes estan representados por medio de símbolos de acordes, que son cuadros pequeños que contienen letras y aparecen arriba de la melodía en cada canción. Para comenzar, usted aprenderá dos acordes, el acorde   C   y el acorde   G 7.

Encienda THE ARRANGER.

Tocando el acompañamiento en . . .

DIMENSION ☐1 Presione el botón de 1-FINGER ACCOMP, que se encuentra en la sección EASY PLAYERS de su órgano Baldwin. Con 1-FINGER ACCOMP, todo lo que usted tiene que hacer es presionar la tecla del manual inferior que corresponda con la letra en el cuadro del acorde. (FIGURA A) El FunMachine tocará automáticamente el bajo.

NOTA: Para cancelar el acompañamiento automático, presione el botón STOP.

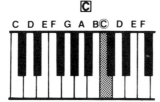 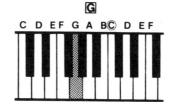

FIGURA A

DIMENSION ☐2 Toque las notas de acorde localizadas a la derecha del símbolo de acorde (FIGURA B). Hay dos formas de obtener las notas del bajo: 1) Tóquelas usted presionando el pedal que tiene el nombre del acorde (FIGURA C). o, 2) presione el FUNCHORDS y haga que estas notas de pedal toquen automáticamente para usted.

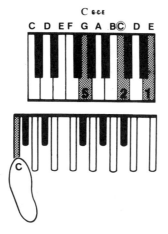 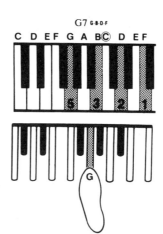

FIGURA B

FIGURA C

DIMENSION ☐3 Figuras D y E, en la siguiente página le mostraremos como leer el pentagrama de la mano izquierda o de acompañamiento.

EL GRAN PENTAGRAMA

De ahora en adelante, cada canción estará escrita en pentagrama doble. El pentagrama doble consiste en dos pentagramas ligados por una línea de barra, como se muestra en la Figura D. Al principio del pentagrama superior se encuentra la clave de sol. Como usted ya sabe, ésto indica que las notas que siguen son tocadas con la mano derecha en la parte superior del teclado. Al principio del pentagrama inferior hay un nuevo símbolo llamado clave de Fa. Este símbolo indica que las notas que siguen son tocadas por la mano izquierda en la parte inferior del teclado o con el pie izquierdo en los pedales.

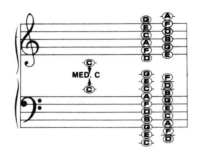

FIGURA D

MED. C

La nota C que aparece en la primera línea suplementaria abajo del pentagrama del atiplado y en la primera línea suplementaria arriba del pentagrama de bajo, es llamada C de enmedio. A pesar de que la C de enmedio puede estar escrita en cualquiera de las dos posiciones, como se muestra en la Figura D, es la misma nota. La C de enmedio en la parte superior del teclado está siempre directamente arriba de la C de enmedio en la parte inferior del teclado. Está representada por medio de la letra C en un círculo, arriba de la ilustración del teclado.

ACORDES EN EL PENTAGRAMA DE BAJO

La Figura E muestra la localización de los acordes y pedales del pentagrama de bajo de C y G7, que usted ha estado tocando. Note la posición de las notas en relación con la C de enmedio. Las letras en las notas le ayudarán a localizar las teclas correctas.

NOTA: Las líneas en curva en **DIMENSION** 3 , que se encuentran en la siguiente página, son llamadas ligaduras — sostenga las notas de ligadura hasta que un nuevo acorde aparezca. Hablaremos sobre las ligaduras más adelante.

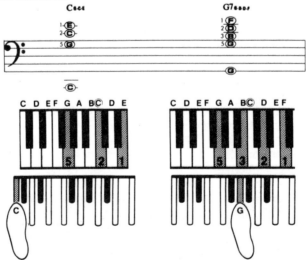

FIGURA E

DIMENSION 1 2 3 Arregle la registración y practique el acompañamiento que se muestra para la dimensión que usted escoja.

DIMENSION 1	DIMENSION 2	DIMENSION 3
THE ARRANGER encendido	THE ARRANGER encendido	THE ARRANGER encendido
1-FINGER ACCOMP. encendido	Para el bajo automático:	
KEY SELECTOR C encendido	FUNCHORDS encendido	
MEMORY apagado	MEMORY apagado	

NOTA: Ciertas características como el KEY SELECTOR no estan proveídas en algunos instrumentos Baldwin. Siempre que encuentre instrucciones en que se requiera una característica que no se encuentre en su isntrumento, simplemente ignore esa instrucción.

TOCANDO CON RITMO

DIMENSIONES [1] [2] [3]

Ritmo es la base de la música. El poder tocar con las características automáticas de Baldwin, será una experiencia muy gratificadora.

Además de indicarle qué tecla tocar, cada tipo de nota tiene un valor de tiempo específico, el cual es medido en compases musicales. La siguiente ilustración muestra los cuatro tipos de notas que estará tocando en las primeras canciones.

Nota negra 1 compas

Nota blanca con puntillo 3 Compases

Nota blanca 2 Compases

Nota redonda 4 Compases

FIGURA F

El siguiente ensayo rítmico de melodía le ayudará a comprender el ritmo.

1. Coordine el ritmo de la melodía con la batería automatica.

2. Coordine tocando acordes con la batería automatica.

3. Coordine tocando juntos la melodía y el acompañamiento.

Ya que usted tocara repetidamente sólo una de la melodía y un acompañamiento de acorde, podrá usar la característica del ritmo automático en cualquier momento. Encienda la batería y escuche . . . note como se relaciona con las notas de la línea de arriba. Si la batería va muy rápido o muy despacio, ajuste la velocidad del ritmo a un tiempo de su agrado. Toque la tecla E con su tercer dedo. A continuación encontrará algunas sugerencias que le ayudarán a tocar las canciones con más facilidad.

Sugerencias para tocar:

1. Toque la música físicamente. Esto involucra la localización correcta de la melodía y las teclas de acorde, observando la combinación sugerida de los dedos, y la incorporación de nueva información musical. Pruebe hacerlo sin quitar los ojos de la música.

2. Toque la música mentalmente. Esto significa leer la música sin tocarla. Trate de escuchar la melodía en su mente e imagínese como suena cada acorde cuando su símbolo aparece en la música. Susurre la melodía, ésto también le ayudará.

3. Observe la música y tóquela mentalmente mientras el RealRhythm está tocando automáticamente. Mientras escucha la música, note la relación con los sonidos de la batería.

4. Físicamente toque la música con el ritmo de la bateria. Para entonces usted estará realmente familiarizado con lo que está tocando.

NOTA: En los organos Baldwin con botones iluminados, al encender una característica, muchas veces causa el que se enciendan automaticamente otras características. En los organos que tengan botones mecanicos de presión, es necesario seleccionar individualmente cada función. Todas las características necesarias para cada registración estan enumeradas; si tiene un instrumento con botones-automáticos iluminados, algnos de ellos se le encenderan automaticamente.

De ahora en adelante, la palabra "on" (encendido) no estara impresa; cualquier característica anotada debera de estar ON (encendida) a lo menos que se indique lo contrario.

Use la siguiente registración para su preparación de la Melodia del Ritmo.

DIMENSIONS [1] [2] [3]

1-FINGER ACCOMP., KEY SELECTOR C (llave o boton selector)
(FANCY) FUNBASS
PRO apagado, MEMORY apagado
THE ARRANGER
REALRHYTHM

FOX TROT
Prepare el TEMPO a una velocidad comoda, como a 3½ o The Conductor = [100.]

Para principiar drums (los bajos) presione STOP.

NOTA: **DIMENSIONS** [1] [2] [3] Use el botón de 1-FINGER ACCOMP para practicar el ritmo de la melodía. (Melody Rhythm Warm-ups). Esto le facilitará concentrarse en cómo el ritmo de la melodía suena con la batería.

Toque con ritmo la canción completa usando la registración apropiada:

DIMENSION ☐1
1-FINGER ACCOMP.

DIMENSION ☐2
Para bajo automático:
FUNCHORDS

DIMENSIONES ☐1 ☐2 ☐3
THE ARANGER
(FANCY) FUNBASS
MEMORY
PRO
REALRHYTHM

FOX TROT
TEMPO 3½/ The Conductor = ☐100

◆ 156

CANCION 2 — CARNIVAL OF VENICE

DIMENSIONES ☐1 ☐2 ☐3

UNA NOTA NUEVA

La nota A es introducida en esta canción como se muestra en la Figura A. al continuar aprendiendo notas de melodía de la mano derecha, use los dedos sugeridos. Esto le ayudará a moverse fuera del margen de las primeras cinco notas sin quedarse "sin dedos para tocar".

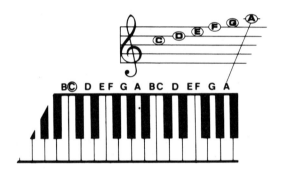

FIGURA A

MEDIDAS

La Figura B ilustra cómo el pentagrama está dividido en secciones iguales por medio del uso de líneas verticales, que son llamadas barras. La sección entre las barras se llamada compás.

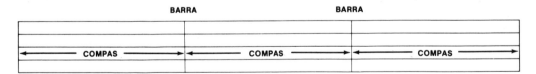

FIGURA B

MEDICION DEL TIEMPO

Los dos números al principio de la canción, son conocidos como medida del tiempo. Vea la Figura C. El número de arriba indica el número de compases en cada medida. El número de abajo indica el tipo de nota que recibe un compás. La canción CARNIVAL OF VENICE tiene 4/4 de medida de tiempo.

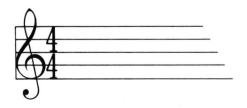

FIGURA C

LIGADURAS

Una línea curva conectando dos notas en la misma línea o en el mismo espacio es llamada ligadura. Una ligadura indica que la primera nota debe ser tocada y sostenida por el tiempo total de las dos notas. En la Figura D, el primer grupo de notas de ligadura es sostenida por un total de cuatro compases y el segundo grupo por un total de seis. NOTA: Porque solo la primera nota en un grupo de ligaduras está tocando, las notas siguientes no tienen letra-nombre adentro.

2   +   2 = 4   4   +   2 = 6   **FIGURA D**

De ahora en adelante, las registraciones estan impresas arriba o sobre la preparación o arriba de la canción. Si el simbolo $\emptyset$ aparece antes o despues del nombre de una característica, ESA CARACTERISTICA DEBERA DE ESTAR APAGADA.

NOTA: No se daran registraciones especiales para las Dimensiones 1, 2, ó 3. De aca en adelante, siga estas instrucciones:

DIMENSION $\boxed{1}$	**DIMENSION** $\boxed{2}$	**DIMENSION** $\boxed{3}$
Agreguele ésto a la registración dada: 1-FINGER ACCOMP. (FANCY) FUNBASS MEMORY opcional REALRHYTHM	Agreguele ésto a la registración dada: (FANCY) FUNBASS MEMORY opcional REALRHYTHM Para bajo autom., tambien agreguele FUNCHORDS	Agreguele ésto a la registración dada: (FANCY) FUNBASS MEMORY opcional REALRHYTHM

El Selector de llave (KEY SELECTOR) indicado para cada canción es para DIMENSION $\boxed{1}$ solamente.

Primero practique el ritmo de melodia, luego toque la canción.

◆ 157

CANCION 3 — MARIANNE

DIMENSION $\boxed{1}$ $\boxed{2}$ $\boxed{3}$

NOTA NUEVA

La canción 3 introduce la nota B.

BC D EF G A BC D EF G A B

NOTA: Observe los compases en las medidas ⑥ al ⑭ .

Practique el ensayo rítmico de la melodía para MARIANNE usando la batería. ◆ 158

Toque la canción usando la registración dada. recuerde la nota sobre Registración (arriba). ◆ 159

CANCION 4 — BORN TO LOSE

DIMENSION ⬛1⬛ ⬛2⬛ ⬛3⬛

LA OCTAVA

En la Figura A, las notas nuevas C, D, E, F, y G son ocho notas mas bajas que C, D, E, F, y G que usted aprendió anteriormente. Este espacio de ocho notas es llamado octava, término que viene de la palabra latina "ocho".

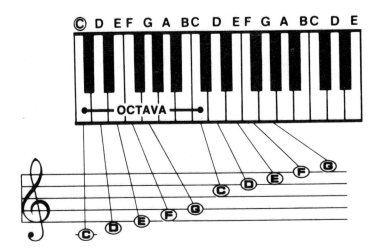

FIGURA A

SUSTITUYENDO LOS DEDOS

Encontrará partes en esta canción en donde verá dos números de dedo abajo de una sola nota (3-1), como mostramos en la Figura B. Estos se llaman dedos de substitución y básicamente le indican que debe presionar la tecla con el dedo indicado por medio del primer número; mientras lo sostiene, cambie al dedo indicado por medio del segundo número. Esto preparará su mano para la siguiente nota.

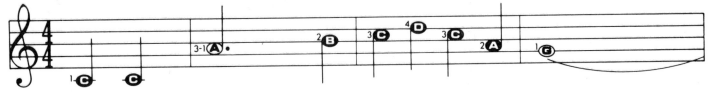

FIGURA B

UN NUEVO ACORDE

El acorde F mayor es ilustrado en las Figuras C, D, y E.

DIMENSION ⬛1⬛

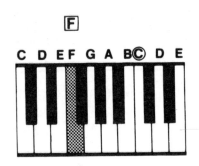

FIGURA C

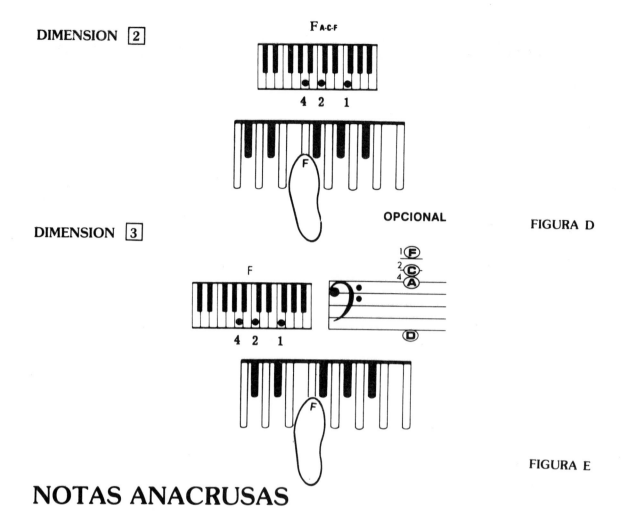

DIMENSION [2]

F A-C-F

4 2 1

DIMENSION [3]

F

4 2 1

OPCIONAL

FIGURA D

¹Ⓕ
²Ⓒ
⁴Ⓐ

Ⓓ

FIGURA E

NOTAS ANACRUSAS

Con frecuencia, una canción comienza con una o mas notas cuyo valor no equivale a una medida completa. Las notas en esta medida incompleta son llamadas anacrusas. Las notas perdidas, se encuentran siempre en la última medida de la canción. En muchos casos, las notas anacrusas son tocadas antes que el acorde de acompañamiento sea tocado.

◆ 160

Practique el ensayo rítmico de melodía para BORN TO LOSE, usando la batería.

◆ 161

CANCION 5 — SKATERS WALTZ

DIMENSION [1] [2] [3]

UN NUEVO COMPAS

La canción número 5, usa una nueva medida de tiempo, 3/4. Como aprendió anteriormente, el 4 le indica que el cuarto de nota tiene una pulsación. El número de arriba, 3, indica tres pulsaciones en cada medida. Esta medida de tiempo o compás indica un ritmo comunmente conocido como vals.

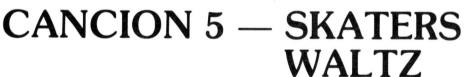

Practique el ensayo rítmico del acompañamiento para SKATERS WALTZ, usando la batería automática.

◆ 162

Toque la canción con la melodia una octova mas alta de la anotada.

◆ 163

CANCION 6 — CHOPSTICKS

DIMENSIONS ☐1 ☐2 ☐3

PAUSAS

La pausa es un símbolo musical que representa un periodo de silencio. El silencio tiene un valor de tiempo igual a su nota correspondiente. En la Figura A, se muestran tres tipos de pausa.

Una nota negra recibe un tiempo.
Una pausa de negra (1) recibe tambien un tiempo.
Una nota blanca recibe dos tiempos.
Una pausa de blanca (2) tambien recibe dos tiempos.
Una nota redonda recibe cuatro tiempos.
Una pausa de redonda (3) recibe cuatro tiempos (o un compas completo).

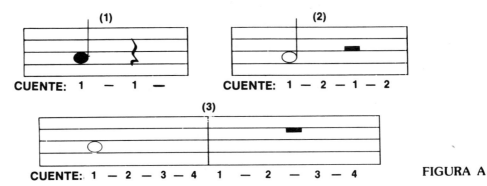

FIGURA A

SIGNOS DE REPETICION

Muchos arreglos musicales requieren que ciertas secciones, o quizás una canción completa sea tocanda dos veces. En vez de imprimir esta sección dos veces, símbolos musicales llamados signos de repetición son usados, los cuales indican la sección que debe ser tocada otra vez.

Los signos de repetición aparecen frecuentemente en pares . . . un signo al principio de la sección que se reperitrá y otras al final.

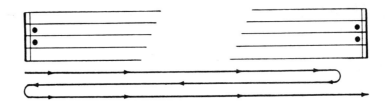

FIGURA B

Cuando esto suceda, toque dos veces todas las medidas que están en el primer signo de repetición. Después todas las medidas que se encuentran en el segundo set de signos de repetición, los cuales deberán ser tocados dos veces. En cada caso, siempre regrese al signo de repetición más cerca.

Ocasionalmente encontrará solo un signo de repetición al final de una sección o canción, como mostramos en la Figura C. Toque hasta el signo, regrese al principio de la canción y toque esa sección otra vez. Si hay mas música después del signo de repetición, simplemente continúe tocando.

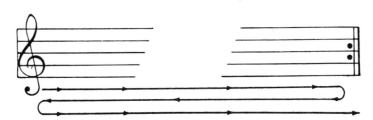

FIGURA C

Una canción puede tener mas de un de signo de repetición, como se muestra en la Figura D.

Cuando esto suceda, toque dos veces todas las medidas que están en el primer símbolo repetición. Despúes todas las medidas que se encuentran en el segundo set de signos de repetición, los cuales deberán ser tocados dos veces. En cada caso, siempre regrese al signo de repetición más cerca.

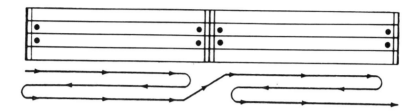

FIGURA D

FINALES DOBLES

CHOPSTICKS contiene signos repetidos en conjunción con otros símbolos musicales. El final doble, que se muestra en la Figura E.

Cuando toque CHOPSTICKS por la primera vez, toque la medida marcada por el primer bloque con el número 1, el primer final. Toque hasta el signo de repetición y regrese hacia el signo de repetición que se encuentra en el principio. Despúes de tocar la canción por la segunda vez, omita el primer final (1) y toque lo marcado por el bloque con el número 2, el segundo final.

FIGURA E

DEDOS CRUZADOS

En los compases ⑫ , ⑬ , ⑰ , y ⑱ , el número de dedos indica lo que se llama cruce de dedos. Mientras sostiene la nota A con el pulgar derecho, (compás ⑫), cruce sobre (➤) con el tercer dedo para tocar la nota G baja en el compás ⑬ . Mientras sostenga la nota F con su dedo índice de la mano derecha (2), compás ⑰ , cruce abajo (➤) con el pulgar, para tocar la nota G mas alta en el compás ⑱ .

TOCANDO NOTAS DOBLES EN LA MELODIA

DIMENSIONS ☐2 ☐3

Cuando usted toca más de una nota al mismo tiempo, se deberán usar diferentes combinaciones de dedos, dependiendo de las notas tocadas y el movimiento relativo de su mano derecha sobre el teclado.

Para su conveniencia y facilidad al tocar, siga los números de dedos sugeridos que aparecen a la par de las notas. Si un patrón melódico similar aparece mas de una vez en la canción, solo el primer patrón indicará cambio de dedos.

Toque la canción con la melodia una octava mas alta de la anotada.

NOTA DE REGISTRACION: Siempre que voces esten anotadas para Pedales Superiores o Inferiores (como hay para CHOPSTICKS), asegurece de apagar THE ARRANGER.

CANCION 7 — CHAMPAGNE POLKA

DIMENSIONS 1 2 3

CHAMPAGNE POLKA es la primera canción en la cual tocará las teclas negras. Las teclas negras son llamadas sostenidos o bemoles. Antes de aprender sobre sostenidos y bemoles, es muy importante para usted que pueda comprender los semitonos e intervalos.

SEMITONOS

El semitono es la distancia entre dos teclas que están adyacentes una a la otra y que no tienen ninguna otra tecla entre ellas. Hay tres maneras de formar un semitono.

1. De una tecla blanca a una tecla negra.
2. De una tecla negra a una tecla blanca.
3. De una tecla blanca a una tecla blanca.

INERVALO

Dos semitonos hacen un intervalo. Hay cuatro maneras de formar un intervalo.

4. De una tecla blanca a una tecla blanca, saltando una tecla negra.
5. De una tecla negra a una tecla negra, saltando una tecla blanca.
6. De una tecla blanca a una tecla negra, saltando una tecla blanca.
7. De una tecla negra a una tecla blanca, saltando una tecla blanca.

La Figura B muestra que siempre habrá una tecla en medio de la formación de un intervalo.

SOSTENIDOS Y BEMOLES

En esta canción y en futuras selecciones, encontrará estos signos frecuentmente (♯) (♭) en el pentragrama antes de ciertas notas. Estos signos son llamados sostenidos y bemoles y son usados para indicar tonos que serán elevados o bajados un semitono.

♯ **Un SOSTENIDO indica que el tono debe ser elevado un semitono.**

♭ **Un BEMOL indica que el tono debe ser bajado un semitono.**

La Figura C muestra algunas notas sostenidas y bemoles y su localización en el teclado.

Cuando un sostenido o un bemol aparecen antes de una nota en un compás dado, afecta todas las notas que son idénticas y que siguen al compas.

RECORDATORIO DE REGISTRACION

De ahora en adelante, los arreglos de registraciones y de tiempo se continuarán encontrando en el título de cada canción. Una vez que los haya probado, no dude en probar otros.

CANCION 8 — LAVENDER'S BLUE

CORCHEAS

Hasta ahora usted ha estado tocando cuatro tipos diferentes de notas: redonda, blanca, blanca con punto y negra. La canción 8 introduce la corchea.

Cuando se encuentra escrita sola, la corchea parece como una negra con una bandera al final de la plica. cuando las notas corcheas están escritas en grupos de dos o mas, las plicas están conectadas por medio de una barra.

El valor del tiempo de una corchea es la mitad de una negra. Entonces dos corcheas de una nota equivalen a una negra.

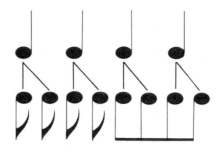

FIGURA A

MEDIO COMPAS Y CONTANDO LAS CORCHEAS

Cuando usted cuenta corcheas, cada compas tendrá que ser dividido en dos partes iguales, un compas mas abajo y un compas mas arriba. Downbeat y upbeat. Esto se puede comprender facilmente si con su pie golpea ligeramente llevando el tiempo de la música. Cada pie golpeará dos partes, un downbeat y un upbeat. Con el propósito de poder contar, al downbeat se le ha asignado un número, y al upbeat se la ha asignado la palabra "y" (&).

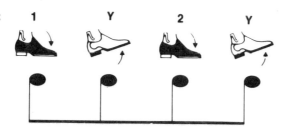

FIGURA B

EJERCICIOS CON CORCHEAS

Practique la Figura C hasta que lo pueda tocar suavemente, y sin dudar. Para ayudarlo a tocar este ejercicio, golpee su pie y cuente en voz alta mientras toca.

UN NUEVO ACORDE

El acorde D7 aparece ilustrado en las Figuras D, E, y F.

DIMENSION 1

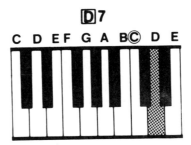

FIGURA D

DIMENSION 2

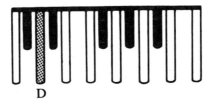

FIGURA E

DIMENSION 3

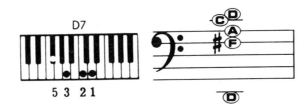

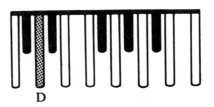

FIGURA F

Toque el ensayo rítmico de melodía para LAVENDER'S BLUE. 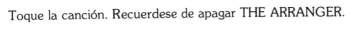 169

Toque la canción. Recuerdese de apagar THE ARRANGER. 170

CANCION 9 — SPANISH EYES

DIMENSIONS [1] [2] [3]

NOTAS NUEVAS

Las notas nuevas usadas en la Canción 9 son A y A♭, y las dos aparecen en la línea suplementaria arriba del pentagrama.

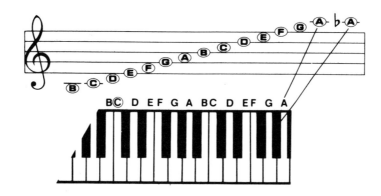

FIGURA A

NUEVO ACORDE

El acorde menor es introducido en esta canción. Los acordes menores están indicados por medio de una "m" que sigue a la letra en el símbolo del acorde.

DIMENSION [1]

Para tocar un acorde menor, simplemente toque la barra MINOR TOUCH con su pulgar mientras toca el acorde de la tecla indicada.

FIGURA B

DIMENSION [2]

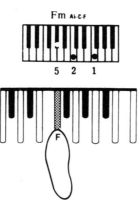

FIGURA C

DIMENSION ③

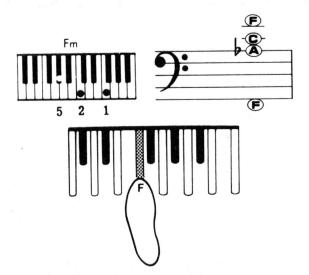

FIGURA D

PRO

Este botón añade automáticamente notas de armonía a la melodía. Las notas de armonía que han sido agregadas, están basadas en los acordes que usted toca.

Toque la canción con la melodia una octava más alta que la anotada.

CANCION 10 — SNOWBIRD

DIMENSION ①

Prepare la registración y toque SNOWBIRD.

RITMOS CON ACORDE DE PEDAL (4/4)

DIMENSIONS ② ③

Un ritmo con acorde de pedal puede ser tocado en canciones que están escritas en tiempo 4/4. esto se muestra en la Figura A. Un pedal es tocado en la primera y tercer compas, mientras el acorde es sostenido.

NOTA: DIMENSION ② — si usted no está usando el bajo automático, toque el acompañamiento de la misma forma en que se muestra en la figura A.

Practique el ensayo rítmico del acompañamiento (Figura B) con la registración.

Cuando usted pueda tocarla con facilidad y sentimiento, practique la melodía, con ensayo de acompañamiento rítmico (Figura C).

Cuando usted pueda tocarla con facilidad y con sentimiento, toque el arreglo completo de SNOWBIRD.

CANCION 11 — AMAZING GRACE

DIMENSION ☐

Prepare la registración para tocar AMAZING GRACE.

ACORDE DE RITMO DE PEDAL (3/4)

DIMENSIONS ☐ ☐

Usted recordará que 3/4 de tiempo significa que hay tres pulsaciones en cada compás. En el patrón de ritmo de vals, un pedal es tocado en la primera pulsación y un acorde en el segundo compás, como se muestra en la Figura A.

NOTA: **DIMENSION** ☐ — Si no está usando el bajo automático, toque el acompañamiento como se muestra en la Figura A.

Practique el Ritmo del Acompañamiento (Figura A). Use la registración dada.

Cuando pueda tocarla facilmente y con sentimiento, toque la canción AMAZING GRACE.

Para un sonido clásico de organo, apague TREMOLO. Pruebe esta canción con y sin ritmo automatico, con y sin PRO.

CANCION 12 — MAKE THE WORLD GO AWAY

DIMENSIONS ☐ ☐ ☐

CLAVE DE LA NOTA

En varias canciones usted encontrará uno o mas sostenidos o bemoles impresos al principio de la música, entre el signo de clave y el signo del compás, como se muestra en la Figura A. Esto es llamado clave de la nota. Por ejemplo, porque una B bemol aparece en la tecla de signatura en MAKE THE WORLD GO AWAY, todas las notas B en la canción están tocadas en la clave B bemol. En el pentagrama de abajo, el bemol que aparece en la clave de la nota después de la clave de fa, se debe aplicar a las Bs en la mano izquierda y a los pedales. Una canción que no tiene sostenidos o bemoles en la clave de la nota, está escrita en la clave de C mayor. Esta canción tiene un bemol, B-bemol, y está en la clave de F mayor.

NOTA: **DIMENSION** ☐ Los botones para hacer la selección están también identificados por el número de sostenidos y bemoles en la clave de nota.

51

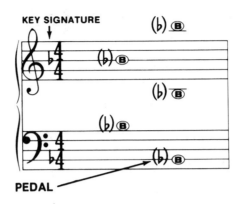

FIGURA A

NUEVO ACORDE

DIMENSION 1

Presione el botón de selección F y toque el acorde.

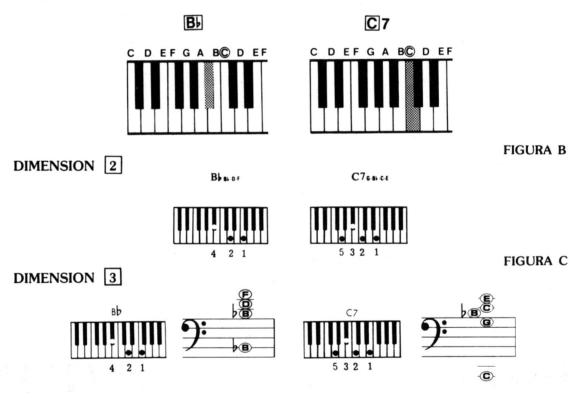

FIGURA B

FIGURA C

FIGURA D

PAUSA DE CORCHEA

Usted ya ha aprendido sobre las notas corchea. La canción 12 usa silencios o pausas de contra parte de las notas corchea, la pausa de corchea. La octava pausa, como la nota corchea, recibe la mitad de un compas. La pausa de corchea es mostrada en la Figura E junto con las otras pausas que usted ya ha aprendido.

PAUSA DE CORCHEA	PAUSA DE NEGRA	PAUSA DE BLANCA	PAUSA DE REDONDA
½ TIEMPO	1 TIEMPO	2 TIEMPOS	4 TIEMPOS

FIGURA E

Toque la canción con y sin PRO.

178

CANCION 13 — THE GAMBLER

DIMENSION ☐1 Arregle la registración y toque la canción THE GAMBLER.

PEDAL-ACORDE-PEDAL-ACORDE DE RITMO (4/4)

DIMENSIONS ☐2 ☐3

Un pedal es tocado en el primer y tercer compas y el acorde es tocado en el segundo y cuarto compas, como se muestra en la Figura A. Recuerde tocar las notas B como B bemol. Practique el pedal de acorde de ritmo en THE GAMBLER, hasta que se sienta bien tocandolo.

NOTA: **DIMENSION** ☐2 — Si no está usando el bajo automático, toque el acompañamiento como se muestra en la Figura A.

◆ 180

CANCION 14 — NADIA'S THEME

DIMENSIONS ☐1 ☐2 ☐3

NUEVOS ACORDES

DIMENSION ☐1

Para tocar el acorde menor de abajo, simplemente toque el MINOR TOUCH con el dedo pulgar mientras toca la llave del acorde indicado. Asegúrese de apagar el Key Selector.

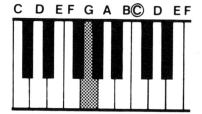
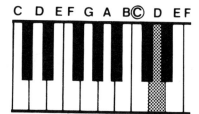
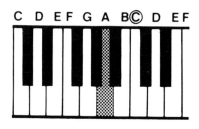

FIGURE A

DIMENSION ☐2

NOTA: Los pedales son opcionales en la **DIMENSION** ☐2

FIGURA B

53

DIMENSION 3

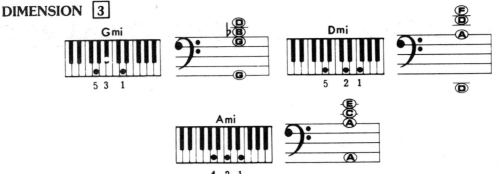

FIGURA C

VARIACION EN RITMO 4/4

DIMENSIONS 2 3

Cuando usted escucha a los organistas profesionales, usted encontrará que no siempre toca el mismo patrón de ritmo en sus acompañamientos. Varios patrones o estilos son mezclados con el ritmo básico, para agregar variedad e interés. NADIA'S THEME usa una variedad en el patrón de acorde de pedal.

NOTA DE REGISTRACIONES: Algunos de los controles anotados en las registraciones posiblemente no se encuentren en su instrumento. Ignore esos controles.

◆182

CANCION 15 — YOU LIGHT UP MY LIFE

NUEVO ACORDE

DIMENSION 1

A7   E

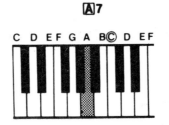
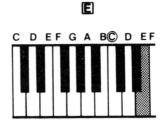

FIGURA A

DIMENSION 2

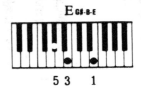

54 2 1   5 3 1

FIGURA B

NOTA: Los pedales son opcionales en la **DIMENSION** 2 .

DIMENSION 3

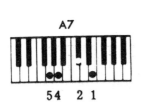

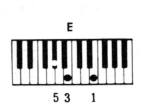
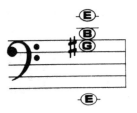

54 2 1   5 3 1

FIGURA C

PEDAL-ACORDE-ACORDE DE RITMO (3/4)

DIMENSIONS [2] [3]

Un pedal es tocado en el primer compas, y el acorde es tocado en el segundo y tercer compas (A).

BECUADROS

DIMENSIONS [1] [2] [3]

Los becuadros aparecen en varios compases en la canción 15, están usados en dos formas, para cancelar los sostenidos y bemoles.

1. En el compas ⑰ , los signos becuadros cancelan la nota anterior de B♭. Toque esta parte de la canción en la clave de C.

2. En otros compases, los becuadros cancelan temporalmente los sostenidos y bemoles en la signatura de la clave. Están en efecto solamente en el compás en en cual aparecen.

DIMENSION [1]

Una nota cuarta de acorde menor, el séptimo menor (m7), es usado en esta canción. Igual que con otros acordes menores, simplemente toque Minor Touch como cuando toca la clave de acorde.

CANCION 16 — FEELINGS

NUEVO ACORDE

DIMENSION [1]

Para tocar un acorde menor, simplemente toque el MINOR TOUCH mientras toca la clave de acorde indicada.

|G| |E|m7 |B|7

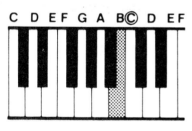

FIGURA A

DIMENSION [2]

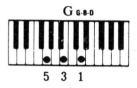
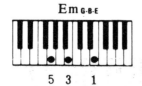
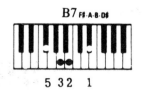

FIGURA B

DIMENSION 3

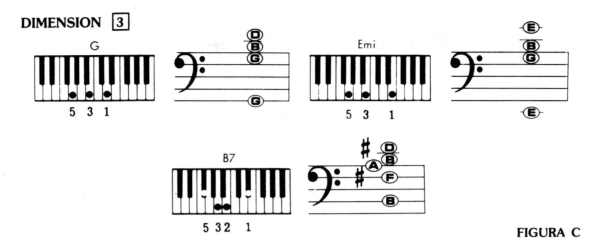

FIGURA C

NOTA: El pedal es opcional en la **DIMENSION** 2 .

NOTA: DIMENSION 3 Algunas veces su mano izquierda toca notas simples en el acompañamiento; esto es llamado contramelodía.

Trate de tocar la melodia para esta canción una octava más alta que la anotada.

187

CANCION 17 — AFTER THE LOVIN'

NUEVO ACORDE

DIMENSION 1

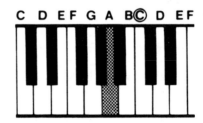

FIGURA A

DIMENSION 2

FIGURA B

NOTA: Los pedales son opcionales en la **DIMENSION** 2 .

DIMENSION 3

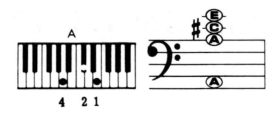

FIGURA C

Toque la melodia para esta canción, una octava más alta que la anotada.

190

CANCION 18 – BREAKING UP IS HARD TO DO

DIMENSIONS ☐1 ☐2 ☐3

RUBATO (Tocando Libremente)

Una palabra italiana que significa "robado", indica libertad con respecto al tiempo y al ritmo de la melodía. El músico puede "robar" de ciertas notas el valor propio por medio de tocarlas un poco más rápido y un poco más lentamente.

En la canción 18, BREAKING UP IS HARD TO DO, toque los primeros ocho compases en rubato. En el noveno compás, presione REALRHYTHM y la batería cesará automáticamente cuando usted presione cualquiera de los pedales o una nota en el teclado inferior.

NUEVO ACORDE

DIMENSION ☐1

Para tocar un acorde menor 1, simplemente toque el MINOR TOUCH CON EL DEDO pulgar, mientras toca el acorde de clave indicado.

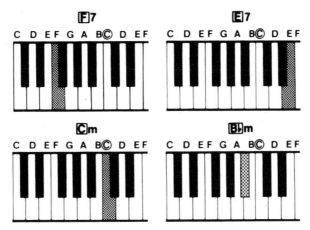

FIGURA A

DIMENSION ☐2

NOTA: Los pedales son opcionales en la **DIMENSION** ☐2 .

FIGURA B

DIMENSION ☐3

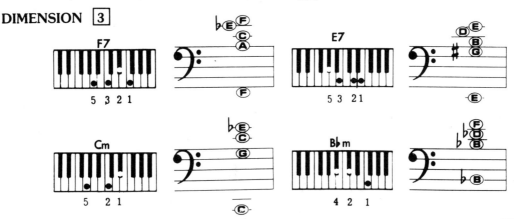

FIGURE C

Toque la melodía para esta canción una octava más alta que la anotada.

193

57

CANCION 19 — YOU ARE THE SUNSHINE OF MY LIFE

DIMENSION [1] Prepare la registración y toque YOU ARE THE SUNSHINE OF MY LIFE.

DIMENSIONS [2] [3]
NOTAS ALTERNADAS DE PEDAL

En todos los acordes que usted ha aprendido hasta ahora, generalmente ha tocado la nota que nombra cada acorde en la parte del pedal; esta nota es generalmente conocida como la raíz del acorde. La Figura A ilustra estos acordes y sus raíces, los cuales están marcados con la letra R.

Para darle mas interes y variedad a su música, debera de saber que otras notas de un acorde pueden ser tocadas con los pedales. La nota que mas se usa se llama la "quinta" ("fifth") del acorde; por ahora, sin embargo, a estas otras notas de acordes nos referimos como a notas alternativas. Las notas alternativas tambien se muestran en la Figura A en la columna marcada A.

ACORDE	R	A
C	C	G
F	F	C
G	G	D
D	D	A
A	A	E
E	E	B
B	B	F♯
B♭	B♭	F

FIGURA A 196

CANCION 20 — COLOUR MY WORLD

DIMENSIONS [1] [2] [3]
TRECILLOS DE CORCHEAS

El trecillo es un grupo de tres notas que se tocan por la misma cantidad de tiempo que tomaría tocar dos notas del mismo tipo. Es fácil reconocer un trecillo porque las tres notas están generalmente unidas al número tres sobre la nota de en medio.

En la Figura A, cada grupo de corcheas (1) y cada trecillo (2) reciben el mismo valor de tiempo, un compas o golpe de pie. Practique (2) hasta que le sea posible tocar el trecillos de corcheas, dándole a cada nota la misma cantidad de tiempo.

Una sugerencia para ayudarlo a tocar (2) parejo: Recite "Hip-pe-ty-Hop-pe-ty, etc." tocando una nota en cada sílaba.

198

La Figura B usa trecillos de corcheas en combinacion con otras notas. Practique la Figura B hasta que pueda tocarla facilmente y sin dudas. En forma de ayuda, golpee con su pie y cuente en voz alta los números arriba del pentagrama.

NUEVO ACORDE

DIMENSION 1

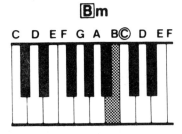

FIGURA C

DIMENSION 2

5 2 1

NOTA: Los pedales son opcionales en la **DIMENSION** 2 .

FIGURA D

DIMENSION 3

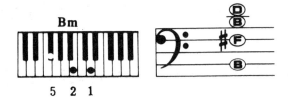

5 2 1

FIGURA E

CANCION 21 — GAMES PEOPLE PLAY

REGISTRACION

DIMENSIONS 1 2 3

Registración — la técnica de hacer cambios de tonalidades musicales — es una de las formas mas sencillas de añadirle interés a las melodías. Es fácil aprender a hacer cambios de registración durante una canción y hacer su ejecución más impresionante. Recuerde estos puntos cuando esté tratando de crea nuevos registros para su música.

1. El cambio debe ser obvio. La nueva registración debe contrastar con el sonido previo.

2. Los cambios de crear nuevos registros para su música.

3. Mantenga el ritmo constante. No ponga una pulsación extra con el propósito de cambiar la registración.

4. Mantenga los movimiento simples. Determine cuanto tiempo tiene, y haga únicamente los cambios que sean posibles de acuerdo a su límite de tiempo. Arregle los movimientos de una nota larga de acuerdo con el ritmo. A veces es necesario "robar" pulsaciones de una nota larga de melodía. Use las pulsaciones "robadas", para presionar las tablillas nuevas, — como regla general, una tablilla por pulsación. Vea la Figura A.

Escrito en esta forma:

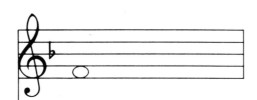

Tocado de esta forma:

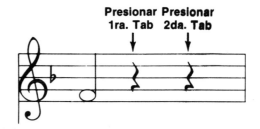

Presionar Presionar
1ra. Tab   2da. Tab

FIGURA A

CUANDO CAMBIAR

Es una buena idea usar diferentes sonidos para tocar una canción, pero no haga ningún cambio, que provoque música confusa. Algunos apropiados lugares para cambiar su registración son:

1. Entre la introducción y el cuerpo de la canción.

2. Entre versos de la canción.

3. Cualquier descanso natural en la canción.

NOTA: La regla número 2 se usa en la Canción 21 en las medidas, ⑦, ⑮, y ㉓.

200

CANCION 22—WONDERLAND BY NIGHT

REGISTRACIONES: CAMBIOS DE RITMO

DIMENSIONS ☐1☐ ☐2☐ ☐3☐

La canción 22 muestra como se le puede agregar variedad a su música, por medio del cambio de ritmos en la canción. En el compás ⑧ agregue BOSSA NOVA, y en el compás ⑯ apague el BOSSA NOVA.

202

RECUERDE: Algunas veces es necesario "robar" pulsaciones de una nota de melodía para poder presionar a tiempo las tablillas del ritmo.

CANCION 23—IT WAS ALMOST LIKE A SONG

DIMENSIONS ☐1☐ ☐2☐ ☐3☐

D.S. AL CODA ⊕

En la canción 23, encontrará la frase *D.S. al CODA* ⊕. Esto le indica que debe regresar al signo (𝄋) que se encuentra al principio de la canción, y que debe repetir todo hasta que se encuentren con signo coda (⊕). Despúes sin parar, vaya directamente al signo de coda y termine la canción. *Coda* es el término italiano para "cola" e indica una sección adicional de la canción la cual es usada como final.

SEMI CORCHEAS

Cuando están escritas solas, la semicorchea se parece a la corchea con una bandera extra agregada a la plica. Cuando las semicorcheas aparecen en grupos de dos o mas, las plicas están unidas por medio de dos barras.

FIGURA A

El valor de tiempo de la semicorchea es la mitad de una corchea y un cuarto de una negra. Usted ya ha aprendido que cada pulsación puede ser dividida en dos partes iguales . . . un número y la palabra "y" . . . para contar la nota corchea con facilidad.

Cuando usted cuenta semicorcheas, cada pulsación puede ser dividida en cuatro partes iguales. Cada parte es indicada por medio de una sílaba, como se muestra en la Figura B.

Toque la Figura B en tiempo lento, mientras cuenta en voz alta y golpea con el pie. Toque cuatro semicorcheas para cada golpe de su pie. Asegúrese de tocarlas uniformes y sin titubear.

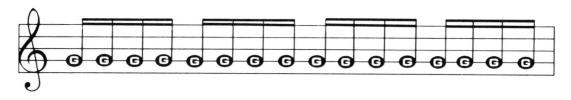

CUENTE:1 — a — & — a   2 — a — & — a   3 — a — & — a   4 — a — & — a

FIGURA B

El siguiente ritmo de práctica incorpora *D.S. al Coda* y semicorcheas. Practique hasta que lo pueda tocar pareja y suavemente.

204
205

CANCION 24— DISCO o BLUES

DIMENSION ☐1☐ ☐2☐ ☐3☐

Además de WALTZ, todos los demás ritmos del FUNMACHINE están basados en tiempos de "cuatro por cuatro". Básicamente la única diferencia musical entre ellos es el "sentido" del ritmo creado por el bajo, acordes y batería. Muchas canciones pueden ser tocadas con diferentes ritmos; esto no significa que la melodía es tocada en forma diferente — una nota completa todavía tiene 4 pulsaciones, y la mitad de la nota dos pulsaciones, etc. . . .

La próxima canción puede tocarse con cualquier ritmo de FunMachine (además del Waltz), sin embargo, Disco, Jazz Rock, y Ballas Rock trabajaran bien con esta canción.

Cuando escuche una canción que lo haga sentir deseos de levantarse a bailar, vaya a su órgano y prepare el ritmo automático a esa velocidad. Escuche la canción y preguntese, "Qué clase de instrumento esta tocando . . . trompeta, saxofón, piano? Qué clase de instrumento está tocando en el fondo? Escuchando sus obras favoritas y haciendose estas preguntas, usted podrá decidir con facilidad qué clase de instrumentos desea en su propio arreglo.

La siguiente canción DISCO o Blues, es una canción divertida; úsela con diferentes ritmos de FunMachine.

207

COMO FORMAR ACORDES

Un acorde es un grupo de notas formadas de ciertos tonos de la escala mayor.

- Acordes mayores están formados por medio de la combinacion de la primera, tercera, y quinta nota de la escala mayor.

- Acordes menores están formados por medio de la combinacion de la primera, tercera baja y la quinta nota de la escala mayor.

- Acorde séptimo por medio de la combinación de las notas primera, tercera, quinta y séptima de la escala mayor.

- Acordes séptimos menores, están formados de la combinación de las notas primera, tercera baja, quinta, séptima bemol de la escala mayor.

Abajo encontrará una lista de todas las escalas mayores:

	1	2	3	4	5	6	7	8
C	C	D	E	F	G	A	B	C
F	F	G	A	Bb	C	D	E	F
Bb	Bb	C	D	Eb	F	G	A	Bb
Eb	Eb	F	G	Ab	Bb	C	D	Eb
Ab	Ab	Bb	C	Db	Eb	F	G	Ab
Db	Db	Eb	F	Gb	Ab	Bb	C	Db
Gb	Gb	Ab	Bb	B	Db	Eb	F	Gb
B	B	C#	D#	E	F#	G#	A#	B
E	E	F#	G#	A	B	C#	D#	E
A	A	B	C#	D	E	F#	G#	A
D	D	E	F#	G	A	B	C#	D
G	G	A	B	C	D	E	F#	G

Ejemplo:

C = 1-3-5 of C Scale = C-E-G

Fm = 1-b3-5 of F Scale = F-Ab-C

G7 = 1-3-5-b7 of G Scale = G-B-D-F

Dm7 = 1-b3-5-b7 of D Scale = D-F♮-A-C♮

INVERSIONES DE ACORDES

Las notas de un acorde pueden ser previamente arregladas y el acorde no perderá su identidad. Este arreglo es conocido como inversión.

Ejemplo:

Acorde C = C - E - G

Inversión del acorde C son: E - G - C y G - C - E

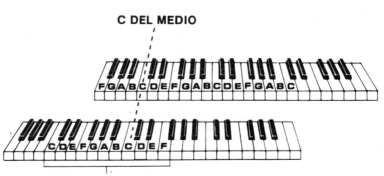

C DEL MEDIO

ACORDE DE ACOMPAÑAMIENTO

El acompañamiento de la mano derecha suena mejor si los acordes están tocando como se muestra en la figura de arriba. También facilita el cambio de un acorde a otro.

SYSTÈME D'APPRENTISSAGE EN TROIS DIMENSIONS

TABLE

BIENVENUE . . .

au système d'apprentissage Baldwin en trois dimensions . . . une nouvelle approche agréable de la musique. Ce système unique vous permet de choisir votre méthode pour apprendre la musique et pour apprendre à jouer de l'orgue Baldwin.

DIMENSION 1 Facile

CLAVIER SUPÉRIEUR ou
SOLO: Votre main droite joue une mélodie à un doigt avec des notes "qui portent leur nom".

CLAVIER INFÉRIEUR ou
ACCOMPAGNEMENT: Votre main gauche joue un accord d'accompagnement à un doigt, représenté par de petits symboles d'accords placés au-dessus de la mélodie (**C**).

PÉDALE: FunMachine de Baldwin joue automatiquement la basse pour vous.

From the Columbia Pictures Release "YOU LIGHT UP MY LIFE"
YOU LIGHT UP MY LIFE

Words and Music by
JOE BROOKS

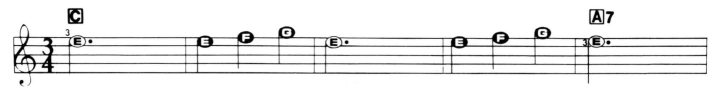

DIMENSION 2 Accord

CLAVIER SUPÉRIEUR ou
SOLO: Votre main droite joue la mélodie écrite en notation traditionnelle. Au fur et à mesure que le cours progresse, la mélodie s'augmentera progressivement de notes supplémentaires et d'expression rythmique.

CLAVIER INFÉRIEUR ou
ACCOMPAGNEMENT: Votre main gauche joue des accords à trois ou quatre notes.

PÉDALE: Soit a) utilisez FunChords de Baldwin pour jouer automatiquement les notes de basse, b) jouez les basses sur les pédales avec votre pied gauche.

From the Columbia Pictures Release "YOU LIGHT UP MY LIFE"
YOU LIGHT UP MY LIFE

Words and Music by
JOE BROOKS

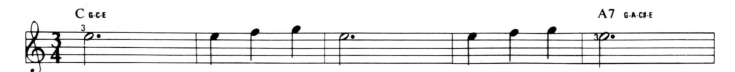

DIMENSION 3 Traditionnelle

SOLO:

Votre main droite joue la même ligne de mélodie que **DIMENSION** 2 .

ACCOMPAGNEMENT
et PÉDALE:

Vous lirez et jouerez la main gauche et les notes de basse. Celles-ci sont écrites avec des notes "qui portent leur nom".

From the Columbia Pictures Release "YOU LIGHT UP MY LIFE"

YOU LIGHT UP MY LIFE

Words and Music by
JOE BROOKS

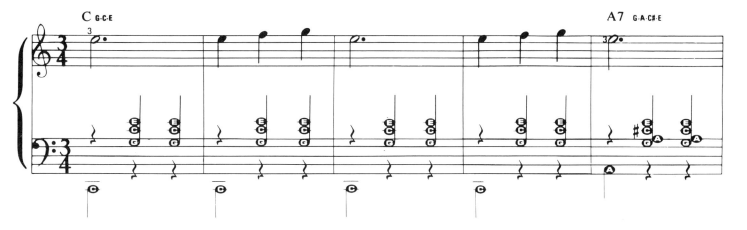

QUELLE DIMENSION CHOISIR?

S'il s'agit de votre première expérience musicale, **DIMENSION** 1 est la plus facile. Vous apprendrez rapidement à jouer vos airs favoris, tout en apprenant la musique.

Si vous avez déjà quelques notions de musique, vous pouvez commencer ce cours par la **DIMENSION** 2 .Vous lirez vos mélodies favorites en notation traditionnelle (pas de lettre dans les notes), et vous apprendrez à créer un accompagnement en formant des accords avec la main gauche.

NOTE: Si vous possédez FunMachine, vous pouvez utiliser **DIMENSION** 1 ou 2 ; ne pas tenir compte de **DIMENSION** 3 .

Si vous êtes capable de lire la musique, ou que vous désirez l'apprendre, choisissez **DIMENSION** 3 Vous déchiffrerez des arrangements pour orgue à deux portées, avec des techniques telles que des motifs pédale — accord, ou l'harmonie à deux parties dans la mélodie, etc.

ET SI JE DÉSIRE ESSAYER
UNE AUTRE DIMENSION?

Ce n'est pas parce que vous commencez avec une **DIMENSION** que vous devez poursuivre avec celle-ci jusqu'à la fin du cours. Si vous décidez d'en essayer une autre, repartez simplement d'un point qui vous semble familier et continuez à partir de là avec la nouvelle **DIMENSION.**

VOTRE ORGUE BALDWIN

Pour vous familiariser avec votre orgue Baldwin, LISEZ le manuel de l'utilisateur. Celui-ci donne une information détaillée et les instructions de fonctionnement pour toutes les caractéristiques et les commandes de votre instrument. Gardez-le sous la main pour pouvoir le consulter fréquemment.

GUIDES DE CLAVIER

Toutes les orgues Baldwin ont des lettres d'identification placées au-dessus des touches blanches. Celles-ci se rapportent aux guides de clavier.

REGISTRATION

L'ARRANGER de Baldwin est une caractéristique étonnante de registration automatique. Lorsque l'ARRANGER est allumé, une registration complète est sélectionnée automatiquement pour vous.

Celle-ci comprend les claviers solo et accompagnement, les voix de basse et les contrôles de mouvement appropriés. L'ARRANGER choisit automatiquement une registration différente et adaptée à chaque rythme choisi. Quand tous les rythmes sont éteints, L'ARRANGER sélectionne un ensemble de flûtes. Lorsque vous arrêtez l'ARRANGER, vous pouvez essayer vos propres registrations. Consultez dans le Manuel de l'utilisateur, la liste des registrations proposées.

NOTE; Les registrations utilisées dans ce livre conviennent à tous les modèles d'orgue Baldwin. Réglez simplement les touches et les effets que vous possédez sur votre orgue et ne vous occupez pas des autres.

EXÉCUTION DES MÉLODIES

Dans un orchestre, la mélodie d'un morceau peut être jouée par des instruments comme la flûte ou la trompette. A l'orgue, celle-ci est généralement jouée de la main droite sur le clavier supérieur ou solo. Les mélodies sont faites de sonorités musicales spécifiques. Pour représenter ces sons, des notes sont placées sur une portée, comme le montre la figure A. La portée se compose de cinq lignes et de quatre interlignes et chacune porte une lettre de A à G. Chaque note qui apparaît sur une des lignes ou dans un interligne est appelée par cette lettre. Ce cours utilise "des notes qui portent leur nom"; associez simplement les lettres des notes aux lettres de votre guide de clavier.

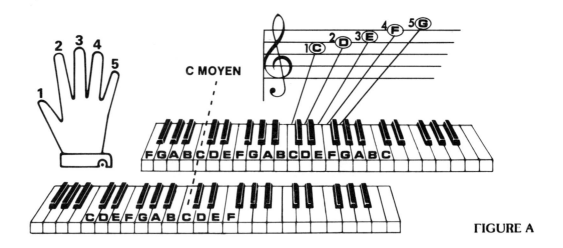

FIGURE A

Le symbole 𝄞 au début de la portée est appelé clé de sol et signifie que toutes les notes doivent être jouées de la main droite. Sont également illustrées les cinq premières notes de mélodie C, D, E, F et G et leurs touches correspondantes. Pour vous aider à jouer ces notes à la main droite, des chiffres sont placés à côté de chaque note, vous indiquant quel doigt utiliser.

Placez votre main droite au-dessus des touches avec votre pouce sur le C qui suit le C moyen, comme l'indique la figure A. Posez doucement vos doigts sur les touches et jouez les cinq notes.

Note: Dans ce cours, le C moyen apparaît dans un cercle .

CHANSON 1 — WHISTLE WHILE YOU WORK

1. Jouez la mélodie suivante sur le clavier solo.

2. Tenez les notes blanches avec les lettres noires un peu plus longtemps que les notes noires avec les lettres blanches . . . nous reparlerons de cela plus tard.

3. Réglez le registration suivante et jouez WHISTLE WHILE YOU WORK dans les **DIMENSION** 1 ou 2 .

EXÉCUTION DE L'ACCOMPAGNEMENT

L'accompagnement sur un orgue consiste généralement en accords joués de la main gauche et leurs notes de basse correspondantes. Les accords sont représentés par des symboles d'accords qui sont de petits cadres contenant des lettres et qui sont placés au-dessus de la mélodie, dans chaque pièce musicale. Pour débuter, vous apprendrez deux accords, l'accord C et l'accord G 7.

Appuyez sur ARRANGER.

Exécution de l'accompagnement en . . .

DIMENSION 1 Enfoncez le bouton 1-FINGER ACCOMP situé dans la section EASY PLAYER de votre orgue Baldwin. Avec 1-FINGER ACCOMP, tout ce que vous avez à faire est d'appuyer sur la touche du clavier accompagnement qui correspond à la lettre du symbole d'accord. (FIGURE A) FunMachine joue automatiquement la basse pour vous.

NOTE: Pour annuler l'accompagnement automatique, appuyez sur le bouton STOP.

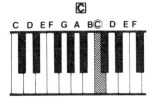
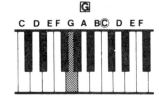

FIGURE A

DIMENSION 2 Jouez les notes d'accord situées à la droite du symbole d'accord (FIGURE B). Il y a deux façons d'obtenir les notes de basse: 1) Jouez-les vous-même en enfonçant la pédale du même nom que l'accord (FIGURE C) ou 2) appuyez sur FUNCHORDS et ces notes de pédale seront jouées automatiquement pour vous.

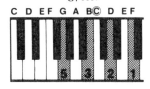

FIGURE B

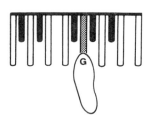

FIGURE C

DIMENSION 3 Les figures D et E de la page suivante vous montrent comment lire la clé de FA.

LA GRANDE PORTÉE

Dorénavant, chaque chanson est écrite sur une grande portée. Celle-ci comprend deux portées réunies par des barres, comme le montre la Figure D. Au début de la portée supérieure se trouve la clé de sol. Comme vous le savez déjà, celle-ci vous indique que les notes qui suivent sont jouées de la main droite sur le clavier solo. Au début de la portée inférieure, il y a un nouveau symbole appelé clé de FA. Celle-ci vous dit que les notes qui suivent sont jouées de la main gauche sur le clavier accompagnement et du pied gauche sur les pédales.

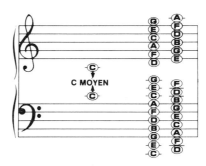

FIGURE D

C MOYEN

La note C qui apparaît sur la première ligne supplémentaire au-dessous de la clé de sol et sur la première ligne supplémentaire au-dessus de la clé de FA est appelée C moyen. Bien que le C moyen puisse être écrit de l'une ou l'autre façon, comme le montre la figure D, il s'agit de la même note. C moyen sur le clavier solo est toujours directement au-dessus de C moyen sur le clavier accompagnement. Il est représenté dans un cercle C sur les illustrations de clavier.

ACCORDS EN CLÉ DE FA

La Figure E montre l'emplacement sur la clé de FA des accords C et G7 et des pédales que vous avez joués. Les lettres des notes vous aident à repérer les touches correctes.

Note: Les lignes courbes dans **DIMENSION** ③ de la page suivante sont appelées liaisons — tenez les notes liées jusqu'à ce qu'un nouvel accord apparaisse.

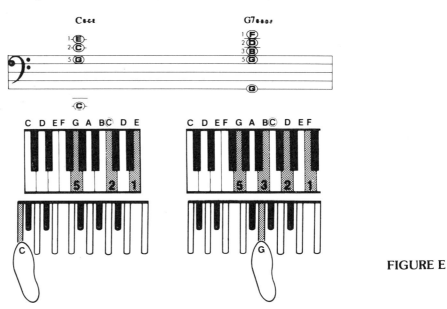

FIGURE E

DIMENSIONS ① ② ③ Réglez la registration et pratiquez l'accompagnement de la page suivante, dans la dimension choisie.

DIMENSION①

L'ARRANGER, allumé
ACCOMPAGNEMENT
   A UN DOIGT, allumé
LE KEY SELECTOR C, allumé
LE MEMORY, fermé

DIMENSION②

L'ARRANGER, allumé
Pour basse automatique:
FUNCHORDS, allumé
MEMORY, fermé

DIMENSION③

L'ARRANGER, allumé

NOTE: Certaines caractéristiques comme le KEY SELECTOR ne sont pas disponibles sur certain instruments Baldwin. Lorsque vous verrez des directives à suivre mais qui ne sont pas applicables à votre instrument, passez tout simplement outre l'instruction en question.

154

JOUER AVEC RHYTHME

DIMENSIONS ☐1 ☐2 ☐3

Le rythme est la base de la musique. Etre capable de jouer avec les caractéristiques automatiques de Baldwin sera une expérience très encourageante.

Outre qu'elle vous indique la touche à jouer, chaque type de note a une valeur de temps spécifique qui est mesurée en temps (ou battements) musicaux. L'illustration suivante montre les quatre types de notes que vous jouerez dans les premiers morceaux.

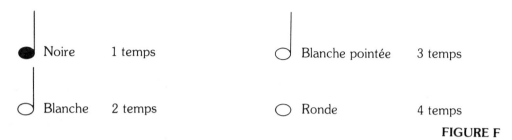

Noire   1 temps   Blanche pointée   3 temps

Blanche   2 temps   Ronde   4 temps

FIGURE F

L'exercice vous aidera à comprendre le rythme:

1. Coordonnez le rythme de la mélodie avec la batterie automatique.

2. Coordonnez l'exécution des accords avec la batterie automatique.

3. Coordonnez l'exécution de la mélodie avec celle de l'accompagnement.

Lorsque vous aurez joué à plusieurs reprises une note de mélodie et un accord d'accompagnement, vous serez à ce moment-là capable d'utiliser le rythme automatique. Allumez la batterie et écoutez... remarquez comme ceci s'apparente aux notes de la ligne du haut. Si la batterie vous paraît trop rapide ou trop lente, réglez la vitesse de rythme à un tempo confortable. Jouez la touche E avec votre troisième doigt. Voici quelques suggestions pour vous aider à jouer plus facilement.

Suggestions pour la pratique:

1. Jouez la musique. Ceci implique de repérer les touches correctes de la mélodie et de l'accompagnement, en observant le doigté conseillé, et en introduisant chaque nouvelle information musicale. Travaillez tout cela sans quitter des yeux la partition.

2. Jouez de nouveau mais mentalement. Cela signifie lire la musique sans la jouer. Essayez d'"entendre" la mélodie dans votre tête et imaginez comment résonne chaque accord lorsque son symbole apparaît dans la musique. Fredonner la mélodie peut aider.

3. Regardez la partition et jouez mentalement en même temps qe le RealRhythm automatique. Lorsque vous "entendez" la musique, remarquez comment elle s'accorde aux sons de la batterie.

4. Rejouez la musique avec la batterie. A ce moment, vous serez familiarisé avec ce que vous êtes en train de jouer.

NOTE: Sur les orgues Baldwin à boutons pressiors allumés, le fait d'allumer un jeu, allume souvent un autre jeu automatiquement. Sur les modèles à boutons mécaniques, il faut choisir chaque fonction individuellement. Totes les touches nécessaires a la régistration sont indiquées; si vous possedez un instrument à boutons pressoirs allumés, certaines touches se mettrons en marche automatiquement.

Dès maintenant, le mot "allumé" (on) ne sera plus indique; toutes les touches ou régistrations indiquées devraient être allumées à moins d'avis contraire.

Servez-vous de la régistration qui suit pour débuter avec le Melody Rhythm.

DIMENSIONS ☐1 ☐2 ☐3

ACCOMPANGNEMENT AU UN DOIGT,

    Le KEY SELECTOR C
(FANCY) FUNBASS
PRO fermé MEMORY fermé
L'ARRANGER
REALRHYTHM

Le FOX TROT
Reglez le tempo à une vitesse
confortable comme 3½ ou
le Conductor = 100

Pour brancher la batterie, pressez
le bouton STOP.

NOTE: **DIMENSIONS** ① ② ③ utilisent le bouton 1-FINGER ACCOMP pour pratiquer les exercices d'échauffement. Ceci vous aidera à vous concentrer sur la façon dont le rythme de la mélodie résonne avec la batterie.

Jouez la pièce musicale au complet avec le rythme, en utilisant la régistration appropriée:

DIMENSION ①	**DIMENSION** ②	**DIMENSIONS** ① ② ③
ACCOMPAGNEMENT A UN DOIGT	Pour basse automatique: FUNCHORDS	L'ARRANGER (FANCY) FUNBASS MEMORY PRO REALRHYTHM FOX TROT TEMPO 3½/ The Conductor - 100

CHANSON 2 — CARNAVAL DE VENISE

DIMENSIONS ① ② ③

UNE NOUVELLE NOTE

La note A est introduite dans ce morceau et est ilustrée à la figure A. Lorsque vous apprenez de nouvelles notes de mélodie pour la main droite, utilisez le doigté suggéré. Ceci vous permet de jouer les cinq premières notes sans que vos doigts se chevauchent.

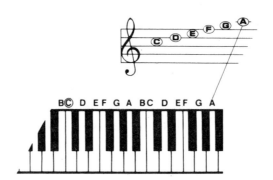

FIGURE A

MESURES

La Figure B montre comment la portée est divisée en sections égales par des lignes verticales appelées barres. Les sections entre les barres sont appelées mesures.

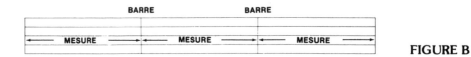

FIGURE B

MESURES À LA CLÉ

Les deux chiffres au début de chaque morceau sont appelés mesures à la clé. Voir Figure C. Le chiffre supérieur indique le nombre de temps dans chaque mesure. Dans la Figure C, le chiffre inférieur indique que chaque noire reçoit un temps. La chanson CARNAVAL DE VENISE a une mesure à 4/4 temps.

FIGURE C

LIAISONS

Une ligne courbe reliant deux notes placées sur la même ligne ou dans le même espace est appelée liaison. Une liaison indique que la première note doit être jouée et tenue pendant un temps égal à la valeur totale des deux notes. Dans la Figure D, le premier groupe de notes liées est tenu pendant une durée totale de quatre temps et le second groupe pendant une durée totale de six temps. NOTE: Etant donné que seule la première note d'un groupe de notes liées est attaquée, les suivantes ne comportent pas de lettre de notation.

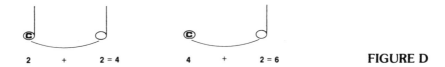

FIGURE D

A compter de maintenant, les régistrations sont indiquées en haut de la "Phase préparatoire" ou au dessus de la pièce musicale. Lorsque le symbole se manifeste avant ou après un jeu, CE JEU NE DOIT PAS ETRE ALLUME.

NOTE: Aucune régistration spéciale ne sera donnée pour Dimensions 1, 2 ou 3. A partir de maintenant, suivez ces directives.

DIMENSION 1

Ajoutez ces jeux aux régistrations suggerées:
ACCOMPAGNEMENT A UN DOIGT
(FANCY) FUNBASS
MEMORY au choix
REALRHYTHM

DIMENSION 2

Ajoutez ces jeux aux régistrations suggerées:
(FANCY) FUNBASS
MEMORY au choix
REALRHYTHM
Pour basse automatique, ajoutez FUNCHORDS

DIMENSION 3

Ajoutez ces jeux aux régistrations suggerées
(FANCY) FUNBASS
MEMORY au choix
REALRHYTHM

Le KEY SELECTOR indique pour chaque chanson n'est que <u>pour DIMENSION 1</u> seulement.

Pratiquez la phase préparatoire dit "MELODY RHYTHM WARMUP" en premier, ensuite jouez la pièce musicale. **157**

CHANSON 3 — MARIANNE

DIMENSIONS 1 2 3

UNE NOUVELLE NOTE

La chanson 3 introduit la note B.

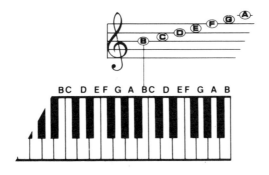

NOTE: Observez le doigté dans les mesures ⑥ et ⑭ .

Pratiquez l'exercice d'échauffement pour MARIANNE en utilisant la batterie automatique. **158**

Jouez la pièce musicale en utilisant la régistration suggerée. Souvenez-vous de la note au sujet de la régistration (plus haut). **159**

CHANSON 4 — BORN TO LOSE

DIMENSIONS ☐1 ☐2 ☐3

OCTAVE

Dans la figure A, les nouvelles notes C, D, E, F et G sont huit notes plus basses que le C, D, E, F et G que vous avez appris auparavant. Cet intervalle de huit notes est appelé OCTAVE, qui vient d'un mot latin qui signifie "huit".

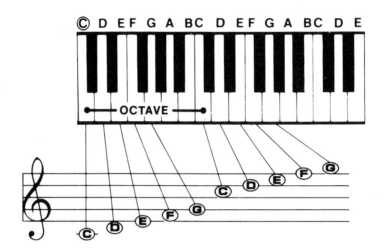

FIGURE A

DOIGTÉ DE SUBSTITUTION

Il y a des endroits dans ce morceau où vous verrez deux chiffre indiquant le doigté, placés sous une seule note (3-1), comme le montre la Figure B. On appelle ceci Doigté de substitution, ce qui signifie qu'il faut d'abord enfoncer la touche avec le doigt indiqué par le premier chiffre, ensuite, tout en tenant la touche abaissée, remplacez votre doigt par celui indiqué par le deuxième chiffre. Cette substitution prépare votre main à attaquer les notes suivantes.

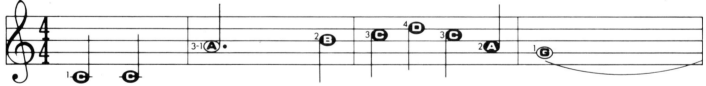

FIGURE B

UN NOUVEL ACCORD

L'accord de F majeur est illustré dans les Figures C, D et E.

DIMENSION ☐1

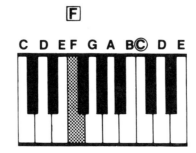

FIGURE C

72

DIMENSION ②

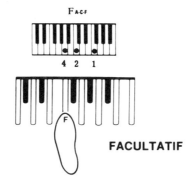

FACULTATIF

FIGURE D

DIMENSION ③

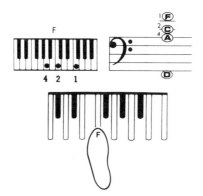

FIGURE E

ANACROUSE

Très souvent, un air commence par une ou plusieurs notes dont la valeur de temps n'équivaut pas à une mesure complète. Les notes de cette mesure incomplète sont appelées ANACROUSE. Les temps manquants se trouvent toujours dans la dernière mesure du morceau. Dans la plupart des cas, les notes de l'anacrouse sont jouées avant d'attaquer l'accord d'accompagnement.

Pratiquez l'exercice d'échauffement pour BORN TO LOSE en utilisant la batterie automatique. ◆ **160**

◆ **161**

CHANSON 5 — VALSE DES PATINEURS

DIMENSIONS ① ② ③

UNE NOUVELLE MESURE DE TEMPS

La chanson 5 utilise une nouvelle mesure à 3/4 temps. Comme vous le savez déjà, le 4 vous dit qu'une noire reçoit un temps. Le chiffre supérieur, 3, indique qu'il y a trois temps dans chaque mesure. Cette mesure de temps représente le rythme de la valse.

Pratiquez l'exercice d'échauffement pour LA VALSE DES PATINEURS en utilisant la batterie automatique. ◆ **162**

Jouez la pièce musicale et la mélodie, un octave plus haut qu'indiqué.

◆ **163** 73

CHANSON 6 — CHOPSTICKS

DIMENSIONS ① ② ③

SILENCES

Un silence est un symbole musical qui représente une période de repos. Les silences ont des valeurs de temps égales à leurs notes correspondantes. Trois types de silences sont montrés à la Figure A.

Une noire dure un temps.
Un soupir reçoit aussi un temps. (1)
Une blanche dure deux temps.
Une demi-pause reçoit aussi deux temps. (2)
Une ronde dure quatre temps.
Une pause (3) reçoit quatre temps (ou une mesure complète).

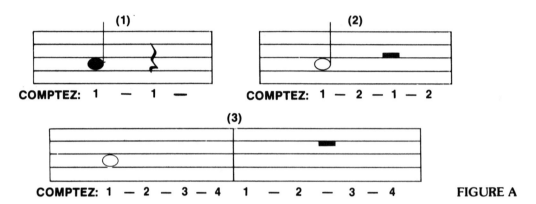

FIGURE A

SIGNES DE REPRISE

Plusieurs arrangements musicaux nécessitent qu'un fragment ou la chanson entière soit joué deux fois. Au lieu de réimprimer ces passages, des symboles musicaux appelés signes de reprise sont utilisés pour indiquer quel fragment est à rejouer.

Les signes de reprise apparaissent le plus souvent par séries de deux . . . un signe au début de la partie à rejouer et un signe à la fin.

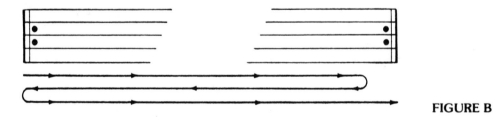

FIGURE B

Quand vous atteignez le second signe de reprise, revenez au premier et répétez toutes les mesures comprises entre les deux signes.

De temps en temps, vous ne trouverez qu'un signe de reprise à la fin d'une partie ou à la fin du morceau, comme le montre la figure C. Jouez jusqu'au signe, revenez au début du morceau et rejouez. S'il y a encore de la musique après le signe de reprise, continuez à jouer.

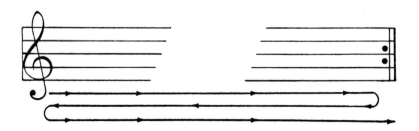

FIGURE C

Une chanson peut aussi contenir plus d'une série de signes de reprise, comme le montre la Figure D.

Lorsque cela se produit, jouez deux fois toutes les mesures comprises entre les deux premiers signes de reprise. Ensuite, jouez deux fois toutes les mesures comprises entre les deux autres signes de reprise. Dans chaque cas, revenez toujours au signe de reprise le plus proche.

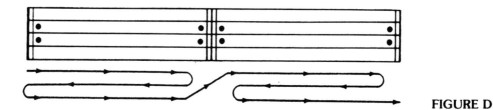

FIGURE D

FINALES DOUBLES

CHOPSTICKS contient des signes de reprise conjugués avec un autre symbole musical, la finale double, ainsi que le montre la Figure E.

Quand vous jouez CHOPSTICKS pour la première fois, exécutez la mesure marquée par le crochet portant le chiffre 1, à savoir, la première finale. Jouez jusqu'au signe de reprise et revenez au signe de reprise du début. Après avoir joué l'air une deuxième fois, sautez la première finale (1) et exécutez les mesures marquées par le crochet portant le chiffre 2, à savoir, la second finale.

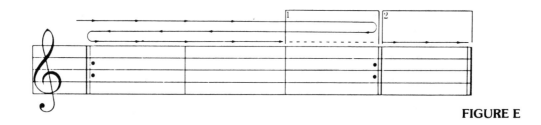

FIGURE E

CROISEMENT DE DOIGTS

Dans les mesures ⑫ , ⑬ , ⑰ et ⑱ , les chiffres de doigté indiquent ce qu'on appelle un croisement de doigts. Lorsque vous tenez la note A avec votre pouce droit (mesure ⑫ , passez pardessus (➤) avec votre majeur pour jouer la note G plus basse de la mesure ⑬ . Lorsque vous tenez la note F avec votre index droit (mesure ⑰ , passez dessous (➤) avec votre pouce pour jouer la note G plus élevée de la mesure ⑱ .

EXÉCUTION DE DOUBLES NOTES DANS LA MÉLODIE

DIMENSIONS ☐2 ☐3

Lorsque vous jouez plus d'une note à la fois, différentes combinaisons de doigts doivent être utilisées, selon les notes jouées et le mouvement correspondant de votre main droite au-dessus de votre clavier.

Pour votre facilité, suivez les chiffres de doigté suggérés à côté des notes. Si un motif mélodique similaire apparaît plus d'une fois dans une chanson, seul le premier motif indiquera le doigté.

Jouez la pièce musicale et la mélodie un octave plus haut qu'indiqué.

NOTE DE REGISTRATION: Lorsque les voix, ou jeux, sont indiqués pour le clavier Supérieur, le clavier Inférieur ou Pédalier (comme pour CHOPSTICKS), assurez-vous que l'ARRANGER est fermé.

◆164

75

CHANSON 7 — CHAMPAGNE POLKA

DIMENSIONS ☐1 ☐2 ☐3

CHAMPAGNE POLKA est le premier morceau dans lequel vous jouerez des touches noires. Celles-ci sont appelées dièses ou bémols. Avant d'étudier les dièses et les bémols, il est très important pour vous, cependant, de comprendre les tons et les demi-tons.

DEMI-TONS

Un demi-ton est la distance entre deux touches adjacentes qui n'ont aucune touche entre elles. Il existe trois manières de former des demi-tons.

1. En reliant une touche blanche à une touche noire.
2. En reliant une touche noire à une touche blanche.
3. En reliant une touche blanche à une touche blanche. 166

TONS

Deux demi-tons égalent un ton. Il y a quatre manières de former des tons.

4. Entre une touche blanche et une touche blanche, en sautant une touche noire.
5. Entre une touche noire et une touche noire, en sautant une touche blanche.
6. Entre une touche blanche et une touche noire, en sautant une touche blanche.
7. Entre une touche noire et une touche blanche, en sautant une touche blanche.

La Figure B montre qu'il y a toujours une touche intermédiaire dans la formation d'un ton. 166

DIÈSES ET BÉMOLS

Dans cette chanson et dans les sélections ultérieures, vous verrez fréquemment ces signes (♯) (♭) placés devant certaines notes sur la portée. ces signes sont appelés dièses et bémols et ils sont utilisés pour indiquer que les tons sont haussés ou abaissés d'un demi-ton.

♯ Un DIÈSE placé devant une note indique que le son de cette note doit être élevé d'un demi-ton.

♭ Un BÉMOL placé devant une note indique que le son de cette note doit être abaissé d'un demi-ton.

La Figure C reproduit quelques notes dièses et bémols ainsi que leur emplacement sur le calvier. 166

Lorsqu'un dièse ou un bémol est placés devant une note dans une mesure donnée, ce signe affecte toutes les notes identiques qui suivent dans cette mesure.

REGISTRATION

A partir de maintenant, les registrations et les réglages de tempo sont encore indiqués sur la page de titre de chaque chanson. Une fois ceux-ci essayés, n'hésitez pas à en essayer d'autres. 167

CHANSON 8 — LAVENDER'S BLUE

DIMENSIONS ☐1 ☐2 ☐3

CROCHES

Jusqu'à présent, vous avez joué quatre différents types de notes: ronde, blanche, blanche pointée et noire. La chanson 8 introduit la croche.

Lorsqu'elle est écrite seule, une croche ressemble à une noire avec un petit drapeau attaché au bout de sa tige. Lorsque les croches sont écrites par groupe de deux ou davantage, les tiges sont reliées par une barre.

Une croche vaut la moitié d'une noire. En conséquence, deux croches sont égales à une noire.

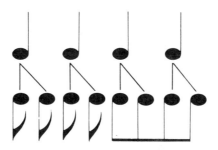

FIGURE A

DEMI-TEMPS ET BATTEMENT DE LA MESURE DES CORCHES

Quand vous battez la mesure des croches, chaque temps simple doit être divisé en deux parties égales, un temps fort et un temps faible. Cette notion peut être plus facilement comprise, si vous pensez à frapper du pied en mesure avec la musique. Chaque frappement de pied se divise en deux parties, un temps fort et un temps faible. Le temps fort est désigné par un chiffre et le temps faible par le mot "et" (&).

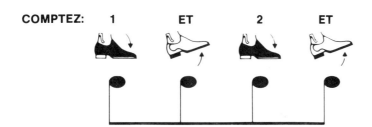

COMPTEZ: 1   ET   2   ET

FIGURE B

EXERCICE DE CROCHES

Pratiquez la figure C jusqu'à ce que vous puissiez le jouer en douceur et régulièrement, sans hésitation. Pour vous aider à exécuter ce premier exercice, frappez du pied et comptez à haute voix pendant que vous jouez.

UN NOUVEL ACCORD

L'accord D7 est illustré dans les Figures D, E, et F.

DIMENSION 1

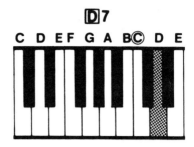

FIGURE D

DIMENSION 2

FIGURE E

DIMENSION 3

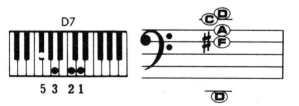

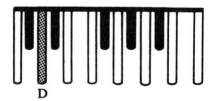

FIGURE F

Jouez l'exercice d'échauffement pour LAVENDER'S BLUE.   ◆ 169

Jouez la pièce musicale. Souvenez-vous que l'ARRANGER doit être fermé.   ◆ 170

CHANSON 9 — SPANISH EYES

DIMENSIONS 1 2 3

NOUVELLES NOTES

Les nouvelles notes utilisées dans la chanson 9 sont A et A♭, et toutes deux figurent sur des lignes supplémentaires au-dessus de la portée.

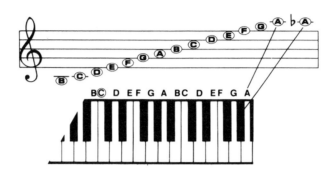

FIGURE A

NOUVEL ACCORD

L'accord mineur est introduit dans ce morceau. Les accords mineurs sont identifiés par un petit "m" qui suit la lettre dans le symbole d'accord.

DIMENSION 1

Pour jouer un accord mineur, effleurez simplement MINOR TOUCH avec votre pouce, tout en jouant la note d'accord indiquée.

FIGURE B

DIMENSION 2

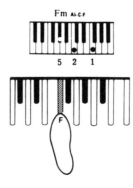

FIGURE C

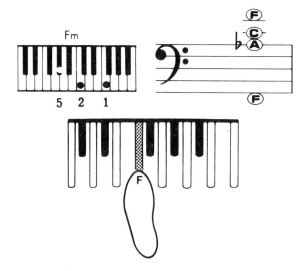

FIGURE D

PRO

Ce bouton ajoute automatiquement des notes d'harmonie à la mélodie. Ces notes d'harmonie sont basées sur les accords que vous jouez.

Jouez la pièce musicale et la mélodie un octave plus haut qu'indiqué.

CHANSON 10 — SNOWBIRD

DIMENSION ①

Mettez la registration en place et jouez SNOWBIRD.

RYTHMES PÉDALE-ACCORD (4/4)

DIMENSIONS ② ③

Un rythme pédale-accord peut être joué dans des morceaux à 4/4 temps. Ceci est illustré à la figure A. Une pédale est jouée sur les premier et troisième temps tandis que l'accord est maintenu.

NOTE: **DIMENSION ②** — Si vous n'utilisez pas la basse automatique, jouez le même accompagnement que celui montré à la figure A.

Pratiquez l'exercice d'échauffement (B) avec la registration.

Quand vous jouerez ce dernier en douceur et avec expression, pratiquez l'exercice (C).

Lorsque vous jouerez celui-ci en douceur et avec expression, attaquez l'arrangement complet de SNOWBIRD.

CHANSON 11 — AMAZING GRACE

DIMENSION 1

Mettez en place la registration et jouez AMAZING GRACE.

RYTHMES PÉDALE-ACCORD (3/4)

DIMENSIONS 2 3

Vous vous rappelez qu'une mesure à 3/4 temps signifie qu'il y a trois temps dans chaque mesure. Dans le motif de rythme de la valse, une pédale est jouée sur le premier temps et un accord sur le second temps, comme le montre la figure A.

NOTE: **DIMENSION** 2 — Si vous n'utilisez pas la basse automatique, jouez l'accompagnement de la figure A.

Pratiquez l'accompagnement (Accompaniment Rhythm Warmup) en phase préparatoire. (FIGURE A). Utilisez la régistration indiquée.

Lorsque vous jouerez ce dernier en douceur et avec expression, pratiquez l'exercice (B).

Quand vous jouerez celui-là en douceur et avec expression, attaquez la chanson AMAZING GRACE.

Pour un son d'orgue classique, fermez le TREMOLO. Essayez cette chanson avec, ou sans, le rythme automatique et avec, ou sans, le PRO.

Jouez la mélodie un octave plus haut qu'indiqué.

CHANSON 12 — MAKE THE WORLD GO AWAY

DIMENSIONS 1 2 3

ARMATURES

Dans la plupart des chansons, vous verrez un ou plusieurs dièses ou bémols imprimés au début de la musique entre le signe de clé et la fraction indiquant la mesure, comme le montre la Figure A. Ceci s'appelle une armature. Par exemple, parce qu'un B bémol apparaît à l'armature de "Make The World Go Away", toutes les notes B du morceau sont jouées sur la touche B bémol. Dans la portée inférieure, le bémol qui apparaît à l'armature après la clé de fa s'applique à tous les B de la main gauche et du pédalier. Une chanson qui n'a ni dièse ni bémol à la clé est écrite dans la gamme de C majeur. Cet air a un bémol, B bémol et il est dans la gamme de F majeur.

NOTE: **DIMENSION** 1 — Les boutons Key Selector sont aussi identifiés par le nombre de bémols ou de dièses de l'armature.

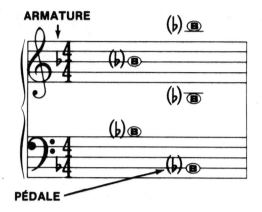

FIGURE A

NOUVEAUX ACCORDS

DIMENSION 1

Enfoncez le Key Selector F et jouez ces notes d'accord.

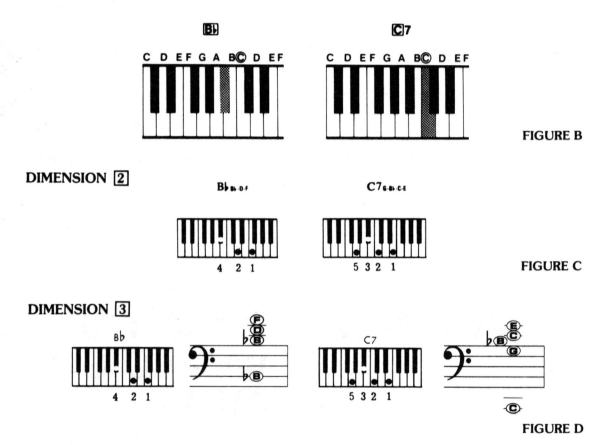

FIGURE B

FIGURE C

FIGURE D

DEMI-SOUPIRS

Vous avez déjà étudié les croches. La chanson 12 utilise la contrepartie silencieuse de la croche, le demi-soupir. Celui-ci, comme la croche, reçoit un demi-temps. Le demi-soupir est illustré à la figure E comme les autres silences déjà étudiés.

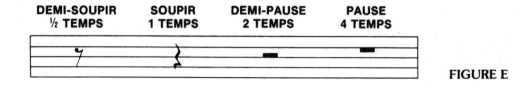

| DEMI-SOUPIR ½ TEMPS | SOUPIR 1 TEMPS | DEMI-PAUSE 2 TEMPS | PAUSE 4 TEMPS |

FIGURE E

Jouez la chanson avec, et sans, le PRO.

178

CHANSON 13 — THE GAMBLER

DIMENSION 1 — Mettez la registration en place et jouez THE GAMBLER.

RYTHME PÉDALE-ACCORD-PÉDALE-ACCORD (4/4)

DIMENSIONS 2 3

Une pédale est jouée sur les premier et troisième temps et l'accord est joué sur les second et quatrième temps, comme le montre la Figure A. N'oubliez pas de jouer les notes B en B bémol. Pratiquez les rythmes pédale-accord dans THE GAMBLER jusqu'à ce que vous les jouiez avec régularité.

◆ 180

NOTE: **DIMENSION** 2 — Si vous n'utilisez pas la basse automatique, jouez l'accompagnement de la Figure A.

CHANSON 14 — THÈME DE NADIA

DIMENSIONS 1 2 3

NOUVEAUX ACCORDS

DIMENSION 1

Pour jouer les accords mineurs ci-dessous, effleurez simplement MINOR TOUCH avec votre pouce tout en jouant la note d'accord indiquée. N'oubliez pas d'éteindre Key Selector.

Gm

Dm

Am

FIGURE A

DIMENSION 2

NOTE: Les pédales sont facultatives avec **DIMENSION** 2.

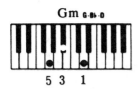

FIGURE B

DIMENSION 3

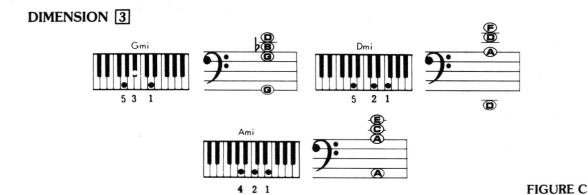

FIGURE C

VARIATION DU RYTHME À 4/4 TEMPS

DIMENSIONS 2 3

Quand vous écoutez un organiste professionnel, vous observerez qu'il ne joue pas toujours les même motifs de rythme dans son accompagnement. Des motifs variés sont mélangés au rythme de base pour ajouter diversité et intérêt. Le THÉME DE NADIA utilise la variété dans les motifs pédale-accord.

NOTE DE REGISTRAITON: Quelques une des touches suggerées dans la régistration ne sont peut être pas disponibles sur votre instrument. Oubliez ces suggestions.

182

CHANSON 15 — YOU LIGHT UP MY LIFE

NOUVEAUX ACCORDS

DIMENSION 1

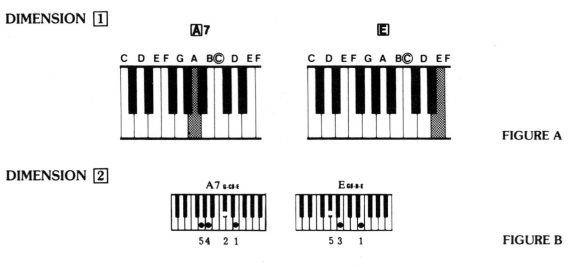

FIGURE A

DIMENSION 2

NOTE: Les pédales sont facultatives avec **DIMENSION 2** .

FIGURE B

DIMENSION 3

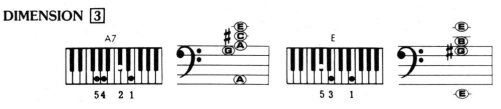

FIGURE C

RYTHME PÉDALE-ACCORD-ACCORD (3/4)

DIMENSION ☒ ☒

Une pédale est jouée sur le premier temps, et l'accord est joué sur les second et troisième temps (A). ◆184

BÉCARRES

DIMENSIONS ☒ ☒ ☒

Les bécarres (♮) apparaissent dans plusieurs mesures de la chanson 15. Ils sont utilisés de deux manières pour supprimer les dièses ou les bémols, à savoir:

1. Dans la mesure ⑰ , les bécarres annulent la précédente armature de B♭. Jouez cette partie de la chanson dans la gamme de C.

2. Dans d'autres mesures, les bécarres annulent temporairement les dièses ou les bémols à la clé. Ils sont effectifs uniquement dans le mesure où ils apparaissent.

DIMENSION ☒

Un accord mineur à quatre notes, l'accord de septième mineure (m7) est introduit dans ce morceau. Lorsque le Key Selector est en place, comme indiqué, FunMachine joue ces accords automatiquement. Comme pour les autres accords mineurs, effleurez simplement Minor Touch lorsque vous jouez la note d'accord. ◆184

CHANSON 16 — FEELINGS

NOUVEAUX ACCORDS

DIMENSION ☒

Pour jouer un accord mineur, effleurez simplement MINOR TOUCH tout en jouant la note d'accord indiquée.

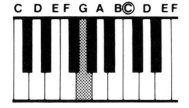

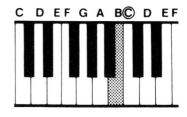

FIGURE A

DIMENSION ☒

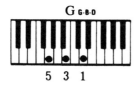

FIGURE B

DIMENSION 3

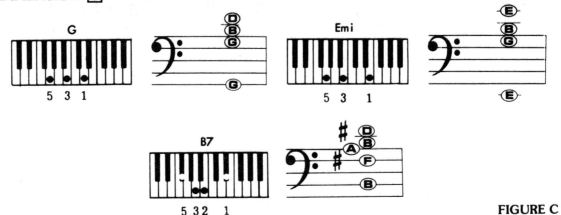

FIGURE C

NOTE: Les pédales sont facultatives avec **DIMENSION** 2 .

NOTE: **DIMENSION** 3 — De temps en temps, votre main gauche joue des notes seules dans l'accompagnement; ceci s'appelle une contre-mélodie.

Essayez de jouer la mélodie de cette pièce musicale, un octave plus haut qu'indiqué.

187

CHANSON 17 — AFTER THE LOVIN'

NOUVEL ACCORD

DIMENSION 1

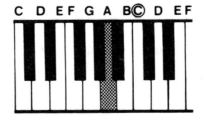

FIGURE A

DIMENSION 2

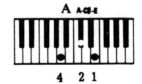

FIGURE B

NOTE: Les pédales sont facultatives avec **DIMENSION** 2 .

DIMENSION 3

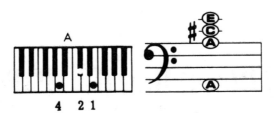

FIGURE C

Jouez la mélodie de cette pièce musicale, un octave plus haut.

190

CHANSON 18 – BREAKING UP IS HARD TO DO

DIMENSIONS ☐1 ☐2 ☐3

RUBATO (Style Libre)

Ce mot italien indique une liberté d'exécution en matière de tempo et de rythme. L'exécutant peut "tricher" sur la propre longueur de certaines notes en les jouant un peu plus vite ou plus lentement.

Dans la chason 18, BREAKING UP IS HARD TO DO, jouez les huit (8) premières mesures *rubato*. A la mesure ⑨, enfoncez REALRHYTHM et la batterie démarrera automatiquement lorsque vous enfoncez soit une pédale, soit une touche du clavier accompagnement.

NOUVEAUX ACCORDS

DIMENSION ☐1

Pour jouer un accord mineur, effleurez simplement MINOR TOUCH avec votre pouce tout en jouant la note d'accord indiquée.

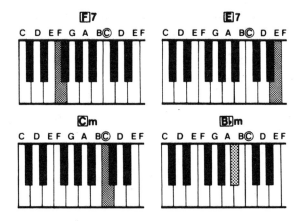

FIGURE A

DIMENSION ☐2

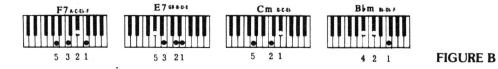

FIGURE B

NOTE: Les pédales sont favultatives avec **DIMENSION** ☐2 .

DIMENSION ☐3

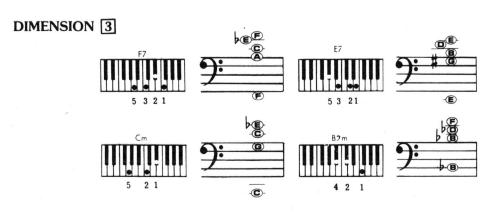

FIGURE C

Jouez la mélodie de cette pièce musicale, un octave plus haut.

CHANSON 19 — YOU ARE THE SUNSHINE OF MY LIFE

DIMENSION [1] — Mettez en place la registration qui suit et jouez YOU ARE THE SUNSHINE OF MY LIFE.

DIMENSIONS [2] [3] .

NOTES DE BASSE ALTERNÉES

Dans tous les accords étudiés jusqu'ici, vous avez joué normalement la note de pédale du même nom que l'accord; cette note est généralement appelée la fondamentale de l'accord. La Figure A illustre ces accords et leurs fondamentales, qui sont sous la rubrique R.

Pour ajouter variété et intérêt à votre jeu, il vous faut savoir que d'autres note d'un accord peuvent aussi être jouées sur les pédales. La note le plus souvent utilisée est appelée la "quinte" de l'accord; à partir de maintenant, cependant, ces autres notes d'accord sont mentionnées comme notes alternées. Celles-ci sont aussi montrées dans la Figure A, colonne A.

ACCORD	R	A
C	C	G
F	F	C
G	G	D
D	D	A
A	A	E
E	E	B
B	B	F♯
B♭	B♭	F

FIGURE A

◆ 196

CHANSON 20 — COLOUR MY WORLD

DIMENSIONS [1] [2] [3]

TRIOLETS DE CROCHES

Un triolet est un groupe de trois notes exécutées pendant le temps nécessaire pour jouer deux notes du même type. Il est facile de reconnaître le triolet parce qu'il y a habituellement un crochet au-dessus des trois notes avec le chiffre 3 au-dessus de la note du milieu.

Dans la Figure A, chaque groupe de deux croches (1) et chaque triolet (2) reçoivent la même valeur de temps, un temps ou un frappement de pied. Exercez-vous (2) jusqu'à ce que vous soyez capable de jouer les triolets de croches, en donnant à chaque note une égale valeur de temps. Un conseil pour vous aider à jouer (2) régulièrement: "Hip-pe-ty-Hop-pe-ty-Hip-pe-ty-Hop-pe-ty, etc." en jouant une note par syllable.

◆ 198

La Figure B utilise des triolets de croches en combinaison avec d'autres notes. Pratiquez celle-ci jusqu'à ce que vous jouiez sans hésitation. Pour vous aider, tapez du pied et comptez à voix haute au moyen des chiffres placés au-dessus de la portée.

NOUVEL ACCORD

DIMENSION 1

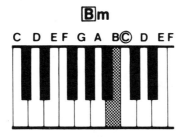

FIGURE C

DIMENSION 2

FIGURE D

NOTE: Les pédales sont facultatives avec **DIMENSION** 2 .

DIMENSION 3

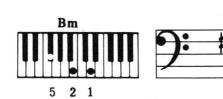

FIGURE E

CHANSON 21 — GAMES PEOPLE PLAY

REGISTRATION

DIMENSIONS 1 2 3

La Registration — technique de changement de tons en musique — est un des moyens les plus simples d'ajouter un intérêt considérable à votre jeu. Il est aisé d'apprendre à changer de registration au milieu d'une chanson et de rendre ainsi votre jeu plus captivant. Ayez toujours en tête les points suivants lorsque vous créez de nouvelles registrations:

1. Les changements doivent être évidents. La nouvelle registration doit contraster avec la sonorité précédente.

2. Les changements doivent refléter l'esprit de la musique.

3. Gardez le rythme à la même vitesse. N'ajoutez pas de temps supplémentaire dans une mesure uniquement pour changer la registration.

4. Jouez très simplement. Déterminez le temps dont vous disposez, et ne faites pas plus de changements que nécessaire. Accordez vos mouvements au rythme. Parfois, il est nécessaire de "voler" des temps à une longue note de mélodie. Utilisez ces temps pour enfoncer de nouvelle touches — en règle générale une touche par temps. Voir Figure A.

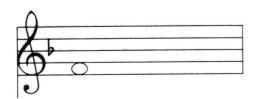

Ecrit comme ceci

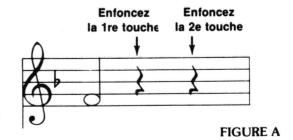

Joué comme ceci

Enfoncez la 1re touche   Enfoncez la 2e touche

FIGURE A

QUAND CHANGER?

C'est une bonne idée d'utiliser différentes sonorités dans une chanson, mais ne créez pas la confusion en faisant trop de changements. Les moments appropriés pour changer votre registration sont:

1. Entre l'introduction et le corps d'un morceau.

2. Entre les couplets d'une chanson.

3. Tout changement naturel dans la musique.

NOTE: La règle 2 est utilisée dans la chanson 21 aux mesures ⑦ , ⑮ et ㉓ .

200

CHANSON 22 — WONDERLAND BY NIGHT

REGISTRATION: CHANGEMENT DE RYTHME

DIMENSIONS ☐1 ☐2 ☐3

La chanson 22 montre comment ajouter de la variété à votre jeu en changeant de rythme au cours d'une chanson. Dans la mesure 8, ajoutez la BOSSA NOVA, et dans la mesure 16, arrêtez la BOSSA NOVA.

202

RAPPEL: Il est parfois nécessaire de "voler" des temps à une note de mélodie pour enfoncer les touches en mesure avec le rythme.

CHANSON 23—IT WAS ALMOST LIKE A SONG

DIMENSIONS ☐1 ☐2 ☐3

D.S. AL CODA⊕

Dans la chanson 23, vous verrez la phrase *D.S. al CODA* ⊕ . Cette expression vous dit de revenir au signe (⊕) au début du morceau et de répéter toutes les mesures jusqu'au signe du coda (⊕). Puis, sans vous arrêter, allez directement jusqu'au *coda* et finissez le morceau. *Coda* est un mot italien qui signifie "queue", employé en musique pour indiquer un fragment supplémentaire d'une chanson, utilisé comme finale.

DOUBLES CROCHES

Lorsqu'elle est seule, une double croche ressemble à une croche avec un drapeau supplémentaire attaché à sa tige. Lorsque des doubles croches sont groupées par deux ou plus, leurs tiges sont reliées par deux barres.

FIGURE A

La valeur de temps d'une double croche est la moitié de celle d'une croche et le quart d'une noire. Vous avez déjà appris que chaque temps peut être divisé en deux parties égales . . . un chiffre et le mot "et" . . . pour faciliter le compte des croches.

Quand vous battez la mesure des doubles croches, chaque temps peut être divisé en quatre parties égales. Chaque partie est indiquée par une syllabe séparée, comme le montre la figure B.

Jouez la Figure B à un tempo lent tout en comptant à voix haute et en tapant du pied. Apprenez à les jouer régulièrement et sans hésitation.

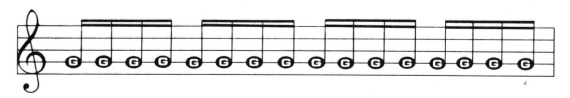

COMPTEZ: 1 — a — & — a   2 — a — & — a   3 — a — & — a   4 — a — & — a

FIGURE B

L'exercice suivant comprend le *D.S. al Coda* et des doubles croches. Exercez-vous jusqu'à ce que vous le jouiez en douceur et régulièrement.

◆ 204
◆ 205

CHANSON 24 — DISCO ou BLUES

DIMENSIONS ① ② ③

Excepté la valse, tous les autres rythmes de FunMachine sont basés sur un rythme à 4/4 temps. Fondamentalement, la seule différence musicale entre eux est la "sensation" rythmique créée par la basse, les accords et la batterie. Plusieurs chansons peuvent être jouées avec différents rythmes; ceci ne signifie pas que la mélodie soit exécutée différemment — une ronde dure toujours quatre temps, une blanche deux temps, etc.

Le morceau suivant peut être joué avec n'importe quel rythme de FunMachine (excepté la valse (WALTZ)), cependant, le Disco, Jazz Rock et Ballad Rock s'accorderont mieux à cet air.

Lorsque vous entendez une chanson qui vous donne envie de vous lever et de danser, installez-vous à votre orgue et réglez le rythme automatique à la même vitesse. Ecoutez le morceau et posez-vous la question, "De quelle sorte d'instrument s'agit-il . . . une trompette, un saxo, un piano? De quelle sorte d'instruments y-a-t'il à l'arrière-plan?" C'est en écoutant vos airs favoris et en vous posant ces questions que vous prendrez conscience des instruments que vous souhaitez dans votre propre arrangement.

Cette chanson DISCO ou BLUES est une chanson gaie; utilisez-la avec différents rythmes de FunMachine.

◆ 207   91

COMMENT FORMER DES ACCORDS

Un accord est un groupe de notes formé à partir de certains tons de la gamme majeure.

- Les accords majeurs sont formés par la combinaison de la première note, de la tierce et de la quinte de la gamme majeure.

- Les accords mineurs sont formés par la combinaison de la première note, de la tierce abaissée d'un demi-ton et de la quinte de la gamme majeure.

- Les accords de spetième sont formés par la combinaison de la première note, de la tierce, de la quinte et de la septième note abaissée d'un demi-ton, de la gamme majeure.

- Les accords de septième mineure sont formés par la combinaison de la première note, de la tierce abaissée d'un demi-ton, de la quinte et de la septième note abaissée d'un demi-ton, de la gamme majeure.

Ci-dessous une liste de toutes les gammes majeures:

	1	2	3	4	5	6	7	8
C	C	D	E	F	G	A	B	C
F	F	G	A	Bb	C	D	E	F
Bb	Bb	C	D	Eb	F	G	A	Bb
Eb	Eb	F	G	Ab	Bb	C	D	Eb
Ab	Ab	Bb	C	Db	Eb	F	G	Ab
Db	Db	Eb	F	Gb	Ab	Bb	C	Db
Gb	Gb	Ab	Bb	B	Db	Eb	F	Gb
B	B	C#	D#	E	F#	G#	A#	B
E	E	F#	G#	A	B	C#	D#	E
A	A	B	C#	D	E	F#	G#	A
D	D	E	F#	G	A	B	C#	D
G	G	A	B	C	D	E	F#	G

Exemple:

C = 1-3-5 de la gamme de C = C-E-G

Fm = 1-b3-5 de la gamme de F = F-Ab-C

G7 = 1-3-5-b7 de la gamme de G = G-B-D-F

Dm7 = 1-b3-5-b7 de la gamme de D = D-F♮-A-C♮

INVERSIONS D'ACCORDS

Les notes d'un accord peuvent être dans un ordre différent et l'accord ne perdra pas son identité. Ceci s'appelle une inversion.

Exemple:

Accord C = C-E-G

Les inversions de l'accord C sont: E-G-C et G-C-E

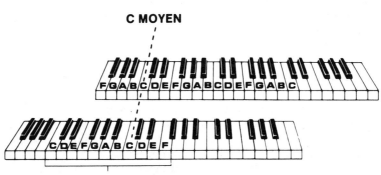

C MOYEN

ACCORD D'ACCOMPAGNEMENT

L'accompagnement de la main gauche résonne mieux si les accords sont joués suivant l'ordre présenté ci-dessus. Cela rend aussi plus facile le passage d'un accord à un autre.

Baldwin
DREI-DIMENSIONALES UNTERRICHTS-SYSTEM

INHALT

HERZLICH WILLKOMMEN . . .

zum Baldwin Unterrichtssystem in drei Dimensionen . . . einer neuen Methode, mit der das Musizieren Spaß macht! Bei diesem einzigartigen System können Sie selbst bestimmen, nach welcher Methode Sie alles über Musik lernen und Ihre Baldwin Orgel spielen wollen.

DIMENSION 1 Leicht

OBERES MANUAL: Mit der rechten Hand spielen Sie Ein-Finger-Melodien. Die Notennamen sind in die Noten eingedruckt.

UNTERES MANUAL: Mit der linken Hand spielen Sie Ein-Finger-Akkorde als Begleitung. Die Namen der Akkorde stehen als kleine Akkord-Symbole über der Melodie (C).

PEDAL: Die Baldwin FunMachine spielt die Baßtöne automatisch.

From the Columbia Pictures Release "YOU LIGHT UP MY LIFE"
YOU LIGHT UP MY LIFE

Words and Music by
JOE BROOKS

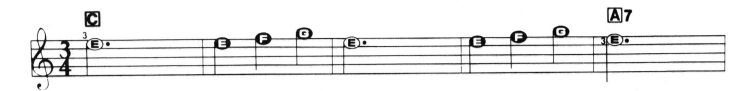

DIMENSION 2 Akkord

OBERES MANUAL: Mit der rechten Hand spielen Sie die Melodie, die in herkömmlicher Weise notiert ist. Im Verlauf des Lehrgangs werden die Melodien durch zusätzliche Noten und rhythmische Phrasierungen interessanter gemacht.

UNTERES MANUAL: Mit der linken Hand spielen Sie drei- und vierstimmige Akkorde.

PEDAL: Entweder verwenden Sie die Baldwin FunChords und die Pedaltöne werden automatisch gespielt, oder Sie spielen die Pedaltöne mit dem linken Fuß.

From the Columbia Pictures Release "YOU LIGHT UP MY LIFE"
YOU LIGHT UP MY LIFE

Words and Music by
JOE BROOKS

DIMENSION ③ Herkömmlich

OBERES MANUAL: Mit der rechten Hand spielen Sie die gleichen Melodienoten wie bei **DIMENSION** ②.

UNTERES MANUAL
und
PEDAL: Sie lesen und spielen die Noten für die linke Hand und für die Pedale. In diese Noten sind Buchstaben eingedruckt.

From the Columbia Pictures Release "YOU LIGHT UP MY LIFE"

YOU LIGHT UP MY LIFE

Words and Music by
JOE BROOKS

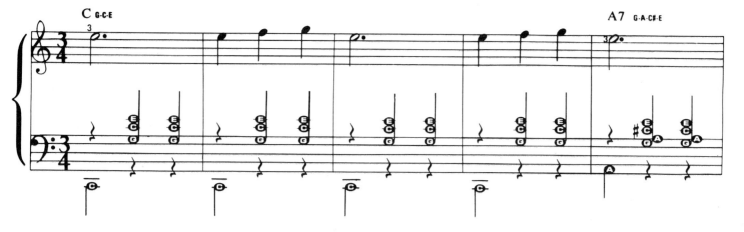

WELCHE DIMENSION SOLL ICH WÄHLEN?

Wenn Sie noch überhaupt keine musikalischen Kenntnisse haben, wäre **DIMENSION** ① am leichtesten für Sie. Sie werden schnell bekannte Melodien spielen können und dazu sehr viel über Musik lernen.

Wenn Sie sich schon mit Musik beschäftigt haben, fangen Sie am besten mit **DIMENSION** ② an. Sie werden die Melodien in der herkömmlichen Notierung lesen (ohne eingedruckte Buchstaben), und Sie werden lernen, wie Sie die Akkord-Begleitung mit der linken Hand nach Noten spielen können.

HINWEIS: Wenn Sie eine FunMachine mit einem Manual besitzen, können Sie entweder **DIMENSION** ① oder **DIMENSION** ② verwenden. Das Material von **DIMENSION** ③ kommt dann für Sie nicht in Frage.

Wenn Sie schon Noten lesen können, oder es lernen möchten, entscheiden Sie sich für **DIMENSION** ③. Sie werden Orgel-Bearbeitungen lesen, die auf doppelten Notensystemen notiert sind, mit BaßAkkord Figuren, zweistimmige Melodie-Passagen usw.

UND WENN ICH EINE ANDERE DIMENSION PROBIEREN MÖCHTE?

Wenn Sie mit einer **DIMENSION** angefangen haben, bedeutet das nicht, daß Sie dann unbedingt auf diese Weise bis zum Ende des Lehrgangs weitermachen müssen. Wenn Sie zu einer anderen **DIMENSION** überwechseln möchten, gehen Sie einfach zurück zu einem Punkt, wo Ihnen das Lernmaterial bekannt und vertraut vorkommt, und machen von dort an in der neuen **DIMENSION** weiter.

IHRE BALDWIN ORGEL

Wenn Sie sich mit Ihrer Baldwin Orgel vertraut machen wollen, LESEN Sie die Gebrauchsanleitung. Da finden Sie ausführliche Erklärungen und Bedienungsanleitungen für alle Vorrichtungen, und Schalter und Regler Ihres Instruments. Halten Sie die Gebrauchsanleitung immer bei der Hand, dann können Sie bequem etwas nachschlagen.

TASTENFÜHRER

Sämtliche Baldwin Orgeln haben Buchstaben über den weißen Tasten. Damit wird das Auffinden der Töne erleichtert.

DAS REGISTRIEREN

Der ARRANGER ist eine wunderbare automatische Registrier-Vorrichtung bei Ihrer Baldwin Orgel. Wenn die ARRANGER eingeschaltet ist, werden die Registrierungen automatisch für Sie eingeschaltet.

Das gilt sowohl für das obere und das untere Manual als auch für das Pedal und die entsprechenden Funktionsregister. Für jeden von Ihnen gewählten Rhythmus schaltet der ARRANGER automatisch eine passende Registrierung ein. Bei ausgeschaltetem Rhythmus schaltet der ARRANGER eine volle Orgel-Registrierung ein. Wenn Sie den ARRANGER ausschalten, können Sie die Registrierungen selbst nach Ihrem Geschmack einstellen. Zur Erleichterung finden Sie in der Gebrauchsanleitung ein Verzeichnis mehrerer Registrierungs-Vorschläge.

HINWEIS: Die bei den Musikstücken in diesem Buch erwähnten Registrierungen können bei den meisten Baldwin Orgelmodellen verwendet werden. Schalten Sie einfach die Register und Effekte ein, die es bei Ihrer Orgel gibt, und berücksichtigen Sie die anderen nicht.

DAS SPIELEN DER MELODIE

Im Orchester wird die Melodie von einem Solo-Instrument wie einer Flöte oder einer Trompete gespielt. Auf der Orgel wird die Melodie meistens mit der rechten Hand auf dem oberen Manual gespielt. Melodien bestehen aus bestimmten Tönen, aus Klänge mit einer bestimmten Tonhöhe. Diese Tönen, aus Klänge mit einer bestimmten Tonhöhe. Diese Töne werden in der Notenschrift durch Noten wiedergegeben. Die Noten werden auf einem System mit fünf Linien notiert, wie in Abbildung A. Das Notenliniensystem hat fünf Linien und vier Zwischenräume. Jede Linie und jedem Zwischenraum ist ein Buchstabe von A bis G zugeordnet. Die Noten tragen jeweils die entsprechenden Namen der Linien oder Zwischenräume. In diesem Lehrgang werden auch Noten mit eingedruckten Buchstaben verwendet. Sie entsprechen den Buchstaben über den weißen Tasten und helfen Ihnen, die richtigen Tasten zu finden.

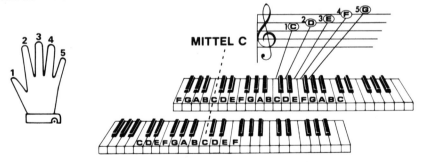

MITTEL C

ABBILDUNG A

Die S-förmige Figur am Anfang des Systems ist der Violinschlüssel, und deutet an, daß diese Noten mit der rechten Hand gespielt werden müssen. Die ersten fünf Noten C, D, E, F und G und die entsprechenden Tasten sind in der Abbildung gezeigt. Damit Sie wissen, mit welchem Finger Sie eine Note spielen sollen, sind neben den Noten kleine Zahlen gedruckt.

Fangen Sie mit der rechten Hand auf den Tasten des oberen Manuals an. Der Daumen kommt auf die Taste C (acht weiße Tasten höher als Mittel Ⓒ , wie in der Abbildung gezeigt). Lassen Sie die Finger locker auf den Tasten ruhen und spielen Sie die fünf Töne der Reihe nach.

HINWEIS: In diesem Lehrgang wird die Taste Mittel-C immer von einem Buchstaben C in einem Kreis Ⓒ angedeutet.

TITEL Nr. 1 – WHISTLE WHILE YOU WORK

Schritt 1: Spielen Sie die Melodie auf dem oberen Manual.

Schritt 2: Halten Sie die weißen Noten mit den schwarzen Buchstaben etwas länger fest als die schwarzen Noten mit den weißen Buchstaben . . . wir kommen darauf noch zurück.

Schritt 3: Schalten Sie die nachstehende Registrierung ein und spielen Sie WHISTLE WHILE YOU WORK entweder in **DIMENSION** ① oder ② .

DAS SPIELEN DER BEGLEITUNG

Bei der Orgel besteht die Begleitung meistens aus Akkorden, die mit der linken Hand gespielt werden, und den entsprechenden Baßtönen. Akkorde werden als Akkord-Symbole notiert. Das sind kleine Kästchen mit einem Buchstaben, die an den entsprechenden Stellen über der Melodie stehen. Für den Anfang lernen Sie zwei Akkorde: den ⊡C⊡ Akkord und den ⊡G⊡ 7 Akkord.

Schalten Sie den ARRANGER ein.

Für das Spielen der Begleitung in . . .

DIMENSION ① Drücken Sie die Taste 1-FINGER ACOMP in der EASY PLAYERS Gruppe Ihrer Baldwin Orgel. Alles was Sie jetzt zu tun haben, ist diejenige Taste auf dem unteren Manual zu drücken, die dem Buchstaben im Akkord-Kästchen entspricht. (ABBILDUNG A). Die FunMachine wird dazu automatisch den Baß spielen.

HINWEIS: Mit der Taste STOP können Sie die automatische Beleitung ausschalten.

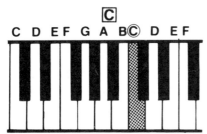
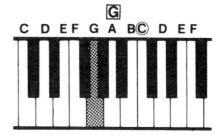

ABBILDUNG A

DIMENSION ② Spielen Sie die Akkordtöne, die neben dem Akkord-Symbol stehen (ABBILDUNG B). Für die Baßtöne gibt es zwei Möglichkeiten: 1) Sie spielen mit dem linken Fuß das Pedal mit dem gleichen Namen wie der Akkord (ABBILDUNG C), oder: 2) Sie drücken die Taste FUNCHORDS. Dann werden die Baßtöne automatisch zu den Akkorden gespielt.

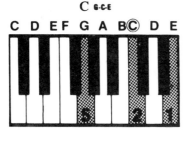
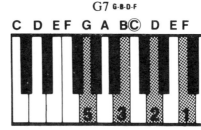

ABBILDUNG B

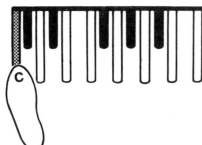
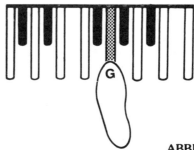

ABBILDUNG C

DIMENSION ③ In den Abbildungen D und E auf der nächsten Seite wird gezeigt, wie der BaßSchlüssel gelesen wird.

DAS DOPPELTE NOTENSYSTEM

Von nun an werden die Musikstücke auf doppeltem Notensystem notiert. Das doppelte Notensystem besteht aus zwei einzelnen Notensystemen, die durch Taktstriche wie im Abbildung D gezeigt verbunden sind. Am Anfang des oberen Systems steht der Violin-Schlüssel. Wie Sie schon wissen, deutet dieser an, daß die Noten auf dem oberen System mit der rechten Hand auf dem oberen Manual gespielt werden müssen. Am Anfang des unteren Notensystems sehen Sie ein neues Zeichen: der BaßSchlüssel. Dieser deutet an, daß die Noten auf dem unteren System mit der linken Hand auf dem unteren Manual gespielt werden müssen.

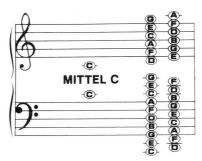

ABBILDUNG D

MITTEL C

Die Note auf der ersten Hilfslinie unter dem oberen System und auf der ersten Hilfslinie über dem unteren System heißt MITTEL C. Obwohl diese Note in zwei verschiedenen Lagen wie in der Abbildung D gezeigt notiert werden kann, ist es die gleiche Note. Die Taste MITTEL C auf dem oberen Manual liegt immer direkt über der Taste MITTEL C vom unteren Manual. In den Zeichnungen wird MITTEL C immer mit einem Buchstaben C im Kreis angedeutet.

AKKORDE IM BAß-SCHLÜSSEL

In der Abbildung E sehen Sie die Noten der Akkorde C und G7, zusammen mit den zugehörigen Baßnoten für die Pedale. Merken Sie sich die Lage dieser Noten, und gehen Sie dabei vom MITTEL C aus. Die Buchstaben in den Noten erleichtern Ihnen das Auffinden der Tasten.

HINWEIS: Die gebogenen Linien in der **DIMENSION** ③ auf der nächsten Seite sind sogenannte Haltebogen. Halten Sie bei den Noten mit einem Haltebogen die Tasten so lange fest, bis ein neuer Akkord kommt. Auf die Haltebogen kommen wir noch zurück.

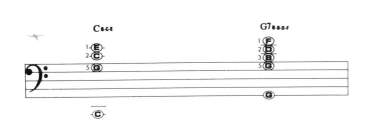

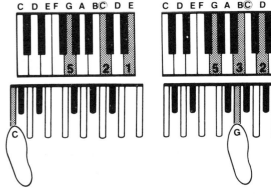

ABBILDUNG E

DIMENSIONEN ① ② ③ Schalten Sie die Register ein und üben Sie die Begleitung je nach der von Ihnen gewählten Dimension.

DIMENSION 1	DIMENSION 2	DIMENSION 3
THE ARRANGER an 1-FINGER ACCOMP. an KEY SELECTOR C an MEMORY aus	THE ARRANGER an Für auto. bass: FUNCHORDS an MEMORY aus	THE ARRANGER an

BEMERKUNG: Bestimmte Bestandteile wie KEY SELECTOR sind an manchen Baldwin Orgeln nicht vorhanden. Wenn Sie deshalb einen Hinweis lesen, wie Sie einen bestimmten Standteil gebrauchen sollten, ihn aber nicht an Ihrer Orgel finden, schenken Sie dem Hinweis keine Beachtung.

DAS SPIELEN MIT DEM RHYTHMUSGERÄT

DIMENSIONEN ① ② ③

Der Rhythmus ist die Grundlage aller Musik. Wenn Sie das Spielen mit dem Baldwin Rhythmus-Gerät beherrschen, haben Sie einen sehr lohnenden Schritt vorwärts getan.

Die Noten deuten nicht nur an, welche Tasten gespielt werden sollen. Je nach ihrer Form haben die Noten auch einen bestimmten Zeitwert, der in der Musik in Taktschlägen gemessen wird. In der nachstehenden Abbildung sehen Sie vier verschiedene Notentypen, die in den nächsten Stücken vorkommen.

♩ Viertelnote	1 Taktschlag	♩. Halbe Note mit Punkt	3 Taktschläge
♩ Halbe Note	2 Taktschläge	○ Ganze Note	4 Taktschläge

ABBILDUNG F

Damit Ihnen das Spielen mit dem Rhytmus-Gerät leichter fällt, sind Melodie/Rhythmus-Vorübungen sehr zu empfehlen:

1. Üben Sie die Melodie zusammen mit dem Rhythmus-Gerät.

2. Üben Sie die Akkorde zusammen mit dem Rhythmus-Gerät.

3. Üben Sie die Melodie und die Begleitung zusammen.

Da Sie bei diesem Stück häufig einen Melodieton und einen Akkord zusammen anschlagen werden, können Sie den automatischen Rhythmus von Anfang an gleich verwenden. Schalten Sie das Rhythmus-Gerät ein und hören Sie zu . . . merken Sie sich den Zusammenhang zwischen den Noten auf dem oberen System und dem Rhythmus. Wenn Ihnen der Rhythmus zu schnell oder zu langsam vorkommt, können Sie das Tempo entsprechend nachstellen. Spielen Sie die Taste E mit dem dritten Finger. Folgende Hinweise werden Ihnen helfen, die Stücke schneller einzuüben:

Hinweise für das Üben:

1. Spielen Sie das Stück am Instrument durch. Dazu sollen Sie die richtigen Melodie- und Akkordtöne suchen, den vorgeschlagenen Fingersatz beachten und die neuen Begriffe kennenlernen. Lassen Sie die Augen nicht von den Noten und arbeiten Sie alles geduldig durch.

2. Spielen Sie das Stück im Kopf durch. Das heißt: Versuchen Sie das Stück zu lesen, ohne es zu spielen. Versuchen Sie, die Melodie im Kopf zu "hören", und wenn ein neues Akkordsymbol erscheint, stellen Sie sich vor, wie dieser Akkord klingen wird. Summen Sie die Melodie, das ist oft eine große Hilfe.

3. Spielen Sie jetzt die Melodie abermals im Kopf durch, schalten Sie dabei das RealRhythm-Gerät ein. Während Sie die Melodie im Kopf "hören", achten Sie darauf, wie die Töne mit dem Schlagzeug zusammentreffen.

4. Spielen Sie jetzt das Stück am Instrument durch, zusammen mit dem Rhythmusgerät. Jetzt haben Sie richtig gelernt, was Sie spielen wollen.

HINWEIS: Wenn man an Baldwin Orgeln mit leuchtenden Knöpfen einen besondesen Teil anstellt, schalten andere automatisch mit ein. An Orgeln mit mechanischem Druckknöpfen, ist es notwendig jede Tätigkeit einzeln zu wählen. Alle Bestandteile notwendig für jede Registration sind aufgeführt; falls Sie ein Instrument mit leuchtenden Knöpfen haben, einige von diesen werden automatisch für Sie eingeschaltet.

Hier beginnend wird das Wort "an" nicht mehr gedruckt werden; irgendwelche Bestandteile solltenals "AN" angesehen werden oder werden anders bemerkt sein.

Gebrauchen Sie folgende Registration vom in den Melodie Rhythmus-Schwung zu kommen.

DIMENSIONEN ☐1 ☐2 ☐3

1-FINGER ACCOMP., KEY SELECTOR C
(FANCY) FUNBASS
PRO aus, MEMORY aus
DER ARRANGER REALRHYTHM

FOX TROT
Setze das TEMPO auf eine beguemliche Zeit
wie z.B 3½ oder The Conductor = 100

Beginn das Schlagzeug, dürcke STOP.

HINWEIS: Für die **DIMENSIONEN** ☐1 , ☐2 und ☐3 sollte bei den Melodie/Rhythmus-Vorübungen die Tasten 1-FINGER ACCOMP eingeschaltet sein. Dann können Sie sich leichter darauf konzentrieren, wie Melodie und Rhythmus zusammenhägen.

Spiele das ganze Lied mit Rhythmus und gebrauche die dazugehörige Registration:

DIMENSION ☐1	DIMENSION ☐2	DIMENSIONEN ☐1 ☐2 ☐3
1-FINGER ACCOMP.	Für auto. bass: FUNCHORDS	THE ARRANGER· (FANCY) FUNBASS MEMORY PRO REALRHYTHM FOX TROT TEMPO 3½/ The Conductor ☐100☐

◆ 155

◆ 156

TITEL Nr. 2 - CARNIVAL OF VENICE
(Der Karneval Von Venedig)

DIMENSIONS ☐1 ☐2 ☐3

EINE NEUE NOTE

In diesem Stück kommt die neue Note A vor, wie in der Abbildung A gezeigt wird. Achten Sie bei den neuen Noten, die Sie lernen, auch auf den Fingersatz. Sonst haben Sie für das Spielen von mehr als fünf Tönen "nicht genügend Finger".

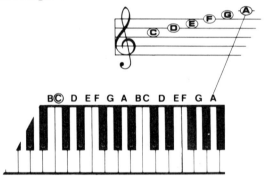

ABBILDUNG A

TAKTE

In Abbildung B wird gezeigt, wie das Notensystem durch vertikale Striche, sogenannte Taktstriche, in gleiche Abschnitte geteilt wird. Die Abschnitte nennt man: TAKTE.

TAKTSTRICH		TAKTSTRICH	
◄——— TAKT ———►	◄——— TAKT ———►	◄——— TAKT ———►	

ABBILDUNG B

TAKTBEZEICHNUNG

Die zwei Zahlen am Anfang eines Stückes nennt man die Taktbezeichnung (Abbildung C). Die obere Zahl deutet die Anzahl der Taktschläge in jedem Takt an. Die untere Zahl deutet an, welcher Notenwert auf einen Taktschlag kommt. In Abbildung C bedeutet die untere Zahl 4, daß auf einen Taktschlag jeweils eine Viertelnote kommt. Das Stück CARNIVAL OF VENICE steht im 4/4 Takt.

ABBILDUNG C

DER HALTEBOGEN

Ein Bogen, der zwei Noten auf der gleichen Notenlinie oder im gleichen Zwischenraum verbindet, nennt man einen Haltebogen. Der Haltebogen bedeutet, daß nur die erste Note angeschlagen werden soll und dann so lange gehalten wird, wie es dem Gesamtzeitwert der beiden Noten entspricht. In der Abbildung D wird die erste Gruppe von Noten mit einem Haltebogen insgesamt vier Taktschläge lang festgehalten. HINWEIS: Da nur der erste Ton angeschlagen werden soll, ist bei der zweiten Note kein Buchstabe eingedruckt.

2   +   2 = 4   4   +   2 = 6

ABBILDUNG D

Von hier an werden die Registrationen über jedem Lied gedruckt. Sollte vor oder hinter der Bestandteilbezeichnung das Zeichen Ø stehen, DAS BESTANDTEIL SOLLTE AUF AUS sein.

HINWEIS: Für die Dimensionen 1, 2 oder 3 werden keine besonderen Registration gegeben werden. Von hier an folgen Sie diese Anleitungen:

DIMENSION ①

Fügen Sie diese zu der angegebenen Registration hinzu:
1-FINGER ACCOMP.
(FANCY) FUNBASS
MEMORY wahlweise
REALRHYTHM

DIMENSION ②

Fügen Sie diese zu der angegebenen Registration hinzu:
(FANCY) FUNBASS
MEMORY wahlweise
REALRHYTHM
Für auto bass, auch
FUNCHORDS hinzu

DIMENSION ③

Fügen Sie diese zu der angebegenen Registration hinzu:
(FANCY) FUNBASS
MEMORY wahlweise
REALRHYTHM

Der KEY SELECTOR für jedes Lied angezeigt ist nur für Dimension ① .

Um in Schwung zu kommen, üben Sie erst die Rhythmus Melodie, dann spielen Sie das Lied.

◆ 157

TITEL Nr. 3 — MARIANNE

DIMENSIONEN ① ② ③

EINE NEUE NOTE

Im Titel Nr. 3 kommt die Note B zum ersten Mal vor.

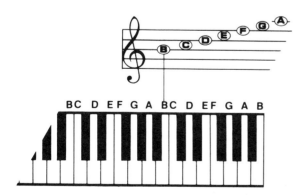

WICHTIGER HINWEIS: Die Noten in diesem Heft sind nach dem international üblichen Notensystem benannt. Dabei ist die Reihenfolge der Töne (nach den weißen Tasten): A B C D E F G. In deutschsprachigen Ländern ist jedoch die Reihenfolge A H C D E F G üblich. Wenn Sie Noten nach dem deutschen System verwenden, sollten Sie also anstelle von B ein H, und anstelle von B ein B lesen!

WICHTIG: Achten Sie in den Takten ⑥ und ⑭ besonders gut auf den Fingersatz.

Machen Sie die Melodie/Rhythmus-Vorübung für MARIANNE mit dem Rhythmus-Gerät.

◆◆ 158

Spiele das Lied und gebrauche die angegebene Registration. Erinnern Sie sich der Bemerkung über die Registration (oben).

◆ 159

TITEL Nr. 4 — BORN TO LOSE

DIMENSIONEN ☐1 ☐2 ☐3

DIE OKTAVE

Die neuen Noten C, D, E, F und G in der Abbildung A liegen acht Töne tiefer als die Noten C, D, E, F und G, die Sie vorher gelernt haben. Einen Abstand von acht Tönen nennt man in der Musik eine "Oktave"; dieses Wort kommt vom lateinischen Wort für "acht".

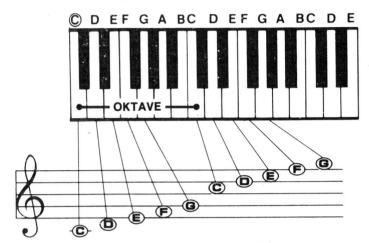

ABBILDUNG A

FINGERWECHSEL

In diesem Stück werden Sie an mehreren Stellen zwei Zahlen für den Fingersatz bei einer Note sehen, z.B. (3 - 1) in der Abbildung B. An diesen Stellen ist ein Fingerwechsel erforderlich. Zuerst schlagen Sie die Taste mit dem Finger an, der von der ersten Zahl angegeben wird, dann wechseln Sie, ohne die Taste loszulassen, zu dem zweiten Fingersatz über. Das bringt die Hand in eine neue Ausgangslage für die folgenden Töne.

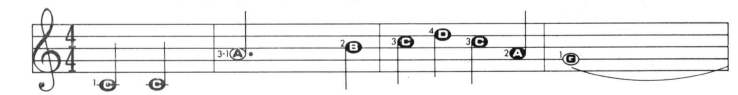

ABBILDUNG B

EIN NEUER AKKORD

Der Akkord von F-Dur wird in den Abbildungen C, D und E gezeigt.

DIMENSION ☐1

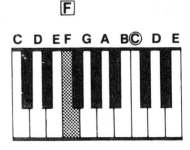

ABBILDUNG C

DIMENSION 2

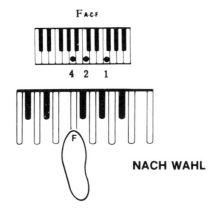

F A-C-F

4 2 1

NACH WAHL

ABBILDUNG D

DIMENSION 3

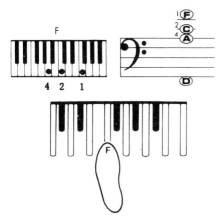

F

4 2 1

ABBILDUNG E

DER AUFTAKT

Oft fängt ein Stück mit ein paar Noten an, deren Gesamtzeitwert keinen vollen Takt ergibt. Einen solchen unvollständigen Takt nennt man: Auftakt. Der letzte Takt eines Stückes mit einem Auftakt wird dann die fehlenden Zeitwerte enthalten und zusammen mit dem Auftakt einen vollen Takt bilden. Meistens werden die Töne vom Auftakt gespielt, bevor die Begleitung einsetzt.

Machen Sie die Melodie/Rhythmus-Vorübung für BORN TO LOSE mit dem Rhythmusgerät.

160
161

TITEL Nr. 5 — SKATERS WALTZ (Die Schlittschuhläufer)

DIMENSIONEN 1 2 3

EINE NEUE TAKTBEZEICHNUNG

Bei diesem Stück lernen Sie eine neue Taktbezeichnung kennen: 3/4. Wie Sie schon vorher gelernt haben, bedeutet die untere Zahl 4, daß auf jeden Taktschlag eine Viertelnote kommt. Die obere Zahl 3 deutet nun, daß jeder Takt drei Schläge hat. Dieser Dreivierteltakt ist der sogenannte Walzer-Rhythmus.

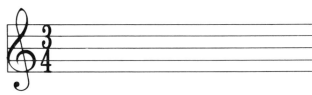

Machen Sie die Melodie/Rhythmus Vorübung für SKATERS WALTZ mit dem Rhythmusgerät.

162

Spiele das Lied mit der Melodie eine Oktave höher als geschrieben.

163

TITEL Nr. 6 — CHOPSTICKS

DIMESNIONEN ⃞1 ⃞2 ⃞3

PAUSEN

Eine Pause deutet an, wann nicht gespielt werden soll. Genauso wie es Noten mit verschiedenen Zeitwerten gibt, haben auch die Pausen unterschiedliche Zeitwerte In der Abbildung A werden drei verschiedene Pausen gezeigt.

Eine Viertelnote dauert einen Taktschlag.
EINE VIERTELPAUSE (1) dauert auch einen Taktschlag.
Eine halbe Note dauert zwei Taktschläge.
EINE HALBE PAUSE (2) dauert auch zwei Taktschläge.
Eine ganze Note dauert vier Taktschläge.
EINE GANZE PAUSE (3) dauert auch vier Taktschläge.

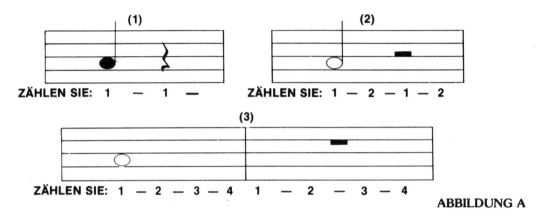

ABBILDUNG A

WIEDERHOLUNGSZEICHEN

Manchmal sollen ganze Passagen eines Stückes oder sogar das ganze Stück wiederholt werden Anstatt das alles noch einmal zu drucken, verwendet man sogenannte Wiederholungszeichen.

Wiederholungszeichen findet man meistens paarweise . . . ein Wiederholungszeichen am Anfang der Passage, die wiederholt werden soll, und das andere Wiederholungszeichen am Ende dieser Passage.

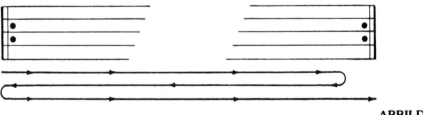

ABBILDUNG B

Wenn Sie bis zum zweiten Wiederholungszeichen gespielt haben, gehen Sie zum Anfang zurück und spielen Sie alle Takte zwischen den beiden Wiederholungszeichen noch einmal.

Manchmal steht auch nur am Ende eines Musikstückes ein einziges Wiederholungszeichen, wie in der Abbildung C gezeigt. Dann spielen Sie das Stück bis zum Wiederholungszeichen, fangen wieder von vorne an und spielen das ganze Stück noch einmal. Wenn nach dem Wiederholungszeichen noch mehr Noten stehen, spielen Sie einfach weiter.

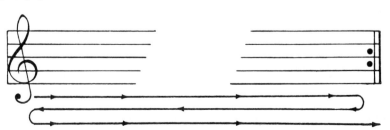

ABBILDUNG C

In einem Stück können auch mehrere Wiederholungszeichen vorkommen, siehe Abbildung D.

In diesem Falle spielen Sie zuerst alle Takte zwischen den ersten Wiederholungszeichen durch. Dann spielen Sie alle Takte zwischen den zweiten Wiederholungszeichen ebenfalls zweimal durch. Sie sollten also immer zum nächstliegenden Wiederholungszeichen zurückgehen.

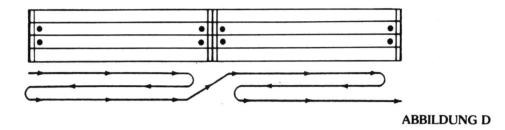

ABBILDUNG D

WIEDERHOLUNG MIT SPRUNG

Im Stück CHOPSTICKS kommt eine andere Art von Wiederholungszeichen vor: die Wiederholung mit Sprung, wie in der Abbildung E gezeigt.

Wenn Sie CHOPSTICHS zum ersten Mal spielen, spielen Sie die Takte unter der Klammer 1. Dann gehen Sie zurück zum ersten Wiederholungszeichen, überspringen die Takte unter der Klammer 1 und spielen die Takte unter der Klammer 2 weiter.

ABBILDUNG E

DAS ÜBER- UND UNTERSETZEN DER FINGER

In den Takten ⑫ , ⑬ , ⑰ und ⑱ kommt das Über- und Untersetzen der Finger vor. Während Sie im Takt ⑫ die Taste A mit dem rechten Daumen festhalten, setzen Sie den dritten Finger über den Daumen, um die tiefere G-Taste im Takt ⑬ zu spielen. Während Sie die Taste F im Takt ⑰ mit dem rechten Zeigefinger (2) festhalten, setzen Sie den Daumen unter, um in Takt ⑱ die höhere G-Taste zu spielen. Das Über- und Untersetzen wird mit Pfeilen (➜) und (➜) angedeutet.

DOPPELGRIFFE IN DER MELODIE

DIMENSIONEN ② ③

Beim Spielen von Doppelgriffen in der Melodie gibt es mehrere Möglichkeiten für den Fingersatz. Das hängt mit den zu spielenden Tasten und der Ausgangslage der Hand zusammen.

Das Spielen von Doppelgriffen wird erheblich erleichtert, wenn Sie sich an den vorgeschriebenen Fingersatz halten. Wenn im Verlauf des Stückes ähnliche Passagen vorkommen, wird der Fingersatz nur beim ersten Mal dazugeschrieben.

Spiele das Lied mit der Melodie eine Oktave höher als geschrieben.

Registrierungs-Bemerkung: Wenn Stimmen für oben, unten und Pedale angegeben sind (wie z.B. für CHOPSTICKS) seien Sie sicher den ARRANGER auszustellen.

TITEL Nr. 7 — CHAMPAGNE POLKA

DIMENSIONEN ☐1 ☐2 ☐3

In dem Stück CHAMPAGNE POLKA werden Sie zum ersten mal die schwarzen Tasten spielen. Schwarze Tasten werden in den Noten durch Kreuze oder B's angedeutet. Bevor wir verstehen können, was es mit den Kreuzen und B's auf sich hat, müssen wir jedoch zuerst etwas über Halbtonschritte und Ganztonschritte wissen.

HALBTONSCHRITTE

Der Abstand zwischen einer Taste und der unmittelbar benachbarten Taste ist ein Halbtonschritt. Auf dem Manual finden wir drei verschiedene Halbtonschritte:

1. Zwischen einer weißen Taste und einer schwarzen Taste.
2. Zwischen einer schwarzen Taste und einer weißen Taste.
3. Zwischen zwei weißen Tasten.

GANZTONSCHRITTE

Zwei Halbtonschritte ergeben zusammen einen Ganztonschritt. Hierbei gibt es sogar vier Möglichkeiten:

4. Zwischen zwei weißen Tasten mit einer schwarzen Taste dazwischen.
5. Zwischen zwei schwarzen Tasten mit einer weißen Taste dazwischen.
6. Zwischen einer weißen und einer schwarzen Taste mit einer weißen Taste dazwischen.
7. Zwischen einer schwarzen und einer weißen Taste mit einer weißen Taste dazwischen.

Aus der Abbildung B geht hervor, daß bei einem Ganztonschritt immer eine Taste in der Mitte liegt. ◀166▶

KREUZE UND B's

In diesem Stück und in allen folgenden werden Sie häufig vor bestimmten Noten diese Zeichen (♯) und (♭) sehen. Diese Zeichen heißen Kreuze und B's und dienen dazu, eine Note um einen Halbtonschritt zu erhöhen oder zu erniedrigen.

♯ **Ein KREUZ erhöht eine Note um einen Halbtonschritt.**

♭ **Ein B ernieddriegt eine Note um einen Halbtonschritt.**

In der Abbildung C sind verschieden erhöhte Noten und die entsprechenden Tasten gezeigt.

Wenn vor einer Note in einem Takt ein Kreuz oder ein B steht, gilt dieses Vorzeichen für alle gleichen Noten in diesem Takt.

NOCHMALS: REGISTRIEREN

Weiterhin werden zu jedem Stück Registriervorschläge und Tempobezeichnungen gegeben. Probieren Sie diese zuerst aus, und versuchen Sie dann auch Ihre eigenen Registrierungen.

TITEL Nr. 8 — LAVENDER'S BLUE

DIMENSIONEN ① ② ③

ACHTELNOTEN

Bis jetzt haben Sie Noten mit vier verschiedenen Werten gespielt: Ganze Noten, halbe Noten, halbe Noten mit einem Punkt und Viertelnoten. Im Stück Nr. 8 lernen Sie die Achtelnote kennen.

Als Einzelnote sieht eine Achtelnote aus wie eine Viertelnote mit einer Flagge am Notenhals. Wenn Achtelnoten in Gruppen von zwei oder mehr vorkommen, werden die Notenhälse durch einen Strich verbunden.

Der Zeitwert einer Achtelnote ist die Hälfte vom Zeitwert einer Viertelnote. Zwei Achtelnoten dauern also genauso lange wie eine Viertelnote.

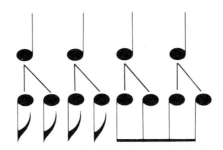

ABBILDUNG A

HALBE TAKTSCHLÄGE UND DAS ZÄHLEN VON ACHTELNOTEN

Um Achtelnoten zählen zu können, muß jeder Taktschlag in zwei gleiche Teile geteilt werden. Wenn Sie mit dem Fuß im Takt stampfen, ist das gar nicht schwierig. Jede vollständige Fußbewegung besteht aus einer Abwärtsbewegung und einer Aufwärtsbewegung. Für das Zählen von Achtelnoten wird zu jeder Abwärtsbewegung eine Zahl gezählt, und bei jeder Aufwärtsbewegung wird das Wort "und" (&) gesprochen.

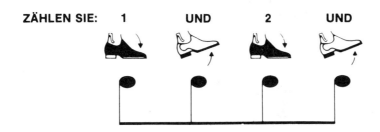

ZÄHLEN SIE: 1 UND 2 UND

ABBILDUNG B

ÜBUNG MIT ACHTELNOTEN

Spielen Sie Abbildung C bis Sie die Achtelnoten fließend und ohne Zögern beherrschen. Stampfen Sie dabei am Anfang mit dem Fuß und zählen Sie laut mit.

◆ 169

EIN NEUER AKKORD

In den Abbildungen D, E, und F sehen Sie den neuen D7-Akkord.

DIMENSION ☐1

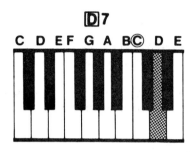

ABBILDUNG D

DIMENSION ☐2

ABBILDUNG E

DIMENSION ☐3

ABBILDUNG F

Spielen Sie die Melodie/Rhythmus-Vorübung für LAVENDER'S BLUE. 169

Spiele das Lied. Vergessen Sie nicht THE ARRANGER auszustellen. 170

TITEL Nr. 9 — SPANISH EYES

DIMENSIONEN ☐1 ☐2 ☐3

NEUE NOTEN

Die neuen Noten im Stück Nr. 9 sind: A und A (As). Beide stehen auf der ersten Hilfslinie über dem Notenliniensystem.

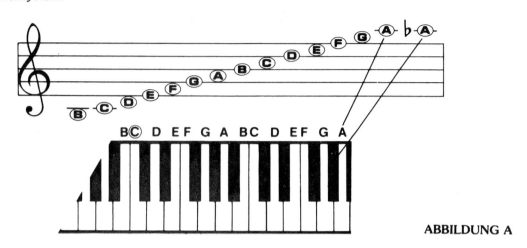

ABBILDUNG A

EIN NEUER AKKORD

In diesem Stück kommt ein sogenannter Moll-Akkord vor. Bei Moll-Akkorden steht hinter dem Buchstaben des Akkordsymbols ein kleiner Buchstabe "m".

DIMENSION ☐1

Für das Spielen von Moll-Akkorden drücken Sie den kleinen Kontaktbalken MINOR TOUCH mit dem Daumen, während Sie die entsprechende Akkordtaste festhalten.

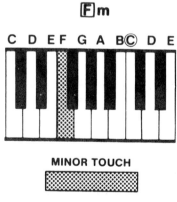

ABBILDUNG B

DIMENSION ☐2

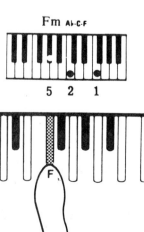

ABBILDUNG C

DIMENSION ③

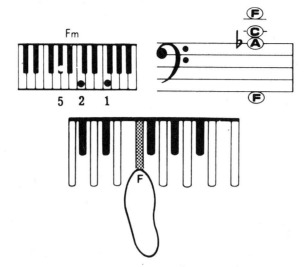

ABBILDUNG D

PRO

Wenn Sie diese Taste einschalten, klingen automatisch die passenden zweiten und dritten Stimmen zu der Melodie. Die Nebenstimmen hägen mit den Akkorden, die Sie spielen, zusammen.

Spiele das Lied mit des Melodie eine Oktave höher als geschrieben.

172

TITEL Nr. 10 — SNOWBIRD

DIMENSION ①

Schalten Sie die Register ein und spielen Sie SNOWBIRD.

PEDAL-AKKORD RHYTHMEN IN 4/4 TAKT

DIMENSIONEN ② ③

In einem Stück im 4/4 Takt können Sie einen interessanten Pedal-Akkord Rhythmus spielen. In der Abbildung A wird das gezeigt. Auf den ersten und auf den dritten TAktschlag wird ein Pedal gespielt. Der Akkord wird den ganzen Takt festgehalten.

174

HINWEIS: **DIMENSION** ② Wenn Sie den automatischen Baß nicht verwenden, spielen Sie die Begleitung wie in der Abbildung A gezeigt.

Spielen Sie die Vorübung für den Rhythmus der Begleitung (B) mit obenstehender Registrierung.

174

Wenn Sie diese Übung locker und fließend spielen können, machen Sie weiter mit der Melodie- und Begleitungsrhythmus-Vorübung (C).

Wenn Sie auch diese Übung beherrschen, spielen Sie die vollständige Bearbeitung von SNOWBIRD.

174

TITEL Nr. 11 — AMAZING GRACE

DIMENSION 1

Schalten Sie die Register ein und spielen Sie AMAZING GRACE.

PEDAL-AKKORD RHYTHMEN IM 3/4 TAKT

DIMENSIONEN 2 3

Sie werden sich erinnern, daß beim 3/4 Takt jeder Takt drei Taktschläge hat. Im Walzerrhythmus wird auf den erste Taktschlag ein Pedalton gespielt. Auf den zweiten und dritten Taktschlag kommt ein Akkord, wie in der Abildung A gezeigt. ◆ **176**

HINWEIS: **DIMENSION** 2 Wenn Sie den automatischen Baß nicht verwenden, spielen Sie die Begleitung wie in der ABBILDUNG A gezeigt.

Um mit dem Rhythmus in den Schwung zu kommen übe die Begleitung (Abbildung A) Gebrauche die ◆ **176** augegebene Registration.

Wenn Sie diese Vorübung fließend spielen können, machen Sie weiter mit der Vorübung für die ◆ **176** Melodie und den Begleitungsrhythmus (B).

Wenn Sie auch diese Vorübung gut und ohne Zögern spielen können, üben Sie das Stück AMAZING ◆ **177** GRACE.

Für einen klassischen Orgel-Sound schalte TREMOLO aus. Übe dieses Lied mit und ohne automatischen Rhythmus, mit und ohne PRO.

Spiele die Melodie dieses Liedes eine Oktave höher als geschrieben. ◆ **177**

TITEL Nr. 12 — MAKE THE WORLD GO AWAY

DIMENSIONEN 1 2 3

FESTE VORZEICHEN

Bei manchen Stücken werden Sie am Anfang jeder Zeile, direkt nach dem Notenschlüssel, ein oder mehrere Vorzeichen (Kreuze oder B's) sehen, wie in der Abbildung A. Das sind sogenannte feste Vorzeichen. Im Stück "Make The World Go Away" zum Beispiel steht ein B als festes Vorzeichen, und deshalb werden alle Noten B in diesem Stück als B gespielt. Das gilt für beide Notensysteme! Im unteren Notensystem sehen Sie das feste Vorzeichen B direkt hinter dem Baß-Schlüssel. Und deshalb müssen auch in der linken Hand und auf den Pedalen alle Noten B als B gespielt werden. Ein Musikstück ohne feste Vorzeichen steht, wie es in der Musik heißt "in der Tonart von C-Dur". Dieses Stück hat ein B als festes Vorzeichen und steht somit in der Tonart von F-Dur.

HINWEIS: **DIMENSION** 1 Die Tasten des KEY SELECTOR sind ebenfalls mit der Anzahl der Kreuze oder B's entsprechend den festen Vorzeichen versehen.

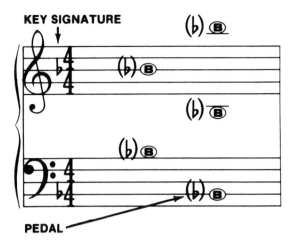

KEY SIGNATURE

PEDAL

ABBILDUNG A

NEUE AKKORDE

DIMENSION ①

Schalten Sie den KEY SELECTOR F ein und spielen Sie die nachstehenden Akkord-Tasten.

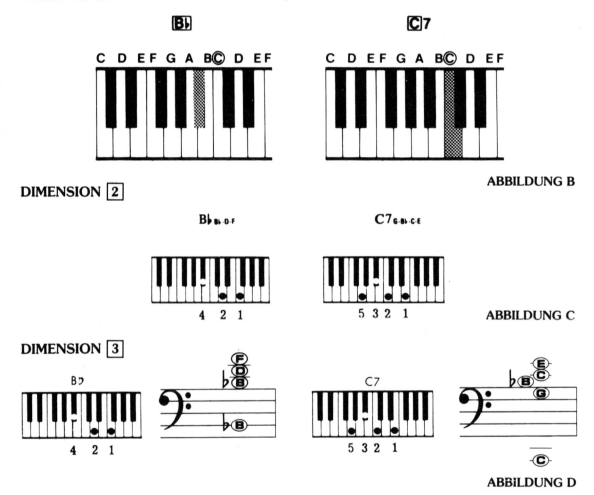

B♭

C7

ABBILDUNG B

DIMENSION ②

B♭ B♭·D·F

C7 G·B♭·C·E

4 2 1

5 3 2 1

ABBILDUNG C

DIMENSION ③

B♭

C7

4 2 1

5 3 2 1

ABBILDUNG D

ACHTELPAUSEN

Die Achtelnoten haben Sie schon gelernt. Im Stück Nr. 12 begegnen Sie nun dem Gegenstück der Achtelnote, der Achtelpause. Diese bekommt, genauso wie die Achtelnote, einen halben Taktschlag. In der Abbildung E sehen Sie die Achtelpause sowie die anderen Pausen, die Sie schon gelernt haben.

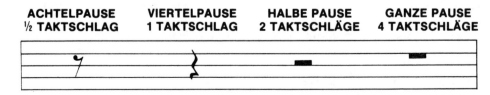

ACHTELPAUSE ½ TAKTSCHLAG	VIERTELPAUSE 1 TAKTSCHLAG	HALBE PAUSE 2 TAKTSCHLÄGE	GANZE PAUSE 4 TAKTSCHLÄGE

ABBILDUNG E

Spiele das Lied mit und ohne PRO.

TITEL Nr. 13 — THE GAMBLER

DIMENSION [1] Schalten Sie die Registrierung ein und spielen Sie THE GAMBLER.

PEDAL-AKKORD-PEDAL-AKKORD RHYTHMUS IM 4/4TAKT

DIMENSIONEN [2] [3]

Bei diesem Rhythmus wird, wie in der Abbildung A gezeigt, auf den ersten und auf den dritten TAktschlag ein Pedal gespielt, und auf den zweiten und den vierten Taktschlag ein Akkord. Denken Sie daran, die Noten B als B zu spielen! Üben Sie den Pedal-Akkord Rhythmus für THE GAMBLER so lange, bis es fließend und fast mühelos gelingt.

180

HINWEIS: **DIMENSION** [2] Wenn Sie den automatischen Baß nicht verwenden, spielen Sie die Begleitung wie in der Abbildung A gezeigt.

TITEL Nr. 14 — NADIA'S THEME

DIMENSIONEN [1] [2] [3]

NEUE AKKORDE

DIMENSION [1]

Für das Spielen untenstehender Moll-Akkorde drücken Sie die MINOR TOUCH Kontaktleiste mit dem Daumen, während Sie die angegebene Akkordtaste festhalten. Vergessen Sie nicht, den KEY SELECTOR auszuschalten.

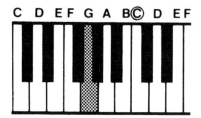

ABBILDUNG A

DIMENSION [2]

HINWEIS: Für **DIMENSION** 2 können Sie die Pedale spielen, wenn Sie das wünschen.

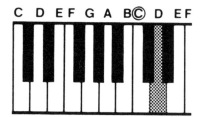

ABBILDUNG B

113

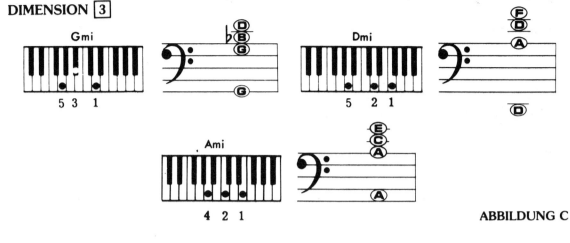

ABBILDUNG C

ÄNDERUNGEN IM 4/4 RHYTHMUS

Wenn Sie einem erfahrenen Organisten zuhören, werden Sie feststellen, daß er nicht immer die gleichen Rhythmusfiguren in der Begleitung spielt. Die Rhythmusfiguren werden manchmal etwas geändert, und diese Variationen machen die Darbietung lebendiger und interessanter. Auch im Stück NADIA'S THEME kommen Variationen in den Pedal/Akkord-Figuren vor.

Registrations-Bemerkung: Einige des angegebenen Kontrollen der Registration sind wahrscheinlich nicht an Ihrem Instrument. Lassen Sie diese unbeachtet.

182

TITEL Nr. 15 — YOU LIGHT UP MY LIFE

NEUE AKKORDE

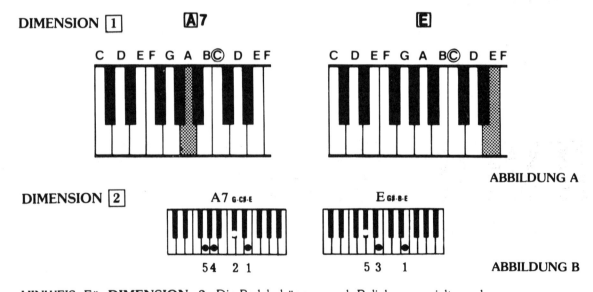

ABBILDUNG A

ABBILDUNG B

HINWEIS: Für **DIMENSION 2** Die Pedale können nach Belieben gespielt werden

DIMENSION ③

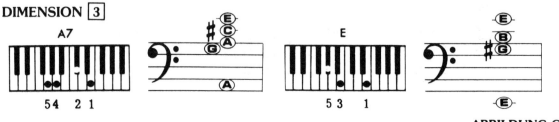

114

ABBILDUNG C

PEDAL-AKKORD-AKKORD RHYTHMUS IM 3/4 TAKT

DIMENSIONEN [2] [3]

Auf den ersten Taktschlag kommt ein Pedalton, auf den zweiten und auf den dritten Taktschlag kommt ein Akkord (A).

◆ **184**

AUFLÖSUNGSZEICHEN

DIMENSIONEN [1] [2] [3]

Auflösungszeichen (♮) finden Sie in verschiedenen Takten beim Stück Nr. 15. Auf zwei Weisen heben diese Auflösungszeichen Kreuze oder B's auf.

1. Im Takt ⑰ hebt das Auflösungszeichen das feste Vorzeichen B auf. Dieser Teil des Stückes muß in der Tonart von C-Dur gespielt werden.

2. In anderen Takten heben die Auflösungszeichen die Kreuze oder B's zeitweilig auf. Auflösungszeichen gelten nur für den Takt, in dem sie vorkommen.

DIMENSION [1]

In diesem Stück erscheint zum ersten Mal ein vierstimmiger Moll-Akkord, der Moll-Septimen-Akkord (m7). Wenn Sie den KEY SELECTOR wie angegeben eingeschaltet haben, wird die FUN MACHINE diesen Akkord automatisch spielen. Genauso wie mit anderen Moll-Akkorden brauchen Sie lediglich die MINOR TOUCH Kontaktleiste zu drücken, wenn Sie die Akkordtaste anschlagen.

◆ **184**

TITEL Nr. 16 — FEELINGS

NEUE AKKORDE

DIMENSION [1]

Für das Spielen der Moll-Akkorde drücken Sie lediglich die MINOR TOUCH Kontaktleiste, während Sie die angegebene Akkordtaste festhalten.

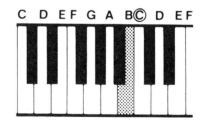

ABBILDUNG A

DIMENSION [2]

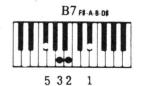

ABBILDUNG B

115

DIMENSION 3

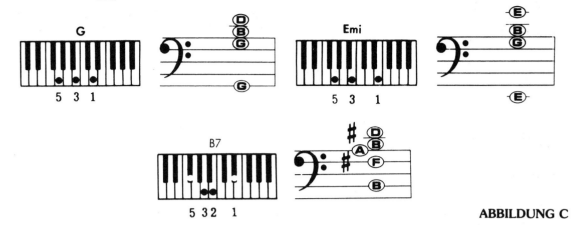

ABBILDUNG C

HINWEIS: Für **DIMENSION** 2 können Sie die Pedaltöne nach Belieben spielen.

HINWEIS: Für **DIMENSION** 3 Manchmal spielt die linke Hand nur Einzeltöne. Diese bilden eine Gegenstimme.

Versuchen Sie die Melodie dieses Liedes eine Oktave höher als geschrieben zu spielen. **187**

TITEL Nr. 17 — AFTER THE LOVIN'

EIN NEUER AKKORD

DIMENSION 1

ABBILDUNG A

DIMENSION 2

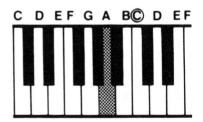

ABBILDUNG B

HINWEIS: Für **DIMENSION** 2 können Sie nach Belieben die Pedale spielen.

DIMENSION 3

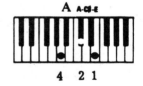

ABBILDUNG C

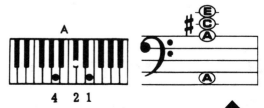

Spiele die Melodie dieser Lieder eine Oktave höher als geschrieben. **190**

TITEL Nr. 18 — BREAKING UP IS HARD TO DO

DIMENSIONEN ☐1 ☐2 ☐3

RUBATO (Freier Vortrag)

"Rubato" ist ein italienisches Wort und bedeutet eigentlich "geraubt". In der Musik bedeutet es: Die Freiheit, das Tempo und den Rhythmus der Melodie beliebig ändern zu dürfen. Der Spieler darf nach seinem Geschmack Noten ihres richtigen Zeitwerts "berauben" und sie mal schneller, mal langsamer spielen.

Spielen Sie beim Stück Nr. 18 BREAKING UP IS HARD TO DO die ersten acht Takte *rubato*, also: frei im Vortrag. Beim Takt ⑨ schalten Sie REALRHYTHM ein. Dann wird das Schlagzeug automatisch einsetzen, sobald Sie ein Pedal oder eine Taste auf dem unteren Manual spielen.

NEUE AKKORDE

DIMENSION ☐1

Für das Spielen von Moll-Akkorden drücken Sie die MINOR TOUCH Kontaktleiste mit dem Daumen, während Sie die angegebene Akkordtaste festhalten.

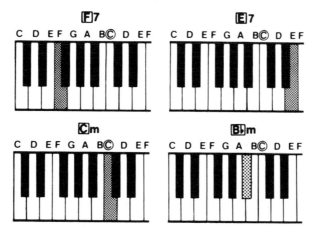

ABBILDUNG A

DIMENSION ☐2

ABBILDUNG B

HINWEIS: Für **DIMENSION** ☐2 Pedale können Sie nach Belieben spielen.

DIMENSION ☐3

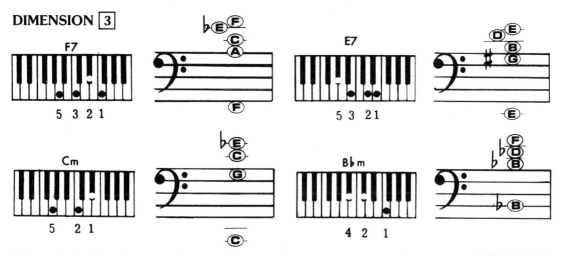

Spiele die Melodie dieses Lieder eine Oktave höher als geschrieben.

ABBILDUNG C ◆ 193

117

TITEL Nr. 19 — YOU ARE THE SUNSHINE OF MY LIFE

DIMENSION [1] Schalten Sie die nachstehende Registrierung ein und spielen Sie YOU ARE THE SUNSHINE OF MY LIFE.

DIMENSIONEN [2] [3]

WECHSELBÄSSE

Zu allen Akkorden, die Sie bis jetzt gelernt haben, wurde der Pedalton mit dem gleichen Namen wie der Akkord gespielt. Diesen Ton nennt man den Grundton vom Akkord. Die Tabelle in Abbildung A zeigt diese Akkorde. In der Spalte G sind die Grundtöne eingetragen.

Sie können auch andere Töne aus dem Akkord im Pedal spielen. Das macht das Spiel attraktiver und interessanter. Meistens wird statt des Grundtons die sogenannte "Quinte" aus dem Akkord als Wechselbaß gespielt. In der Spalte W in Abbildung A sehen Sie die Wechselbässe für die bisher gelernten Akkorde.

AKKORD	G	W
C	C	G
F	F	C
G	G	D
D	D	A
A	A	E
E	E	B
B	B	F#
Bb	Bb	F

ABBILDUNG A

196

TITEL Nr. 20 — COLOUR MY WORLD

DIMENSIONEN [1] [2] [3]

ACHTEL-TRIOLEN

Eine Triole ist eine Gruppe von drei Noten, die in der gleichen Zeit gespielt werden, in der normalerweise zwei Noten vom gleichen Notenwert gespielt werden. man kann die Triole bequem erkennen, da sie meistens mit einer Klammer versehen ist, über der die Zahl 3 steht.

In der Abbildung A hat jede Gruppe von zwei Achtelnoten (1) und jede Triole (2) den gleichen Zeitwert: Ein Taktschlag. Üben Sie die Zeile (2), bis Sie die Achtel-Triolen gleichmäßig spielen können und alle Noten den gleichen Zeitwert haben.

Eine kleine "Eselsbrücke": Sprechen Sie ganz gleichmäßig ein dreisilbiges Wort, z.B. "Klei-nig-keit, Klei-nig-keit, Klei-nig-keit", und spielen Sie zu jeder Silbe einen Ton.

198

In der Abbildung B finden Sie Achtel-Triolen zusammen mit anderen Notenwerten. Üben Sie Abbildung B, bis Sie die ganze Passage fließend spielen können. Stampfen Sie dazu mit dem Fuß und zählen Sie laut mit.

EIN NEUER AKKORD

DIMENSION 1

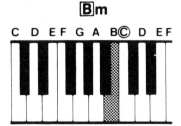

ABBILDUNG C

DIMENSION 2

5 2 1

ABBILDUNG D

HINWEIS: Für **DIMENSION** 2 können Sie die Pedale nach Belieben spielen.

DIMENSION 3

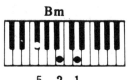

5 2 1

ABBILDUNG E

TITEL Nr. 21 — GAMES PEOPLE PLAY

DAS REGISTRIEREN

DIMENSIONEN 1 2 3

Das Registrieren — das Ändern der Klangfarben in der Musik — ist die einfachste Art, das Spiel interessanter und lebendiger zu nachen. Dabei ist es gar nicht schwer, im Verlauf eines Stückes Registerwechsel vorzunehmen. Dadurch macht Ihr Spiel einen viel besseren Eindruck auf die Zuhörer. Wenn Sie während des Spielens einen Registerwechsel machen wollen, sollten Sie folgende Punkte beachten:

1. Der Registerwechsel soll deutlich sien. Die neue Registrierung soll zur vorangehenden einen Kontrast bilden.

2. Die Registrierungen sollen dem Charakter des Stückes entsprechen.

3. Bleiben Sie im Takt. Machen Sie keine Pausen oder halten Sie die Noten nicht länger an, wenn Sie die Registrierung umschalten.

4. Machen Sie es nicht zu kompliziert. stellen Sie fest, wieviel Zeit Sie haben und nehmen Sie sich nicht mehr Registerwechsel vor, als Sie in der Zeit schaffen können. Passen Sie die Umschaltungen dem Rhythmus an. Manchmal ist es unvermeidlich, einem langen Melodieton ein oder zwei Taktschläge zu "stehlen". In dieser "gestohlenen" Zeit können Sie die Register umschalten, bei jedem Taktschlag eine Umschaltung. Siehe Abbildung A.

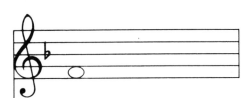

So notiert:

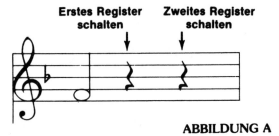

Wird so gespielt:

Erstes Register schalten   **Zweites Register schalten**

ABBILDUNG A

REGISTERWECHSEL . . . ABER WANN?

Es ist an sich gut, in einem Stück viele Klangfarben verwenden zu wollen. Passen Sie jedoch auf, daß es nicht verwirrend wirkt. Die geeigneten Stellen für einen Registerwechsel sind:

1. Zwischen der Einleitung und dem eigentlichen Anfang eines Stückes.

2. Zwischen Couplet und Kehrreim eines Stückes.

3. Bei längeren Pausen oder Übergängen.

HINWEIS: Im Stück Nr. 21 sind die Registerwechsel in den Takten ⑦ , ⑮ und ㉓ nach obenstehender Regel Nr. 2 vorgesehen.

TITEL Nr. 22 — WONDERLAND BY NIGHT

REGISTRIEREN: RHYTHMUSWECHSEL

DIMENSIONEN ☐1 ☐2 ☐3

Im Stück Nr. 22 wird gezeigt, wie ein Rhythmuswechsel im Verlauf des Stückes den Vortrag beleben kann. Im Takt Nr. ⑧ schalten Sie den BOSSA NOVA Rhythmus ein, und im Takt ⑯ schalten Sie den BOSSA NOVA Rhythmus wieder aus.

ERINNERN SIE SICH: Es ist manchmal unvermeidlich, einem Melodieton einen oder zwei Taktschläge zu "stehlen", damit Sie die Schalterknöpfe im Takt mit dem Rhythmus betätigen können.

TITEL Nr. 23 — IT WAS ALMOST LIKE A SONG

DIMESNIONEN ☐1 ☐2 ☐3

D.S. AL CODA ⊕

Im Stück Nr. 23 begegnen Sie dem Begriff *D.S. al CODA* ⊕. Es bedeutet, daß Sie zurückgehen müssen zum Zeichen (𝄋) am Anfang des Stückes, und dann alle Takte noch einmal spielen bis zum Zeichen CODA ⊕. Von dort springen Sie ohne Unterbrechung auf die Zeile über, wo am Anfang wieder CODA steht. Das Wort *CODA* ist der italienische Ausdruck für Schwanz oder Schweif, und bezeichnet eine zusätzliche Schlußwendung bei einem Musikstück.

SECHZEHNTELNOTEN

Als Einzelnote sieht die Sechzehntelnote aus wie eine Achtelnote mit zwei Fähnchen am Notenhals. Wo Sechzehntelnoten in Gruppen von zwei oder mehr vorkommen, werden die Notenhälse mit zwei Strichen zusammengefaßt.

ABBILDUNG A

Der Zeitwert einer Sechzehntelnote ist die Hälfte des Zeitwerts einer Achtelnote und ein Viertel des Zeitwerts einer Viertelnote. Sie haben schon gelernt, daß jeder Taktschlag in zwei Teile unterteilt werden kann. Zum Zählen verwendet man dann eine Zahl und die Zwischensilbe "und".

Beim Zählen von Sechzehntelnoten muß der Taktschlag in vier Teile unterteilt werden. Jeder Teil bekommt nun eine eigene Silbe, wie in der Abbildung B dargestellt.

Spielen Sie die Übung von der Abbildung B langsam durch. Zählen Sie dazu laut mit und stampfen Sie mit dem Fuß. Sie müssen zu jeder Fußbewegung vier Sechzehntelnoten spielen. Üben Sie das, bis Sie es fließend und ohne zu stocken können.

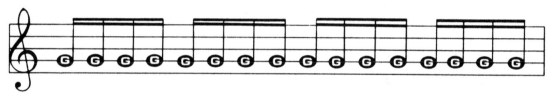

ZÄHLEN SIE: 1 — te — & — te   2 — te — & — te   3 — te — & — te   4 — te — & — te

ABBILDUNG B

Die nachstehende Rhythmus-Vorübung enthält die *D.S. al CODA* Zeichen sowie Sechzehntelnoten. Spielen Sie diese Übung, bis Sie sie fließend und gleichmäßig beherrschen.

204

205

TITEL Nr. 24 — DISCO oder BLUES

DIMENSIONEN ☐1☐ ☐2☐ ☐3☐

Mit Ausnahme des Walzers sind alle Rhythmen der FunMachine im 4/4 Takt. Der einzige grundsätzliche Unterschied zwischen den verschiedenen Rhythmen liegt in der Reihenfolge, in der die Baßtöne, Akkorde und Schlaginstrumente erklingen. Viele Stücke können mit verschiedenen Rhythmen gespielt werden. Das heißt aber nicht, daß sich an der Melodie etwas ändert. nach wie vor bekommt eine ganze Note vier Taktschläge, eine halbe Note zwei Taktschläge usw.

Das nachstehende Stück kann mit sämtlichen FunMachine Rhythmen (außer WALTZ) gespielt werden. DISCO, JAZZ ROCK und BALLAD ROCK werden jedoch am besten klingen.

Wenn Sie ein Musikstück hören, das Sie buchstäblich zum Tanzen auffordert, schalten Sie Ihre Orgel ein und stellen Sie das TEMPO des Rhythmusgeräts auf die gleiche Geschwindigkeit ein. Hören Sie auf die Musik und versuchen Sie festzustellen, welches Instrument die Melodie spielt . . . eine Trompete, ein Saxophone, ein Klavier? Und welche Instrumente spielen im Hintergrund? Wenn Sie auf diese Weise Ihren Lieblingsliedern aufmerksam zuhören und sich selbst dabei diese Fragen stellen, werden Sie bald herausbekommen, welche Instrumente und Klangfarben für Ihr eigenes Spiel am besten geeignet wären.

Das nächste Stück DISCO oder BLUES ist ein musikalischer Spaß. Verwenden Sie bei diesem Stück verschiedene FunMachine Rhythmen.

207

DAS AUFBAUEN VON AKKORDEN

Ein Akkord ist eine Gruppe von Tönen, die einer Tonleiter entnommen sind.

- Dur-Akkorde bestehen aus dem ersten, dritten und fünften Ton der Dur-Tonleiter.

- Moll-Akkorde bestehen aus dem ersten, dem erniedrigten dritten und den fünften Ton der Dur Tonleiter.

- Septimen-Akkorde bestehen aus dem ersten, dritten, fünften und erniedrigten siebenten Ton der Dur-Tonleiter.

- Moll-Septimen-Akkorde bestehen aus dem ersten, dem erniedrigten dritten, dem fünften und dem erniedrigten siebenten Ton der Dur-Tonleiter.

Untenstehend finden Sie sämtliche Dur-Tonleitern in Form einer Tabelle:

	1	2	3	4	5	6	7	8
C	C	D	E	F	G	A	B	C
F	F	G	A	B♭	C	D	E	F
B♭	B♭	C	D	E♭	F	G	A	B♭
E♭	E♭	F	G	A♭	B♭	C	D	E♭
A♭	A♭	B♭	C	D♭	E♭	F	G	A♭
D♭	D♭	E♭	F	G♭	A♭	B♭	C	D♭
G♭	G♭	A♭	B♭	B	D♭	E♭	F	G♭
B	B	C#	D#	E	F#	G#	A#	B
E	E	F#	G#	A	B	C#	D#	E
A	A	B	C#	D	E	F#	G#	A
D	D	E	F#	G	A	B	C#	D
G	G	A	B	C	D	E	F#	G

ZUM BEISPIEL:

C = 1-3-5 der C-Dur Tonleiter = C-E-G

Fm = 1-♭3-5 der F-Dur Tonleiter = F-A♭-C

G7 = 1-3-5-♭7 der G-Dur Tonleiter = G-B-D-F

Dm7 = 1-♭3-5-♭7 der D-Dur Tonleiter = D-F♮-A-C♮

AKKORD-UMKEHRUNGEN

Die Reihenfolge der Noten eines Akkords kann geändert werden, ohne daß der Akkord hierdurch seine Funktion verliert. Die Änderung der Reihenfolge nennt man die Umkehrung eines Akkords.

ZUM BEISPIEL:

Der C-Akkord = C-E-G

Die Umkehrungen sind: E-G-C und G-C-E

MITTEL C

AKKORD-BEGLEITUNG

Die Akkordbegleitung für die linke Hand klingt am besten in dem in obenstehender Abbildung gezeigten Bereich des unteren Manuals. Hier ist der Wechsel von Akkord zu Akkord auch leichter.

Baldwin

LES-SYSTEEM IN DRIE DIMENSIES

INHOUD

HARTELIJK WELKOM . . .

bij het Baldwin Orgelles-Systeem in drie dimensies . . . een nieuwe manier om op prettige wijze muziek te leren. Met dit unieke systeem kunt u zelf bepalen, hoe u alles over muziek kunt leren en uw Baldwinorgel kunt leren bespelen.

DIMENSIE [1] Gemakkelijk

BOVENMANUAAL: Met uw rechterhand speelt u de melodie in enkele tonen. De melodienoten hebben ingedrukte notennamen om het notenlezen te vergemakkelijken.

ONDERMANUAAL: Met uw linkerhand speelt u de akkoorden met één vinger. De akkoordsymbolen staan boven de melodie: ([C]).

PEDAAL: De Baldwin "FunMachine" speelt de pedalen automatisch mee.

From the Columbia Pictures Release "YOU LIGHT UP MY LIFE"
YOU LIGHT UP MY LIFE

Words and Music by
JOE BROOKS

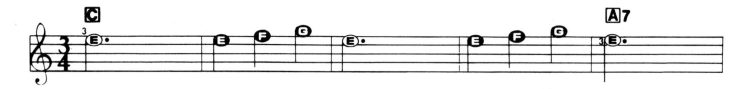

DIMENSIE [2] Akkoorden

BOVENMANUAAL: Met uw rechterhand speelt u de melodie, die op de gebruikelijke wijze geschreven is. In het verdere verloop van de kursus worden extra-noten en ritmische fraseringen toegevoegd.

ONDERMANUAAL: Met uw linkerhand speelt u drie- en vierstemmige akkoorden.

PEDAAL: Twee mogelijkheden: a) Bij ingeschakelde "FunChords" worden de bastonen automatisch gespeeld, of: b) U speelt zelf de bastonen met uw linkervoet.

From the Columbia Pictures Release "YOU LIGHT UP MY LIFE"
YOU LIGHT UP MY LIFE

Words and Music by
JOE BROOKS

DIMENSIE [3] De gebruikelijke methode

BOVENMANUAAL: Met uw rechterhand speelt u de melodie, precies zo als bij **DIMENSIE** [2].

ONDERMANUAAL
en PEDAAL: U leest en speelt de noten voor uw linkerhand en voor het pedaal. Voor het gemak zijn de namen van de noten erin gedrukt.

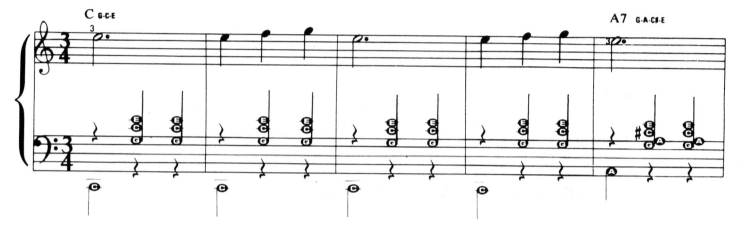

WELKE DIMENSIE ZAL IK KIEZEN?

Wanneer u nog nooit iets aan muziek gedaan hebt, zal **DIMENSIE** [1] u het gemakkelijkst vallen. Daarmee leert u snel leuke songs spelen, en u leert een heleboel over muziek in het algemeen.

Wanneer u vroeger als eens een instrument geleerd hebt, is **DIMENSIE** [2] de aangewezen weg. U leert op de gebruikelijke manier notenlezen voor de melodie (zonder ingedrukte letters), en u leert de begeleiding in akkoorden met uw linkerhand te spelen.

OPMERKING: Wanneer u een Baldwin FunMachine met één manuaal hebt, kunt u **DIMENSIE** [1] of **DIMENSIE** [2] volgen. **DIMENSIE** [3] komt dan voor u niet in aanmerking.

Wanneer u reeds noten kunt lezen (of wanneer u dat goed zoudt willen leren) kunt u **DIMENSIE** [3] nemen. Daarmee leert u orgel-bewerkingen op twee notenbalken spelen, met pedaal/akkoord figuren, dubbelgrepen in de melodie, enz.

EN WANNEER U VAN DE ENE OP DE ANDERE DIMENSIE WILT OVERGAAN?

Wanneer u eenmaal bij één **DIMENSIE** begonnen bent, hoeft u dat niet met alle geweld tot het einde toe door te maken. Zoudt u liever op een andere **DIMENSIE** willen overschakelen, gaat u heel eenvoudig terug naar een punt waar het theoretische materiaal en de aanwijzingen u bekend voorkomen, en leert u van daar af aan verder in een andere **DIMENSIE**.

UW BALDWIN-ORGEL

Uw Baldwin-orgel kunt u het beste leren kennen, wanneer u de gebruiksaanwijzing aandachtig DOORLEEST. In de gebruiksaanwijzing worden alle registers en schakelaars uitvoerig beschreven. Houdt u deze gebruiksaanwijzing bij de lessen steeds bij de hand, zodat u, waar nodig, alles snel kunt naslaan.

TOETSENWIJZERS

Bij alle Baldwin-orgels zijn boven de witte toetsen letters aangebracht. Dat noemen we toetsenwijzers.

HET REGISTREREN

De zogenaamde ARRANGER maakt u het registereren bij uw Baldwin-orgel heel gemakkelijk. Met de ARRANGER kunt u een bepaalde register-kombinatie (een bepaalde "registratie") automatisch instellen.

De ARRANGER stelt de registers voor het bovenmanuaal, voor het ondermanuaal en voor het pedaal in, en ook de niet-sprekende registers die de klank van de sprekende registers beinvloeden. Bij ieder ritme dat u inschakelt kiest de ARRANGER een passende registratie. Wanneer geen ritme ingeschakeld is, kiest de ARRANGER een volle orgel-registratie. Wanneer u de ARRANGER uitschakelt, kunt u zelf naar eigen smaak registreren. In de gebruiksaanwijzing vindt u een lijst met aanbevolen registraties om het u makkelijker te maken.

OPMERKING: De registraties bij de stukken in dit boek kunnen bij de meeste Baldwin-modellen gebruikt worden. Schakelt u de voorgeschreven registers in voorzover deze op uw orgel voorkomen, en laat u de andere achterwege.

HET SPELEN VAN DE MELODIE

In een orkest wordt de melodie (het "wijsje" van een muziekstuk) door instrumenten zoals fluit of trompet gespeeld. Bij het orgel wordt de melodie meestal op het bovenmanuaal met de rechterhand gespeeld. Melodieën bestaan uit verschillende tonen. Die tonen worden voorgesteld door noten, die op een notenbalk geschreven worden. Zie afb. A. Een notenbalk bestaat uit vijf lijnen en vier tussenruimten, die met de letters van A tot en met G benoemd worden. Iedere noot op een bepaalde lijn of in een bepaalde tussenruimte wordt naar die letter benoemd. Bij dit les-systeem worden noten met ingedrukte letters gebruikt, om het u gemakkelijk te maken. Alles wat u te doen heeft, is de toetsen aan te slaan waarboven dezelfde letters als in de noten staan.

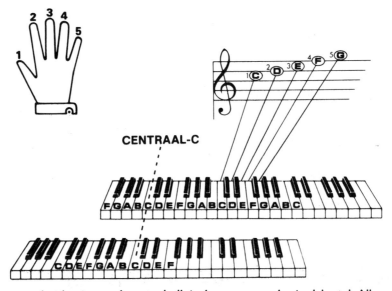

CENTRAAL-C

Afb. A

De S-vormige figuur aan het begin van de notenbalk is de zogenaamde vioolsleutel. Alle noten op deze notenbalk worden met de rechterhand gespeeld. In afbeelding A ziet u de eerste vijf melodienoten C, D, E, F en G en de daarbij behorende toetsen. Bij de noten staan kleine cijfertjes, die aangeven, met welke vinger u de toetsen moet spelen (vingerzetting).

Begint u met uw rechterhand op het bovenmanuaal, met uw duim op de toets C boven Centraal-C, zoals in de afbeelding A is aangegeven. Zet uw vingers losjes op de toetsen en speelt u de vijf tonen uit afb. A.

OPMERKING: Bij dit les-systeem staat overal de noot Centraal-C in een cirkeltje:

SONG 1 — WHISTLE WHILE YOU WORK

*1 Speelt u de volgende melodie op het bovenmanuaal.

*2 Houdt u bij de witte noten met zwarte letters erin de toetsen een beetje langer vast dan bij de zwarte noten met de witte letters . . . we komen hier later nog op terug.

*3 Schakelt u de onderstaand aangegeven registers in en speelt u WHISTLE WHILE YOU WORK naar keuze in **DIMENSIE** ☐1 of ☐2 .

HET SPELEN VAN DE BEGELEIDING

Bij het orgelspel bestaat de begeleiding meestal uit akkoorden die met de linkerhand gespeeld worden, en de daarbij passende bastonen. Akkoorden worden door zogenaamde akkoordsymbolen aangeduid. Akkoordsymbolen zijn kleine vierkante hokjes met een letter erin, die boven de melodie staan. Om te beginnen leren we twee akkoorden kennen: Het akkoord van ☐C en het akkoord van ☐G 7.

Schakelt u THE ARRANGER in

Om de begeleiding te spelen in . . .

DIMENSIE ☐1 schakelt u de knop 1-FINGER ACCOMP van de EASY PLAYER sectie op uw Baldwin-orgel in. Alles wat u nu nog te doen hebt, is op het ondermanuaal de toets met dezelfde letter als in het akkoordsymbool aan te slaan. (Zie afb. A). De FunMachine speelt dan automatisch de bas.

OPMERKING: Om het automatische ritme uit te schakelen, drukt u de toets STOP in.

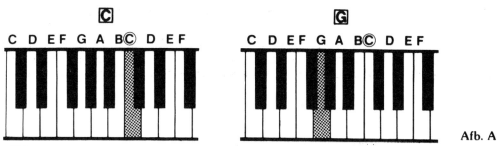

Afb. A

DIMENSIE ☐2 speelt u akkoordtonen die naast het hokje met het akkoordsymbool staan, zoals in afb. B. Voor de bastonen zijn er twee mogelijkheden: 1) U kunt ze zelf spelen, waarbij u de pedaaltoets met dezelfde letter als het akkoordsymbool speelt (Afb. C), of: 2) u schakelt FUNCHORDS in, en uw orgel speelt automatisch de juiste bastonen.

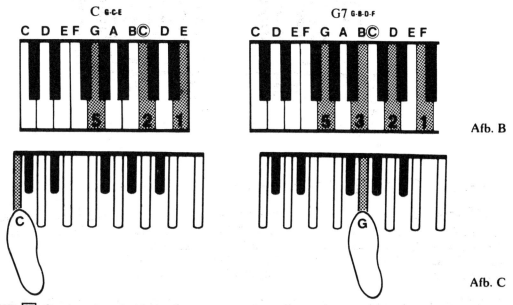

Afb. B

Afb. C

DIMENSIE ☐3 Op de volgende bladzijde ziet u in de afbeeldingen D en E hoe u de bassleutel kunt lezen.

HET NOTENBALKEN-SYSTEEM

Van hier af aan is elke song op een zogenaamd systeem geschreven. Een systeem bestaat uit twee notenbalken, die door vertikale maatstrepen met elkaar verbonden zijn, zoals in afb. D. Aan het begin van de bovenste balk staat een vioolsleutel. Zoals u weet, betekent dit, dat de noten op deze balk met de rechterhand op het bovenmanuaal gespeeld moeten worden. Aan het begin van de onderste notenbalk vindt u een nieuwe sleutel, de zogenaamde bassleutel. Deze duidt aan, dat de noten op de onderste balk met de linkerhand op het ondermanuaal en met de linkervoet op het pedaal gespeeld moeten worden.

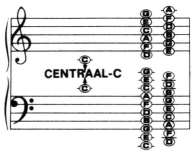

Afb. D

CENTRAAL-C

De noot C op de eerste hulplijn onder de bovenste notenbalk en op de eerste hulplijn boven de onderste notenbalk heet Centraal-C. Hoewel deze noot zowel op de ene als op de andere manier geschreven kan worden (zie afb. D) is het één en dezelfde noot. Centraal-C op het bovenmanuaal ligt altijd direkt boven Centraal-C op het ondermanuaal. In de kleine tekeningetjes van de toetsen wordt Centraal-C overal in een cirkeltje getekend.

AKKOORDEN IN DE BASSLEUTEL

In afbeelding E ziet u, hoe de akkoorden van C en G7 en de bijbehorende basnoten voor het pedaal in de bassleutel geschreven worden. Let u op de ligging van de akkoordtonen ten opzichte van CentraalC. De letters in de noten maken het opzoeken van de juiste toetsen erg gemakkelijk.

Opmerking: De gebogen lijnen tussen de noten bij **DIMENSIE** 3 op de volgende bladzijde betekenen, dat de akkoorden overgebonden zijn. Houdt u de overgebonden akkoorden zolang vast, totdat u aan een nieuw akkoord komt. We komen op overgebonden noten later nog terug.

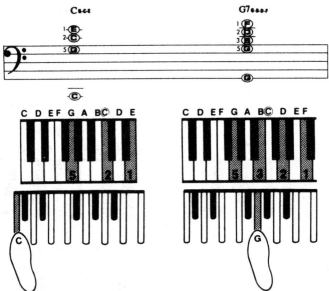

Afb. E

DIMENSIES 1 2 3 : Schakelt u de registratie in en oefent u de begeleiding.

DIMENSIE 1	DIMENSIE 2	DIMENSIE 3
ARRANGER ingeschakeld	ARRANGER ingeschakeld	ARRANGER ingeschakeld
1-FINGER ACCOMP. ingeschakeld	Voor De Bas Pedalen:	
KEY SELECTOR C ingeschakeld	FUNCHORD ingeschakeld	
MEMORY uitgeschakeld	MEMORY uitgeschakeld	

OPMERKING: De Registraties bij de melodieën in dit boek kunnen bij de meeste Baldwin - Modellen gebruikt worden. Schakelt u de voorgeschreven registers in voorzover deze op uw orgel voorkomen, en laat de andere achterwege.

154

HET SPELEN MET RITME

DIMENSIES ① ② ③

Ritme is de basis van alle muziek. Wanneer u met de Baldwin begeleidingsautomaat kunt spelen, brengt dat u een heel stuk verder.

Een muzieknoot duidt niet alleen aan, welke toets u moet aanslaan; de vorm van de muzieknoten geeft ook aan, hoe lang de noten duren. De tijdsduur van een toon wordt in de muziek in maatslagen gemeten. In onderstaande afbeelding ziet u vier verschillende notentypen, die in de volgende songs voorkomen:

Kwartnoot   1 Maatslag   Halve noot met punt   3 Maatslagen

Halve noot   2 Maatslagen   Hele noot   4 Maatslagen   **Afb. F**

Om het spelen met de ritme-automaat en de begeleidingsautomaat makkelijker te maken, zijn de volgende oefeningen zeer aan te bevelen:

1. Eerst het ritme van de melodie met de ritme-automaat samen instuderen.

2. Dan de akkoorden voor de begeleiding samen met de ritme-automaat instuderen.

3. Dan melodie en begeleiding samen met de ritme-automaat instuderen.

Daar u bij dit stuk dikwijls een melodietoon en een begeleidings-akkoord samen moet spelen, kunt u de ritme-automaat direct van het begin af aan gebruiken. Schakelt u de ritme-automaat direct van het begin af aan gebruiken. Schakelt u de ritme-automaat in en luistert u goed . . . gaat u na, hoe de noten op de bovenste balk met het ritme samenvallen. Als het ritme u tel snel of te langzaam gaat, kunt u dat met de TEMPO-regelaar nastellen. Speelt u de toets E met uw derde vinger (uw middelvinger). Hier volgen nog een paar tips om u het instuderen te vergemakkelijken:

Tips voor het instuderen:

1. Speelt u het stuk eerst aan het orgel door. Dat wil zeggen: Zoekt u de juiste melodienoten en de juiste akkoorden, let u daarbij op de vingerzetting en op eventuele nieuwe dingen. Blijft u, terwijl u dit alles doet, voortdurend op het muziekblad kijken.

2. Speelt u het stuk "in gedachten" door. Probeert u het stuk te lezen, zonder het te spelen. U moet de melodie in gedachten kunnen "horen", en u voor kunnen stellen, hoe elk akkoord bij een nieuw akkoordsymbool klinkt. Als u het makkelijker vindt, kunt u de melodie ook meezingen of meeneuriën.

3. Speelt u het stuk nu in gedachten door, samen met de RealRhythm automaat. Probeert u te "horen" hoe de noten samenvallen met het ritme.

4. Eerst dan kunt u het stuk weer op het orgel spelen. Ditmaal samen met de ritme-automaat. Dan zult u zien, dat u het stuk op deze manier werkelijk geleerd hebt.

OPMERKING: Alle Registraties worden aangegeven bij elke melodie. Op Baldwin orgels met verlichte registreer knoppen worden bepaalde registraties automatisch ingesteld. Op Baldwin orgels met mechanische drukknoppen moet men alle registreer knoppen individueel indrukken.

Van nu aan, wordt het woord ingeschakeld achter een register knop niet meer gebruikt, als er een register wordt aangegeven betekent dat ingeschakeld.

Gebruin de volgende registratie voor de Melodie Ritme Oefening.

DIMENSIE ① ② ③

1-FINGER ACCOMP., KEY SELECTOR C
(FANCY) FUNBASS
PRO uitgeschakeld, MEMORY uitgeschakeld
ARRANGER
REALRHYTHM

FOX TROT
Stel de TEMPO regelaar in op 3½ of The Conductor = ⎍100⎍.
Om de drums in te schakelen, stel in STOP.

OPMERKING: Voor **DIMENSIES** 1 2 en 3 wordt bij deze melodie-ritme oefeningen de knop 1-FINGER ACCOMP ingeschakeld. Dan kunt u zich makkelijker op het samenvallen van melodie en ritme concentreren.

155

Speel de complete melodie met ritme, gebruik de juiste registratie.

DIMENSIE 1	**DIMENSIE** 2	**DIMENSIES** 1 2 3
1-FINGER ACCOMP.	Voor De Bas Pedalen: FUNCHORDS	ARRANGER (FANCY) FUNBASS MEMORY PRO REALRHYTHM FOX TROT TEMPO 3½/ The Conductor = 100

156

SONG 2 — CARNIVAL OF VENICE

DIMENSIES 1 2 3

EEN NIEUWE NOOT

Als nieuwe noot komt in dit stuk een A voor. Zie afb. A. Naarmate u meer nieuwe melodienoten voor uw rechterhand leert, moet u heel precies de voorgeschreven vingerzetting spelen. Dat maakt het makkelijker, in een groter bereik dan vijf tonen te spelen, zonder dat u "vingers to kort komt".

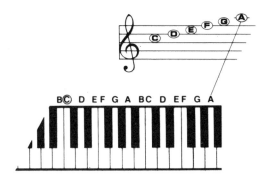

Afb. A

MATEN

In afbeelding B ziet u, hoe de notenbalk door vertikale lijnen in gelijke afdelingen verdeeld wordt. Deze afdelingen heten "maten", de vertikale lijnen heten "maatstrepen".

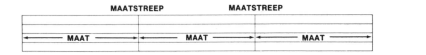

Afb. B

MAATTEKENS

Vóór aan de notenbalk, direkt na de sleutels, staan bij een muziekstuk twee getallen, zoals in afbeelding C. Dat zijn de maattekens. Het bovenste getal geeft aan, hoeveel tellen elke maat heeft. Het onderste getal geeft aan, wat voor een noot (hele, halve, kwart, enz.) er op iedere tel komt. In afbeelding C duidt het onderste getal 4 aan, dat er op iedere tel (op iedere maatslag dus) een kwartnoot komt. Het stuk CARNIVAL OF VENICE staat in 4/4 maat ("in vierkwartsmaat").

Afb. C

OVERGEBONDEN NOTEN

Wanneer twee of meer gelijke noten door een gebogen lijn ("een boog") verbonden zijn, wordt de toets slechts éénmaal aangeslagen. Daarmee kunnen we dus tonen opschrijven die lang aangehouden moeten worden. In afbeelding D wordt de eerste groep van overgebonden noten vier tellen lang vastgehouden, en de tweede groep zes tellen lang. OPMERKING: Omdat bij overgebonden noten alleen de eerste noot aangeslagen moet worden, drukken we in de tweede noot geen letter.

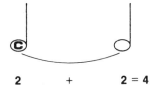 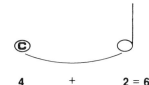

| 2 | + | 2 = 4 | | 4 | + | 2 = 6 | Afb. D |

Van nu af aan worden registraties boven de oefeningen of melodie geplaatst. Als u het symbool ∅ ziet voor of na een register betekent dit dat het register uitgeschakeld moet zijn.

OPMERKING: Van nu al aan worden en geen speciale registraties aangegeven voor Dimensies 1, 2, 3.

DIMENSIE 1

Voeg deze aan de aangegeven registratie toe:
1-FINGER ACCOMP.
(FANCY) FUNBASS
MEMORY optie
REALRHYTHM

DIMENSION 2

Voeg deze aan de aangegeven registratie toe:
(FANCY) FUNBASS
MEMORY optie
REALRHYTHM
Voor het spelen van Debassen FUNCHORDS

DIMENSIE 3

Voeg deze aan de aangegeven registraties toe:
(FANCY) FUNBASS
MEMORY optie
REALRHYTHM

De KEY SELECTOR wordt aangegeven alléén voor DIMENSIE 1

Daarna speelt u de compleete melodie.

SONG 3 — MARIANNE

DIMENSIES 1 2 3

EEN NIEUWE NOOT

In Song 3 komt als nieuwe noot een B voor.

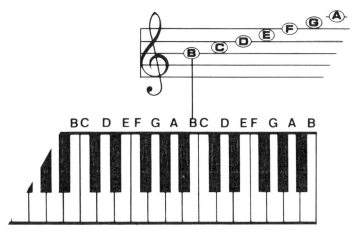

Let u in maat ⑥ en maat ⑭ goed op de vingerzetting.

Studeert u de melodie/ritme oefening voor MARIANNE met de ritme-automaat in.

Speel de melodie met de aangegeven registratie. Vergeet niet de opmerking over Registraties in de vorige les.

SONG 4 — BORN TO LOSE

DIMENSIES ☐1 ☐2 ☐3

OKTAVEN

De nieuwe noten C, D, E, F en G in afbeelding A liggen acht tonen lager dan de noten C, D, E, F en G die u al eerder hebt leren kennen. Een afstand van acht tonen heet een "oktaaf". Dit woord is afgeleid van het latijnse woord voor "acht".

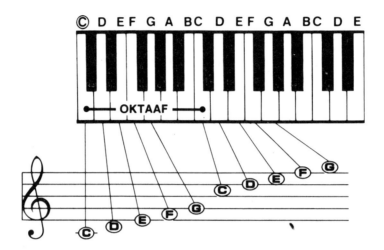

Afb. A

VINGERWISSELEN

Op sommige plaatsen in dit stuk staan er bij een noot twee cijfertjes voor de vingerzetting, bijvoorbeeld 3-1 in afbeelding B. Dat betekent, dat u de toets eerst met uw derde vinger (3) moet aanslaan, en dan, zonder de toets los te laten, naar uw duim (1) moet wisselen. Daardoor komt uw hand in de juiste uitgangspositie voor de volgende tonen.

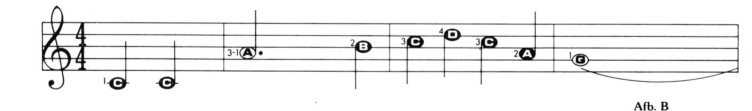

Afb. B

EEN NIEUW AKKOORD

In de afbeelding C, D en E vindt u het nieuwe akkoord van F majeur.

DIMENSIE ☐1

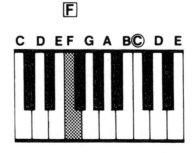

Afb. C

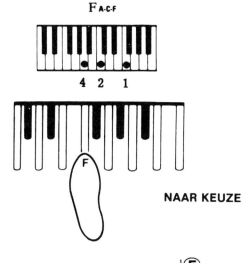

NAAR KEUZE

Afb. D

DIMENSIE 3

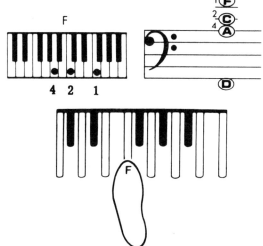

Afb. E

OPMAAT

Dikwijls begint een song met één of meer noten die samen geen volle maat vormen. Zo'n onvolledige maat aan het begin heet een OPMAAT. Aan het eind van het stuk vindt u dan weer een onvolledige maat; bij een stuk dat met een opmaat begint zijn de opmaat en de allerlaatste maat samen weer één volledige maat. Meestal begint bij stukken met opmaat de begeleiding pas bij de eerste volledige maat.

Speelt u de melodie/ritme oefening voor BORN TO LOSE samen met de ritme-automaat. ◆160 ◆161

SONG 5 — DE SCHAATSENRIJDERS WALS

DIMENSIES 1 2 3

EEN NIEUW MAATTEKEN

Bij Song 5 vindt u een nieuw maatteken: 3/4, de driekwartsmaat. Zoals u al eerder geleerd hebt, duidt het cijfer 4 aan, dat er op iedere tel een kwartnoot komt. Het bovenste cijfer 3 betekent nu, dat er in elke maat 3 tellen voorkomen. De driekwartsmaat is het bekende walsritme.

Studeert u de melodie/ritme oefening voor DE SCHAATSENRIJDERS WALS met de ritmeautomaat. ◆162

Speel de melodie één oktaaf hoger. ◆163

SONG 6 — CHOPSTICKS ("De Biefstukwals")

DIMENSIES ☐1 ☐2 ☐3

RUSTEN

Rusten geven aan, wanneer er niet gespeeld moet worden. Rusten komen in dezelfde waarden voor als noten. In afbeelding A ziet u drie verschillende rusttekens.

Een kwartnoot duurt één tel.
Een KWARTRUST (1) duurt ook één tel.
Een halve noot duurt twee tellen.
Een HALVE RUST (2) duurt ook twee tellen.
Een hele noot duurt vier tellen.
Een HELE RUST (3) duurt ook vier tellen (of een hele maat).

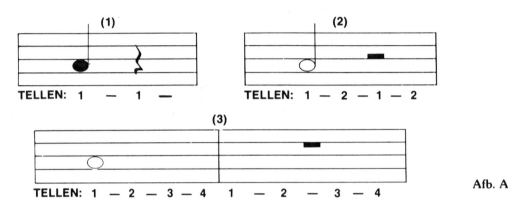

Afb. A

HERHALINGSTEKENS

Dikwijls moet een gedeelt van een muziekstuk of het hele stuk nog eens gespeeld worden. In plaats van dat alles nog eens op te schrijven, gebruiken we zogenaamde "herhalingstekens".

Herhalingstekens komen meestal in paren voor . . . één herhalingsteken aan het begin van het gedeelte dat herhaald moet worden, en één herhalingsteken aan het einde.

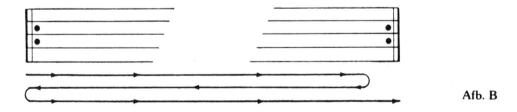

Afb. B

Wanneer u bij het tweede herhalingsteken komt, gaat u terug naar het eerste teken en speelt u alle maten tussen beide herhalingstekens nog een keer.

Soms staat er ook alleen maar aan het einde van een song een herhalingsteken, zoals in afbeelding C. Dan speelt u tot aan het herhalingsteken, u gaat terug naar het begin van de song en speelt dat gedeelte nog een keer. Als er na het herhalingsteken nog meer muziek komt, speelt u gewoon verder.

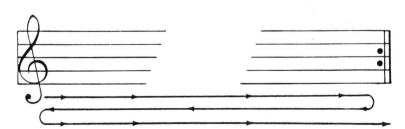

Afb. C

In een song kunnen ook verschillende gedeelten voor zich herhaald moeten worden, zoals in afbeelding D.

In dat geval speelt u eerst alle maten tussen het eerste paar herhalingstekens tweemaal. Dan komen alle maten tussen het tweede paar herhalingstekens ook tweemaal. In beide gevallen gaat u dus terug naar het dichtstbijzijnde herhalingsteken.

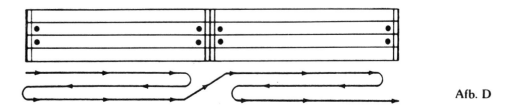

Afb. D

GEDEELTELIJKE HERHALING

Bij CHOPSTICKS komt nog een ander soort herhaling voor, de zogenaamde gedeeltelijke herhaling, ook herhaling met sprong genoemd. Zie afbeelding E.

Eerst speelt u CHOPSTICKS tot aan het herhalingsteken in de maat met het nummer 1 erboven. Dan gaat u terug naar voren, speelt alles nog eens, maar u slaat de maat onder het cijfer 1 over en speelt onder het cijfer 2 verder.

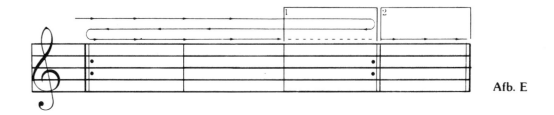

Afb. E

OVER- EN ONDERZETTEN

In maat ⑫ , ⑬ , ⑰ en ⑱ vereist de vingerzetting het zogenaamde over- en onderzetten. Terwijl u de toets A in maat ⑫ met uw rechterduim vasthoudt, zet u uw derde vinger over uw duim (➡) om de toets G in maat ⑬ te spelen. Terwijl u in maat ⑰ met uw rechterwijsvinger (2) de toets F vasthoudt, zet u uw duim onder uw hand (➡) om de toets G in maat ⑱ te spelen.

DUBBELGREPEN IN DE MELODIE

DIMENSIES ☐2 ☐3

Bij het spelen van dubbelgrepen zijn er verschillende mogelijkheden voor de vingerzetting. Wat de beste vingerzetting is hangt ervan af, welke noten aangeslagen moeten worden en in welke richting uw hand zich over het manuaal beweegt.

Het eenvoudigste is, de vingerzetting te gebruiken die bij de noten staat. Wanneer dezelfde passage meermaals in een stuk voorkomt, wordt de vingerzetting alleen bij de eerste keer geschreven.

Speel de melodie één oktaaf hoger.

REGISTRATIE OPMERKING: Als er registraties aangegeven worden voor boven manuaal, beneven manuaal of pedalen, gebruiw dan niet THE ARRANGER

164

SONG 7 — CHAMPAGNE POLKA

DIMENSIES [1] [2] [3]

De CHAMPAGNE POLKA is het eerste stuk, waarbij u zwarte toetsen moet spelen. Voordat we de zwarte toetsen leren kennen is het beslist noodzakelijk, iets te leren over halve en hele toonsafstanden.

HALVE TONEN

De afstand tussen twee toetsen die direkt naast elkaar liggen, dus zonder een andere toets ertussen, heet een halve toon. Dat is heel wat anders dan een halve noot. Er zijn drie soorten van halve toonsafstanden:

1. Tussen een witte toets en een zwarte toets.
2. Tussen een zwarte toets en een witte toets.
3. Tussen twee witte toetsen.

HELE TONEN

Een hele toonsafstand bestaat uit twee halve tonen. (Ook hier geldt weer: dat is heel wat anders dan een hele noot!) Er zijn vier soorten van hele toonsafstanden:

1. Tussen een witte toets en een witte toets, met een zwarte toets ertussen.
2. Tussen een zwarte toets en een zwarte toets, met een witte toets ertussen.
3. Tussen een witte en een zwarte toets, met een witte toets ertussen.
4. Tussen een zwarte en een witte toets, met een witte toets ertussen.

Zoals u in afbeelding B kunt zien, ligt er bij een hele toon altijd een toets tussenin.

KRUISEN EN MOLLEN

Bij deze song, en ook verderop in dit boek, zult u dikwijls voor bepaalde noten deze tekens zien: (♯) en (♭). Deze tekens zijn kruisen en mollen, en duiden aan, dat de betreffende noten een halve toonsafstand hoger of lager gespeeld moeten worden.

♯ **EEN KRUIS betekent, dat de noot een halve toon hoger gespeeld moet worden.**

♭ **EEN MOL betekent, dat de noot een halve toon lager gespeeld moet worden.**

In afbeelding C ziet u verschillende noten met een kruis en met een mol. Ook ziet u daar de ligging van deze tonen op het manuaal.

Wanneer er voor een noot een kruis of een mol staat, geldt dit teken voor alle gelijke noten die in diezelfde maat voorkomen.

NOG EEN OPMERKING OVER HET REGISTREREN

Ook in de volgende stukken staan aan het begin telkens de registraties en de instellingen voor het tempo. Probeert u deze eerst uit, en probeert u daarna gerust eens andere registerkombinaties door.

SONG 8 — LAVENDER'S BLUE

DIMENSIE 1 2 3

ACHTSTE NOTEN

Totdusver hebt u vier verschillende notenwaarden leren kennen: Hele noten, halve noten, halve noten met een punt erachter, en kwartnoten. Bij song 8 krijgen we voor het eerst achtste noten te spelen.

Een enkele achtste noot lijkt op een kwartnoot met een vlaggetje aan de notenhals. Wanneer achtste noten in groepen van twee of meer voorkomen, worden de notenhalzen door een dikke streep verbonden.

Een achtste noot duurt de helft van een kwartnoot. En dus duren twee achtste noten samen net zo lang als één kwartnoot.

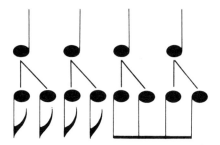

Afb. A

HALVE TELLEN EN HET TELLEN VAN ACHTSTE NOTEN

Om achtste noten uit te tellen, moet u elke tel in twee gelijke delen verdelen: de tel zelf, en een tussentel. Dat is minder moeilijk dan het lijkt, wanneer u met uw voet "in de maat stampt". Iedere voetbeweging kunt u in twee delen onderverdelen: Naar beneden en naar boven. Om te tellen geeft u nu iedere beweging naar beneden een getal, en iedere beweging naar boven een lettergreep daartussen: E - ne, twee - je enzovoorts.

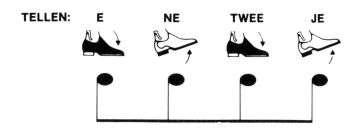

Afb. B

OEFENING MET ACHTSTE NOTEN

Studeert u afb. C totdat u deze vlot en zonder haperen kunt spelen. In het begin kunt u met uw voet de maat meestampen en hardop tellen.

169

137

EEN NIEUW AKKOORD

In de afbeeldingen D, E, en F ziet u het akkoord van D7.

DIMENSIE [1]

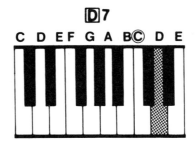

Afb. D

DIMENSIE [2]

Afb. E

DIMENSIE [3]

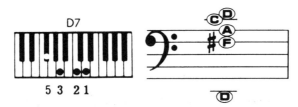

Afb. F

Speelt u de melodie/ritme oefening voor LAVENDER'S BLUE. **169**

Speel deze melodie. Vergeet niet THE ARRANGER uit te schakelen. **170**

SONG 9 — SPANISH EYES

DIMENSIES ① ② ③

NIEUWE NOTEN

In song 9 komen als nieuwe noten A en A (As) voor. Deze beide noten staan op hulplijntjes boven de notenbald.

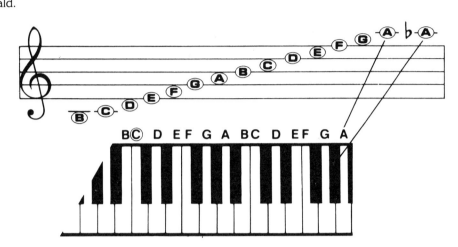

Afb. A

EEN NIEUW AKKOORD

In deze song komt voor het eerst een zogenaamd mineur-akkoord voor. Mineur-akkoorden worden in het symbool aangeduid door een kleine letter "m" achter de letter van het akkoordsymbool.

DIMENSIE ①

Om een mineur-akkoord te spelen, drukt u de MINOR TOUCH kontaktstrip met uw duim in terwijl u de aangegeven akkoordtoets aanslaat.

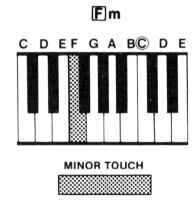

Afb. B

DIMENSIE ②

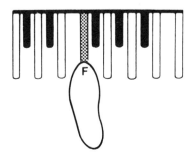

Afb. C

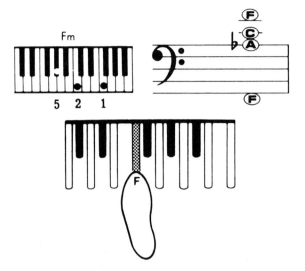

Afb. D

PRO

Wanneer u deze drukknop inschakelt, klinkt de melodie automatisch meerstemmig. De extrastemmen passen bij de akkoorden die u speelt.

Speel de melodie één oktaaf hoger. 172

SONG 10 — SNOWBIRD

DIMENSIE ①

Schakelt u de registers in en speelt u SNOWBIRD door.

PEDAAL-AKKOORD RITME IN 4/4 MAAT

DIMENSIES ② ③

Bij muziekstukken in 4/4 maat kan men een pedaal-akkoord ritme spelen. Dit wordt in afbeelding A verduidelijkt. Op de eerste en de derde tel van de maat wordt een pedaal gespeeld. Het akkoord wordt de hele maat lang vastgehouden. 174

OPMERKING: DIMENSIE ② : Wanneer u de automatische bas niet inschakelt, speelt u de begeleiding zoals in afbeelding A.

Studeert u de begeleidings-ritme oefening met de registratie (B). 174

Wanneer u deze oefening vlot en gemakkelijk kunt spelen, gaat u verder met de melodie-begeleiding ritme oefening met afbeelding C. 174

Wanneer u dit vlot en met gevoel kunt spelen, speel de complete arrangement van SNOWBIRD.

SONG 11 — AMAZING GRACE

DIMENSIE 1

Schakelt u de registratie voor AMAZING GRACE in.

PEDAAL-AKKOORD RITME IN 3/4 MAAT

DIMENSIES 2 3

U zult zich herinneren, dat het maatteken 3/4 aanduidt, dat elke maat drie tellen heeft. In een walsritme komt op de eerste tel een pedaal, en op de tweede tel komt een akkoord. Zie afbeelding A.

OPMERKING: **DIMENSIE** 2 : Wanneer u de automatische bas niet inschakelt, speelt u de begeleiding zoals in afbeelding A.

Oefen de begeleiding ritme oefening. Figuur A. Gebruin de aangegeven registratie.

Wanneer u de voorgaande oefening vlot en zonder haperen kunt spelen, gaat u verder met onderstaande melodie/begeleiding/ritme vooroefening (B).

En wanneer deze oefening ook vlot en moeiteloos gaat, kunt u AMAZING GRACE spelen.

Voor een klassieke orgel registratie, schakel de TREMOLO uit. Probeer dese melodie met en zonder ritme automatiek ook met en zonder PRO.

Speel de melodie één oktaaf hoger.

SONG 12 — MAKE THE WORLD GO AWAY

DIMENSIES 1 2 3

VASTE VOORTEKENS

Bij verschillende stukken staan vóór aan de sleutel kruisen of mollen, direkt na de viool- en bassleutel. Zie afbeelding A. Deze noemen we "vaste voortekens". Bij de song MAKE THE WORLD GO AWAY ziet u bijvoorbeeld een mol als vast voorteken. Dat betekent nu, dat alle noten B in dit stuk als B (Bes) gespeeld moeten worden. Voor de onderste notenbalk geldt dit ook. In de linkerhand en in het pedaal moeten ook alle noten B als B (Bes) gespeeld worden. Wanneer een muziekstuk geen kruisen of mollen vóóraan de notenbalk heeft, wanneer het stuk dus geen vaste voortekens heeft, zegt men dat dat stuk in de toonsoort van C-majeur geschreven is. Het volgende stuk heeft één mol als vast voorteken, en is dus in de toonsoort van F-majeur geschreven.

OPMERKING: **DIMENSIE** 1 : Bij de KEY SELECTOR drukknoppen is ook het aantal kruisen of mollen als vast voorteken aangegeven.

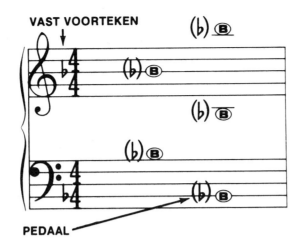

Afb. A

NIEUWE AKKOORDEN

DIMENSIE [1]

Schakelt u de KEY SELECTOR op F en speelt u de volgende akkoordtoetsen:

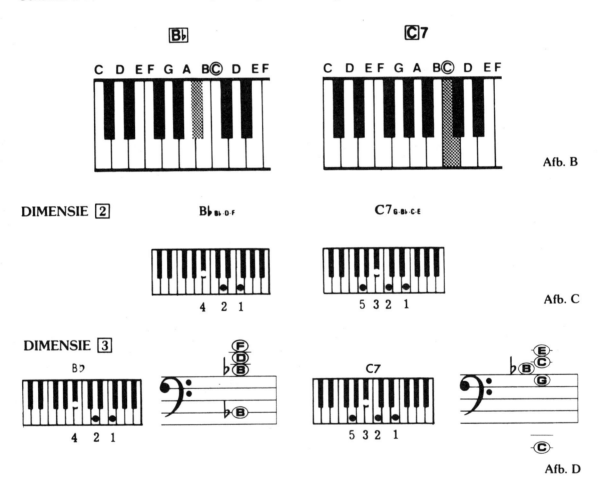

Afb. B

Afb. C

Afb. D

ACHTSTE RUSTEN

Achtste noten heeft u al leren kennen. In song 12 komt nu de achtste rust voor. Evenals de achtste noot duurt de achtste rust een halve tel. In afbeelding E ziet u de achtste rust, samen met de andere rusten die u al geleerd hebt.

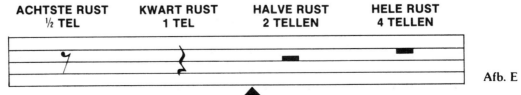

Afb. E

Speel dese melodie eerst met dan zonder PRO. **178**

SONG 13 — THE GAMBLER

DIMENSIE [1] Schakelt u de registratie in en speelt u THE GAMBLER.

PEDAAL-AKKOORD-PEDAAL-AKKOORD RITME IN 4/4 MAAT

DIMENSIES [2] [3]

Op de eerste en de derde tel van ieder maat komt een pedaal, op de tweede en de vierde tel komt een akkoord, zoals in afbeelding A. Denkt u er aan, alle noten B als B (Bes) te spelen! Oefent u dit pedaalakkoord ritme voor de song THE GAMBLER totdat het vlot en gemakkelijk gaat.

◆ 180

OPMERKING: **DIMENSIE** [2] :Wanneer u de automatische bas niet inschakelt, speelt u de begeleiding zoals in afbeelding A.

SONG 14 — NADIA'S THEME

DIMENSIES [1] [2] [3]

NIEUWE AKKOORDEN

DIMENSIE [1]

Om de onderstaande mineur-akkoorden te spelen, drukt u de MINOR TOUCH strip met uw linkerduim in terwijl u de aangegeven akkoordtoets aanslaat. Denkt u eraan, de KEY SELECTOR uit te schakelen.

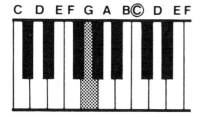

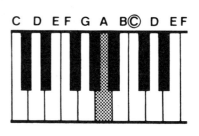

Afb. A

DIMENSIE [2]

OPMERKING: Voor **DIMENSIE** [2] kunt u de pedalen naar keuze spelen.

Gm G-B♭-D   Dm A-D-F   Am A-C-E

5 3 1   5 2 1   4 2 1

Afb. B

DIMENSIE ③

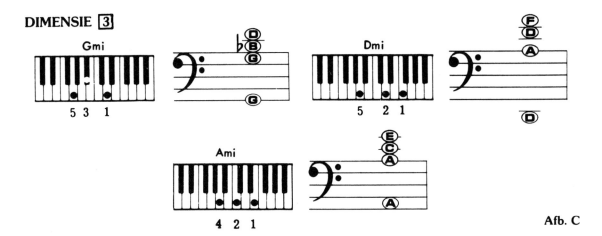

Afb. C

VARIATIES IN 4/4 MAAT

DIMENSIES ② ③

Wanneer u een ervaren organist hoort spelen, zal het u opvallen, dat hij in de begeleiding niet voortduren dezelfde ritmische figuren speelt. De ritmische figuren worden dikwijls tijdens het spelen een beetje veranderd, om het stuk interessanter en levendiger te maken. Bij de song NADIA'S THEME komen ook variaties in het pedaal/akkoord ritme voor.

REGISTRATIE OPMERKING: Schakel u de voorgeschreven registrs in voorzover deze op uw orgel ◆182 voorkomen, en laat u de andere achterwege.

SONG 15 — YOU LIGHT UP MY LIFE

NIEUWE AKKOORDEN

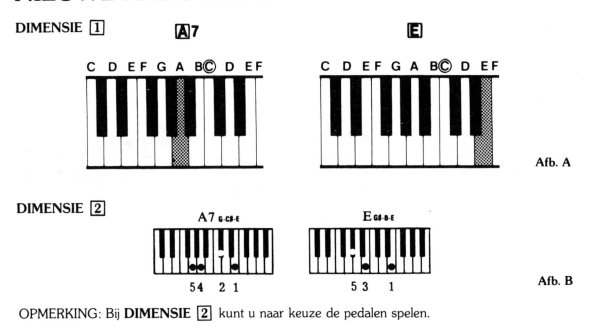

OPMERKING: Bij **DIMENSIE** ② kunt u naar keuze de pedalen spelen.

PEDAAL-AKKOORD-AKKOORD RITME
IN 3/4 MAAT

DIMENSIE 2 3

Op de eerste tel van iedere maat komt een pedaal; op de tweede en de derde tel komt een akkoord (A). **184**

HERSTELLINGSTEKENS

DIMENSIES 1 2 3

In song 15 staat voor verschillende noten een zogenaamd herstellingsteken (♮). Deze herstellingstekens heffen een kruis of mol op.

1. In maat ⑰ heft het herstellingsteken het vaste voorteken (twee mollen) op. Dit gedeelte van de song moet u dus in de toonsoort van C-majeur spelen.

2. Op verschillende andere plaatsen heffen herstellingstekens een kruis of een mol voor een noot op. Dat geldt dan alleen voor die maat waarin het herstellingsteken voorkomt.

DIMENSIE 1

In deze song komt een vierstemmig mineur-septiemakkoord (m7) voor. Wanneer u de KEY SELECTOR zoals aangegeven hebt ingeschakeld, speelt de FUN MACHINE dit akkoord automatisch. Zoals bij alle andere mineur-akkoorden moet u alleen even de MINOR TOUCH kontaktstrip indrukken terwijl u de akkoordtoets aanslaat. **184**

SONG 16 — FEELINGS

NIEUWE AKKOORDEN

DIMENSIE 1

Om de mineur-akkoorden te spelen, drukt u de MINOR TOUCH kontaktstrip in terwijl u de aangegeven akkoordtoets aanslaat.

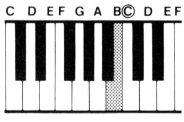

Afb. A

DIMENSIE 2

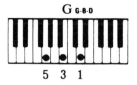
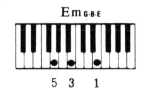

Afb. B

DIMENSIE 3

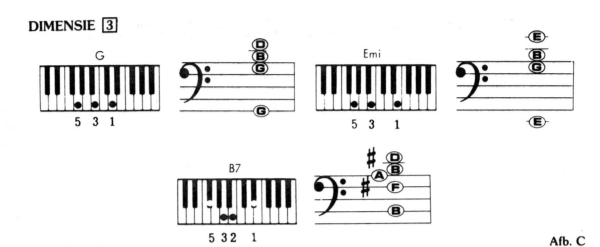

Afb. C

OPMERKING: Bij **DIMENSIE** 2 kunt u naar keuze de pedalen spelen.

OPMERKING: **DIMENSIE** 3 : Af en toe komen er in de linkerhand enkele noten als begeleiding voor. Men noemt dit een tegenmelodie.

Speel de melodie één oktaaf hoger.

SONG 17 — AFTER THE LOVIN'

EEN NIEUW AKKOORD

DIMENSIE 1

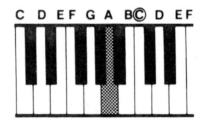

Afb. A

DIMENSIE 2

Afb. B

OPMERKING: Bij **DIMENSIE** 2 kunt u naar keuze de pedalen spelen.

DIMENSIE 3

Speel de melodie één oktaaf hoger.

Afb. C

SONG 18 — BREAKING UP IS HARD TO DO

DIMENSIES ☐1 ☐2 ☐3

RUBATO (Vrij in tempo spelen)

"Rubato" is een italiaans woord, dat eigenlijk "beroofd" betekent. Hiermee wordt aangeduid, dat de speler in het tempo en in het ritme van de melodie vrij is. De speler kan bepaalde noten een beetje van hun waarde "beroven" en ze iets sneller of iets langzamer spelen.

In song 18 BREAKING UP IS HARD TO DO kunt u de eerste acht maten *rubato* spelen. Pas bij maat ⑨ schakelt u REALRHYTHM in, dan begint het ritme automatisch zodra u eens toets op het ondermanuaal of een pedaal aanslaat.

NIEUWE AKKOORDEN

DIMENSIE ☐1

Om een mineur-akkoord te spelen, drukt u de MINOR TOUCH kontaktstrip met uw linkerduim in terwijl u de aangegeven akkoordtoets aanslaat.

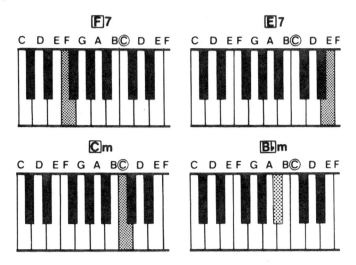

Afb. A

DIMENSIE ☐2

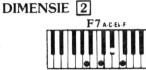

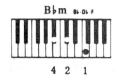

OPMERKING: Bij **DIMENSIE** ☐2 kunt u de pedalen naar keuze spelen.

Afb. B

DIMENSIE ☐3

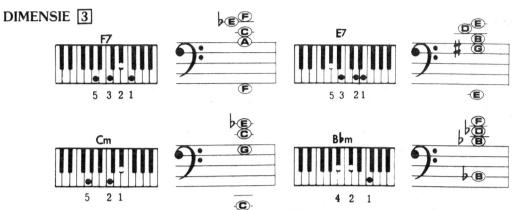

Afb. C

Speel de melodie één oktaaf hoger. ▼193

SONG 19 — YOU ARE THE SUNSHINE OF MY LIFE

DIMENSIE ☐1 : Stelt u de aangegeven registratie in en speelt u YOU ARE THE SUNSHINE OF MY LIFE.

DIMENSIES ☐2 ☐3

WISSELBASSEN

Bij alle akkoorden die u totdusver hebt geleerd, hebt u een pedaaltoon met dezelfde naam als het akkoord gespeeld. Deze toon noemt men de grondtoon van het akkoord. In afbeelding A ziet u deze akkoorden; in de kolom G staan de grondtonen.

U kunt echter ook andere tonen uit een akkoord als pedaaltonen spelen. Dat maakt uw spel interessanter en prettiger. De meestgebruikte toon is hierbij de zogenaamde "Quint" uit het akkoord. In de kolom W in afbeelding A staan deze tonen, die als "wisselbas" gespeeld kunnen worden, vermeld.

AKKOORD	G:	W:
C	C	G
F	F	C
G	G	D
D	D	A
A	A	E
E	E	B
B	B	F♯
B♭	B♭	F

Afb. A ◆196

SONG 20 — COLOUR MY WORLD

DIMENSIES ☐1 ☐2 ☐3

ACHTSTE TRIOLEN

Een "triool" is een groepje van drie noten, die gespeeld worden in de tijd waarin normaal twee noten met dezelfde waarde gespeeld worden. De triool is makkelijk te herkennen, want de drie noten worden meestal onder een haakje of onder een boogje geschreven waarboven het getal 3 staat.

In afbeelding A duren de groepjes van twee achtste noten (1) net zo lang als de groepjes van drie achtste noten (de achtste triolen) (2). Oefent u het spelen van achtste triolen zolang, totdat u ze precies in de maat kunt spelen, waarbij elke noot even lang duurt.

Nog een tip om de tweede regel (2) gelijkmatig te leren spelen: Telt u (hardop) mee: "Ap-pel-tije, ap-pel-tje" enz., en speelt u bij elke lettergreep een toon.

◆198

In afbeelding B ziet u achtste triolen samen met andere noten. Oefent u afbeelding B zolang totdat u de beide regels vlot en zonder haperen kunt spelen. Stampt u daarbij rustig met uw voet de maat en telt u hardop.

EEN NIEUW AKKOORD

DIMENSIE 1

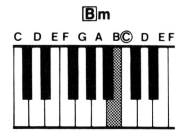

Afb. C

DIMENSIE 2

Afb. D

DIMENSIE 3

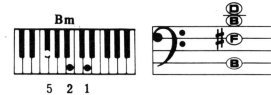

Afb. E

OPMERKING: Bij **DIMENSIE** 2 kunt u naar keuze de pedalen spelen.

SONG 21 — GAMES PEOPLE PLAY

REGISTRATIE

DIMENSIES 1 2 3

Registratie — de kunst van het instellen en wisselen van de verschillende klankkleuren van een orgel — is de eenvoudigste manier om uw spel interessant en levendig te maken. Het wisselen van registratie in het verloop van een muziekstuk is helemaal niet zo moeilijk, en uw spel maakt daarmee een veel betere indruk. Bij het instellen van nieuwe registraties in een stuk moet u de volgende punten in het oog houden:

1. Een registerwisseling moet duidelijk zijn. De nieuwe registratie moet met de vorige registratie in kontrast staan.

2. Registerwisselingen moeten bij de stemming van het stuk passen.

3. Blijf in de maat spelen. Geen extra tellen in een maat inlassen om registers te wisselen!

4. Houdt u de verschillende schakelgrepen eenvoudig. Gaat u na hoeveel tijd u voor een registerwisseling hebt, en verandert u niet meer registers dan in die tijd mogelijk is. Schakelt u de registers in het ritme van het stuk om. Hier en daar is het onvermijdelijk, van een lang-aangehouden melodietoon iets "af te moeten knijpen". In de zo gewonnen tijd kunt u de nieuwe registers inschakelen — als regel één register op iedere tel. Zie afbeelding A.

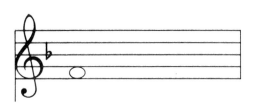

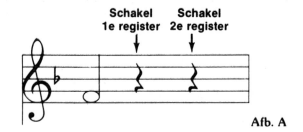

Afb. A

WANNEER EN WAAR U MOET WISSELEN

Het is op zich zelf een goed idee, in een stuk veel verschillende registraties toe te passen. Zorgt u er echter voor, dat het niet teveel wordt, waardoor het verwarrend werkt. De beste momenten voor een registerwisseling zijn:

1. Tussen de inleiding en het eigenlijke begin van een song.

2. Tussen de coupletten of herhalingen van een song.

3. Overal waar in het verloop van een stuk natuurlijke pauzes voorkomen.

OPMERKING: Bij song 21 is in de maten (7) , (15) en (23) regel nr. 2 toegepast. **200**

SONG 22 — WONDERLAND BY NIGHT

REGISTRATIE: RITME WISSELEN

DIMENSIES 1 2 3

In song 22 ziet u, hoe u afwisseling in een stuk kunt brengen door in het verloop van het stuk het ritme te veranderen. In maat (8) schakelt u de BOSSA NOVA in, in maat (16) schakelt u de BOSSA NOVA weer uit. **202**

DENKT U ERAAN: Soms is het onvermijdelijk, van een melodietoon een beetje "af te moeten knijpen" om de schakelaars precies in de maat te kunnen bedienen.

SONG 23 — IT WAS ALMOST LIKE A SONG

DIMENSIES ① ② ③

D.S. AL CODA⊕

In song 23 ontmoet u de uitdrukking: *D.S. al CODA* ⊕ .Dat betekent: Gaat u terug naar het teken (𝄋) aan het begin van de song, en herhaalt u alle maten tot aan het *coda* teken (⊕). Dan speelt u zonder onderbreking verder bij het *coda* tot het einde van het stuk. *Coda* is een italiaans woord, dat eigenlijk "staart" betekent, en gebruikt wordt om een extra slot van een stuk aan te duiden.

ZESTIENDE NOTEN

Als enkele noot ziet een zestiende noot eruit als een achtste noot met een extra vlaggetje. In groepen van twee of meer worden de notenhalzen van zestiende noten door twee dikke strepen verbonden.

Afb. A

Een zestiende noot duurt half zo lang als een achtste noot, en een kwart van de tijdsduur van een kwartnoot. U hebt al geleerd, dat iedere tel in twee gelijke delen verdeeld kan worden . . . een getal, en de lettergreep "-ne", "je" of "re". Daarmee wordt het tellen makkelijker gemaakt.

Wanneer u zestiende noten uit wilt tellen, moet u elke tel in vier gelijke delen verdelen. Ook darrbij kunnen hardop getelde tussenlettergrepen u goed op weg helpen, zoals u in afbeelding B kunt zien.

Speelt u afbeelding B heel langzaam door, telt u hardop en stampt u met uw voet in de maat mee. U moet bij iedere voetbeweging vier zestiende noten spelen. Oefent u dit zolang, totdat u het vlot en zonder haperen kunt.

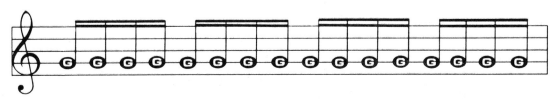

TELLEN: 1 — he — ne — he   2 — he — je — he   3 — he — je — he   4 — he — re — he

Afb. B

Bij de volgende ritme-oefening vindt u ook de uitdrukking *D.S. al Coda* en zestiende noten. Oefent u zolang, totdat alles vlot en gelijkmatig gaat.

SONG 24 — DISCO of BLUES

DIMENSIES 1 2 3

Behalve WALTZ is ieder ritme van de FunMachine op de vierkwartsmaat gebaseerd. Eigenlijk bestaat het verschil alleen in de volgorde waarin de bastonen, de akkoorden en de slaginstrumenten spelen. Vele songs kunnen met verschillende ritmische begeleidingen gespeeld worden. Dat wil niet zeggen, dat de melodie dan anders gespeeld wordt — een hele noot duurt altijd vier tellen, een halve noot twee tellen, enzovoorts.

De volgende song kan letterlijk met ieder gewenst ritme van de FunMachine (behalve WALTZ) gespeeld worden. Het beste klinken Disco, Jazz Rock en Ballad Rock.

Wanneer u een song hoort waarbij u op zou willen staan en dansen, gaat u dan eens aan uw orgel zitten en regelt u het tempo van de ritme-automaat op dezelfde snelheid. Luistert u eens aandachtig naar de song en vraagt u zich eens af: "Wat voor een instrument speelt daar de melodie . . . trompet, saxofoon, piano? Welke instrumenten spelen de begeleiding?" Wanneer u aandachtig naar uw lievelings-songs luistert en zich deze dingen afvraagt, zult u al heel spoedig ontdekken, welke instrumenten u bij uw eigen spel het beste kunt toepassen.

De volgende song DISCO of BLUES is een grappig muziekstuk. Probeert u het maar eens uit met verschillende FunMachine ritmes.

HOE AKKOORDEN OPGEBOUWD ZIJN

Een akkoord is een samenklank van bepaalde tonen uit een toonladder.

- Majeur-akkoorden bestaan uit de eerste, de derde en de vijfde toon van een majeur-toonladder.

- Mineur-akkoorden bestaan uit de eerste, de verlaagde derde en de vijfde toon van een majeur-toonladder.

- Dominant-septiemakkoorden bestaan uit de eerste, de derde, de vijfe en verlaagde zevende toon van een majeur-toonladder.

- Mineur-septiemakkoorden bestaan uit de eerste, de verlaagde derde, de vijfde en de verlaagde zevende toon van een majeur-toonladder.

Onderstaand vindt u een lijst van alle majeur-toonladders:

	1	2	3	4	5	6	7	8
C	C	D	E	F	G	A	B	C
F	F	G	A	Bb	C	D	E	F
Bb	Bb	C	D	Eb	F	G	A	Bb
Eb	Eb	F	G	Ab	Bb	C	D	Eb
Ab	Ab	Bb	C	Db	Eb	F	G	Ab
Db	Db	Eb	F	Gb	Ab	Bb	C	Db
Gb	Gb	Ab	Bb	B	Db	Eb	F	Gb
B	B	C#	D#	E	F#	G#	A#	B
E	E	F#	G#	A	B	C#	D#	E
A	A	B	C#	D	E	F#	G#	A
D	D	E	F#	G	A	B	C#	D
G	G	A	B	C	D	E	F#	G

Bijvoorbeeld:

C = 1-3-5 uit de C-toonladder = C-E-G

Fm = 1-♭3-5 uit de F-toonladder = F-A♭-C

G7 = 1-3-5-♭7 uit de G-toonladder = G-B-D-F

Dm7 = 1-♭3-5-♭7 uit de D-toonladder = D-F♮-A-C♮

AKKOORD-OMKERINGEN

De volgorde van de tonen van een akkoord kan veranderd worden, zonder dat het akkoord daardoor zijn karakter verliest. Deze verandering in de volgorde van de akkoordtonen noemt men "omkering".

Bijvoorbeeld:

Het akkoord van C = C-E-G

De omkeringen van dit akkoord zijn: E-G-C en G-C-E.

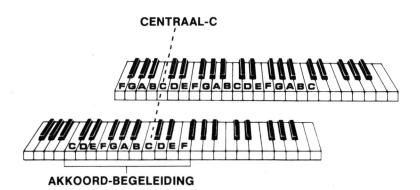

CENTRAAL-C

AKKOORD-BEGELEIDING

De begeleidings-akkoorden voor de linkerhand klinken het beste, wanneer deze in het in afbeelding A aangegeven bereik van het ondermanuaal gespeeld worden. In dat bereik zijn de overgangen van het ene akkoord naar het andere ook gemakkelijker te spelen.

WHISTLE WHILE YOU WORK

Music by
FRANK CHURCHILL

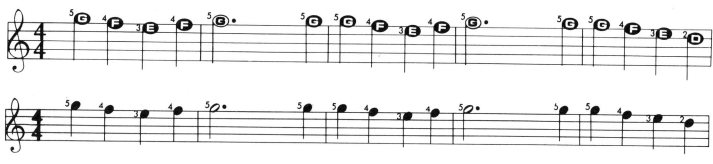

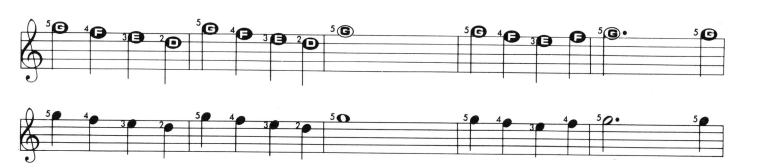

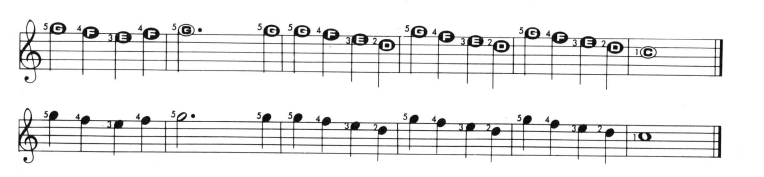

WHISTLE WHILE YOU WORK

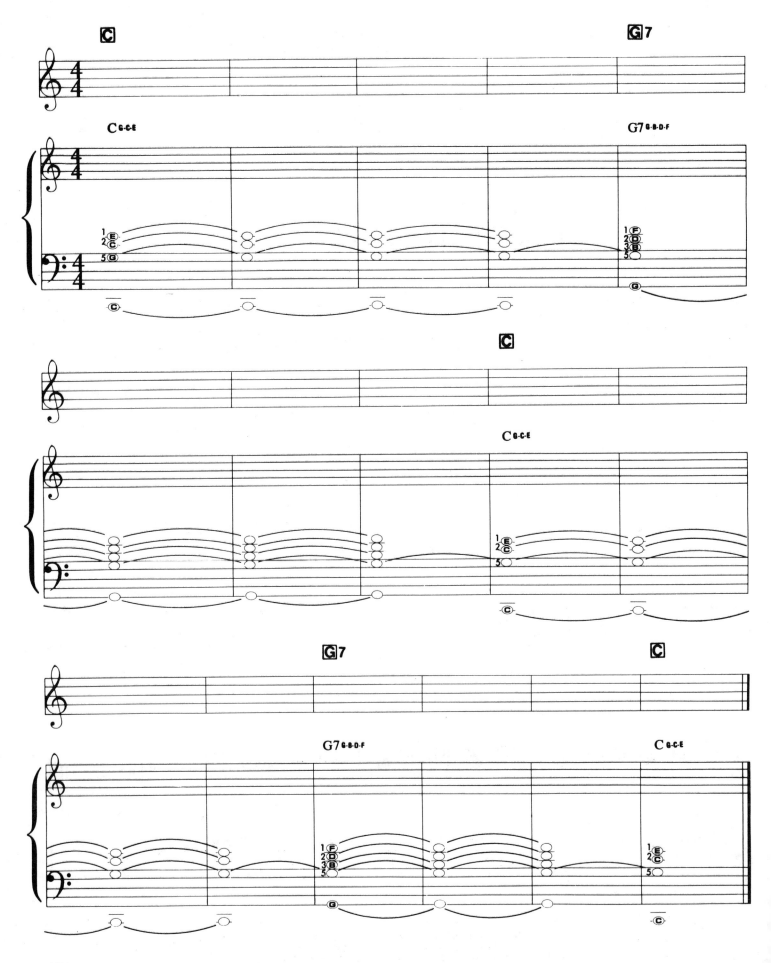

WHISTLE WHILE YOU WORK

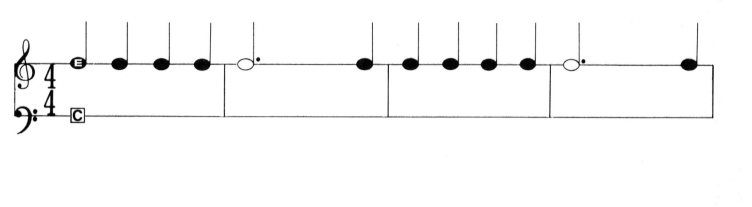

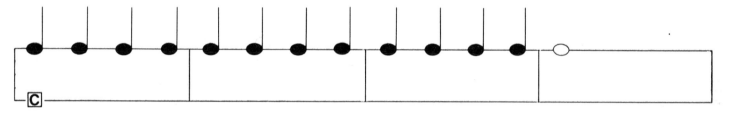

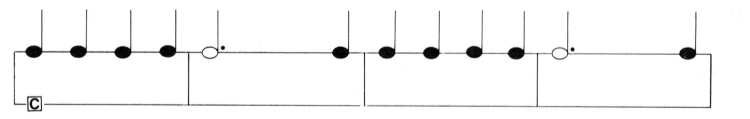

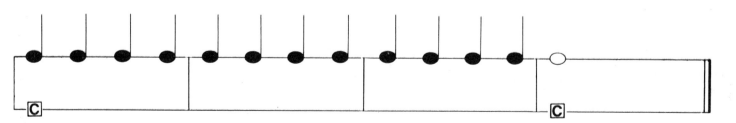

Note: To stop DRUMS, Press STOP.

WHISTLE WHILE YOU WORK

Music by
FRANK CHURCHILL

CARNIVAL OF VENICE

Ø = off/apagado/éteindre/aus/uit

THE ARRANGER
Ø PRO
Ø MEMORY

SWING
TEMPO 4/ The Conductor [120]

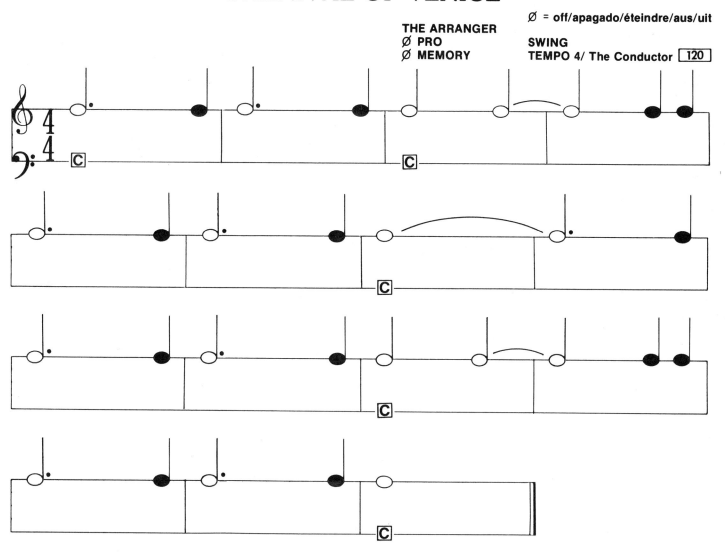

CARNIVAL OF VENICE

THE ARRANGER
Ø PRO

SWING
TEMPO 4/ The Conductor [120]

(KEY SELECTOR C)

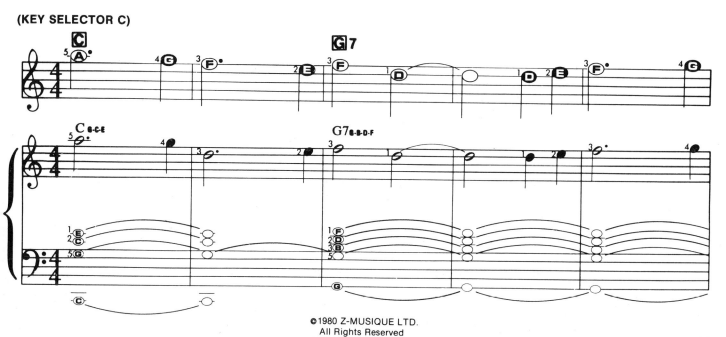

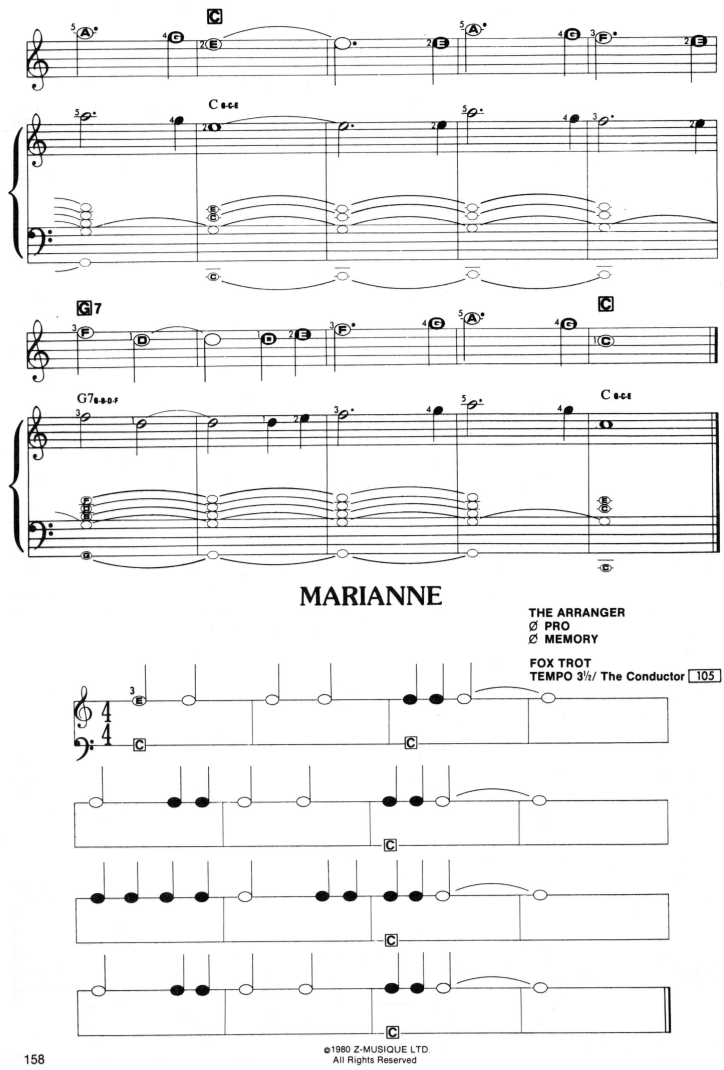

MARIANNE

THE ARRANGER
Ø PRO
Ø MEMORY

FOX TROT
TEMPO 3½/ The Conductor 105

MARIANNE

THE ARRANGER
∅ PRO

FOX TROT
TEMPO 3½/ The Conductor 105

(KEY SELECTOR C)

BORN TO LOSE

Words & Music by
TED DAFFAN

THE ARRANGER
Ø **PRO**
Ø **MEMORY**

COUNTRY (FOX TROT)
TEMPO 4½/ The Conductor ⌐130⌐

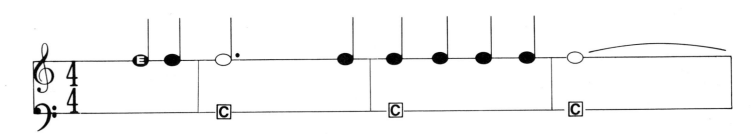

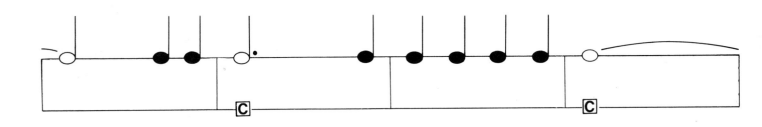

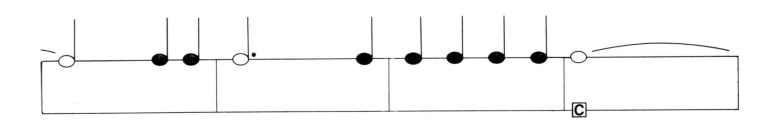

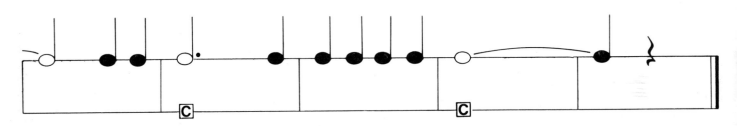

BORN TO LOSE

Words & Music by
TED DAFFAN

THE ARRANGER

COUNTRY (FOX TROT)
TEMPO 4½/ The Conductor 130

(KEY SELECTOR C)

SKATERS WALTZ

THE ARRANGER
Ø **PRO**
Ø **MEMORY**

WALTZ
TEMPO 4½/ The Conductor [130]

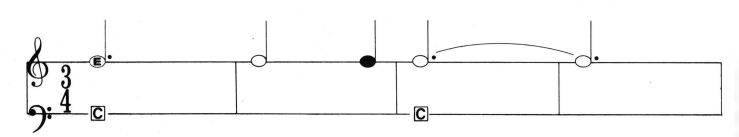

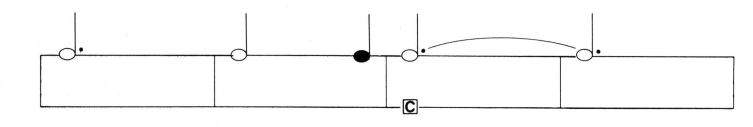

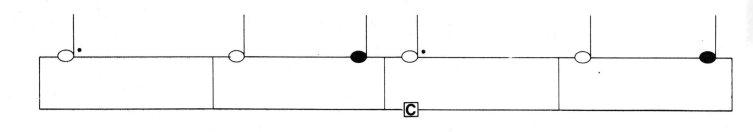

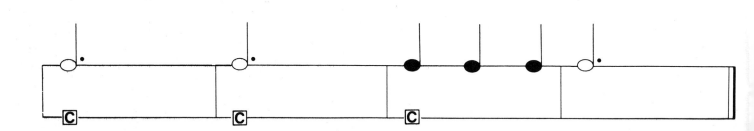

SKATERS WALTZ

THE ARRANGER

WALTZ
TEMPO 4½/ The Conductor 130

(KEY SELECTOR C)

CHOPSTICKS

Ø THE ARRANGER
UPPER: Piano
LOWER: Piano
PEDALS: String Bass

WALTZ
TEMPO 5½/ The Conductor [150]

(KEY SELECTOR C)

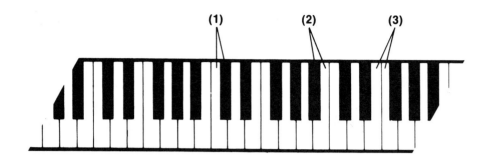

(A)

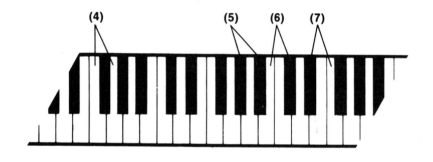

(B)

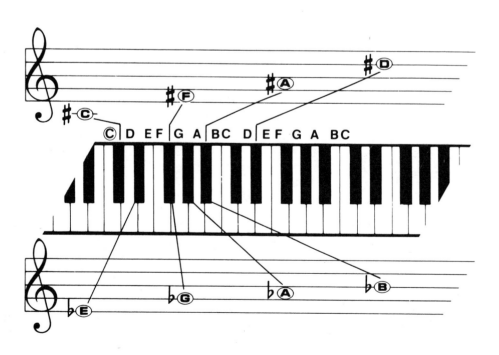

(C)

CHAMPAGNE POLKA

Music by
LAWRENCE WELK

THE ARRANGER

POLKA/MARCH
TEMPO 8½/ The Conductor 280

(KEY SELECTOR C)

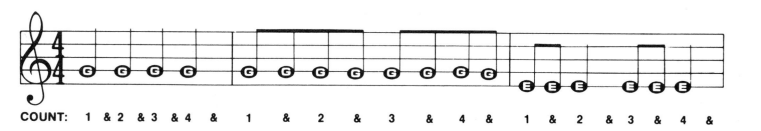

COUNT: 1 & 2 & 3 & 4 & 1 & 2 & 3 & 4 & 1 & 2 & 3 & 4 &

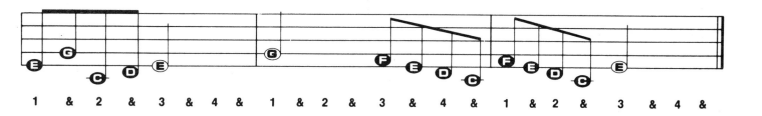

1 & 2 & 3 & 4 & 1 & 2 & 3 & 4 & 1 & 2 & 3 & 4 &

(C)

LAVENDER'S BLUE

THE ARRANGER

FOX TROT
TEMPO 3½/ The Conductor [105]

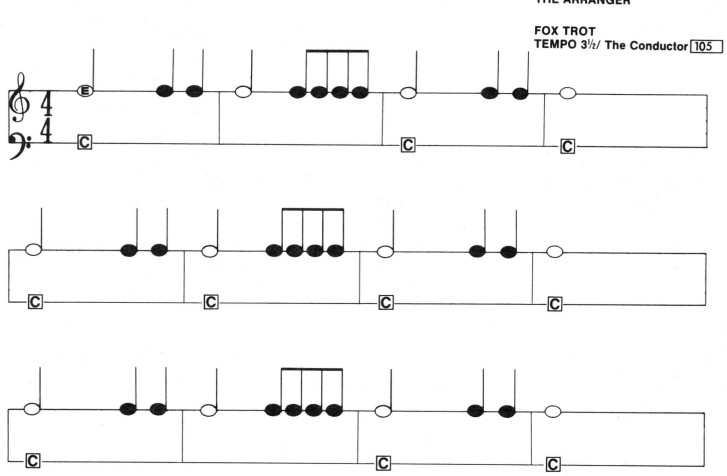

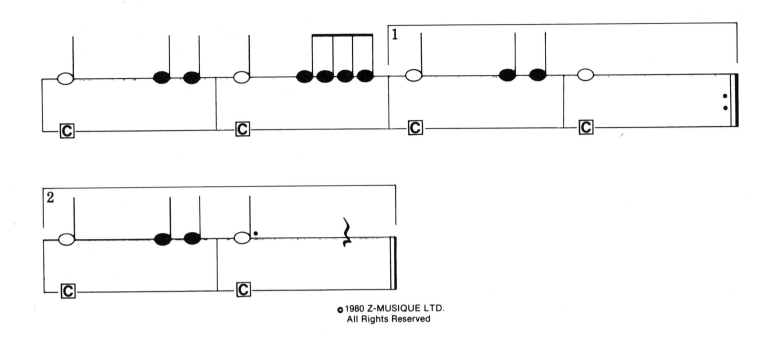

LAVENDER'S BLUE

UPPER: Flute 8', 4'
Accordion
LOWER: Flute 8', Guitar
PEDALS: String Bass
MOTION: Tremolo

FOX TROT
TEMPO 3½/ The Conductor 105

(KEY SELECTOR C)

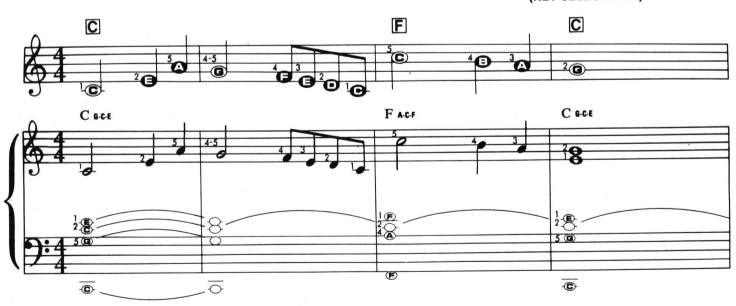

SPANISH EYES

THE ARRANGER

RHUMBA
TEMPO 5/ The Conductor 145

(KEY SELECTOR C)

172

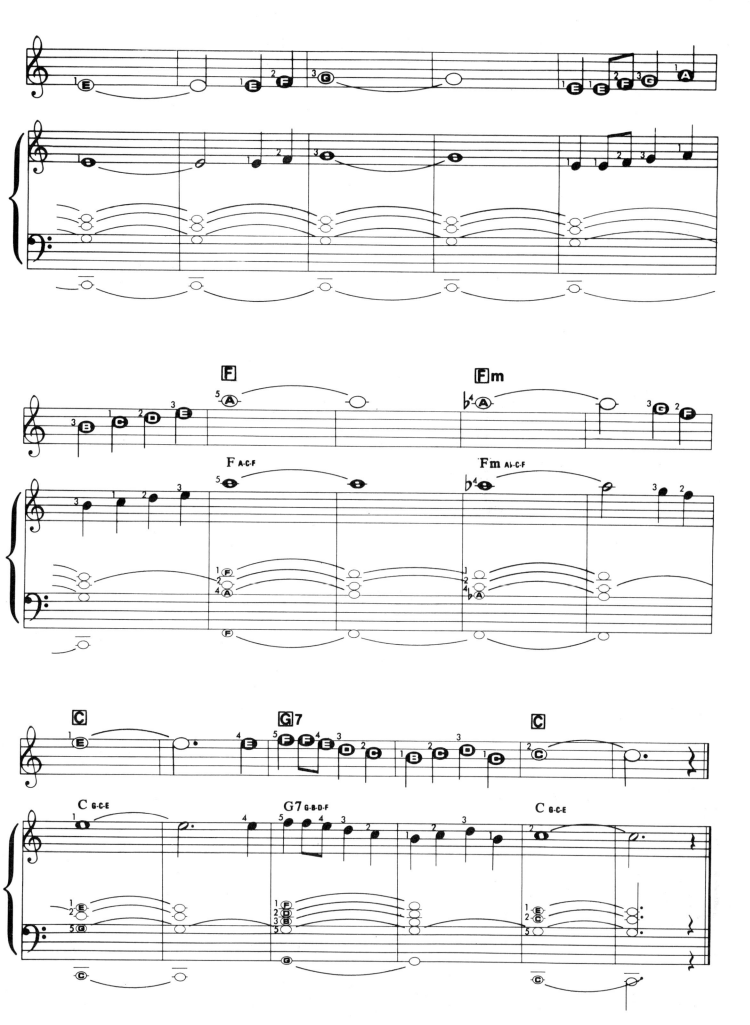

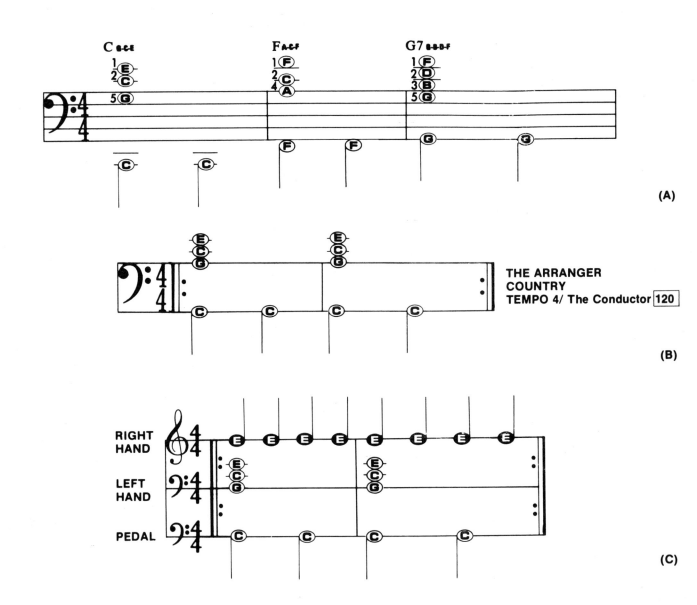

(A)

(B)

**THE ARRANGER
COUNTRY
TEMPO 4/ The Conductor** 120

(C)

SNOWBIRD

Words and Music by
GENE MacLELLAN

THE ARRANGER

**COUNTRY
TEMPO 5/ The Conductor** 160

(KEY SELECTOR C)

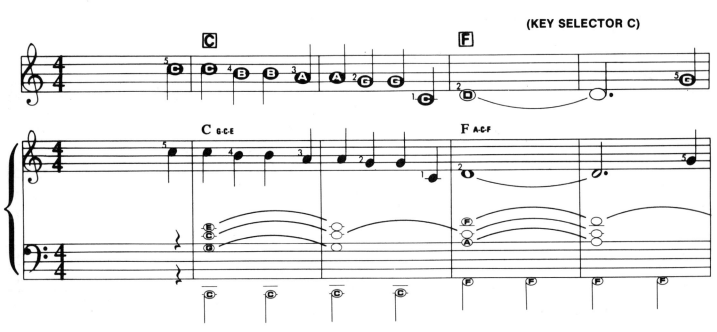

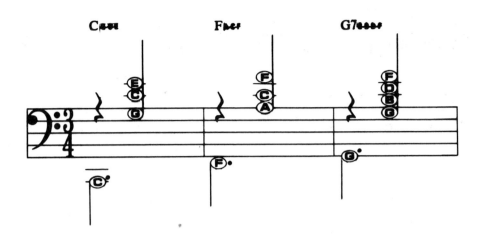

(A)

UPPER: Flute 16′, 8′, 4′
LOWER: Flute 8′, Piano
PEDALS: Flute 8′
MOTION: Tremolo

WALTZ
TEMPO 2½/ The Conductor [80]

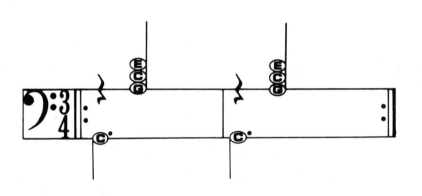

(B)

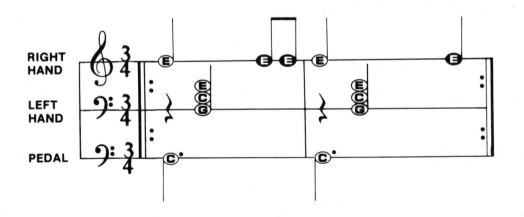

(C)

AMAZING GRACE

UPPER: Flute 16′, 8′, 4′
LOWER: Flute 8′, Piano
PEDALS: Flute 8′
MOTION: Tremolo

WALTZ
TEMPO 2½/ The Conductor 80

MAKE THE WORLD GO AWAY

Words and Music by
HANK COCHRAN

UPPER: Piano
LOWER: Flute 8′, Guitar
PEDALS: String Bass
MOTION: Tremolo

JAZZ ROCK
TEMPO 3½/ The Conductor 105

(KEY SELECTOR F)

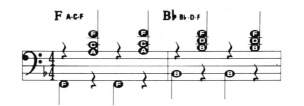

(A)

THE GAMBLER

Words and Music by
DON SCHLITZ

THE ARRANGER

COUNTRY
TEMPO 5½/ The Conductor 160

(KEY SELECTOR F)

180

A Screen Gems T.V. Serial

NADIA'S THEME
(The Young And The Restless)

By
BARRY DE VORZON and
PERRY BOTKIN, Jr.

UPPER: Flute 16', 4', 1'
      Sustain
LOWER: Cello 8', Piano
PEDALS: Flute 8'
MOTION: String Chorus

BOSSA NOVA
TEMPO 2½/ The Conductor 90

(KEY SELECTOR Ø)

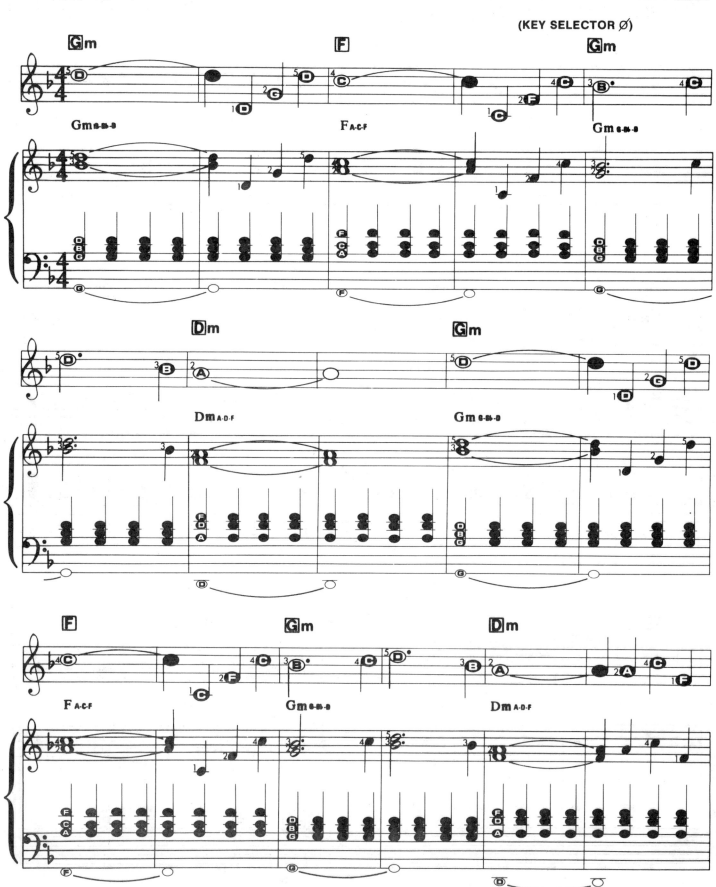

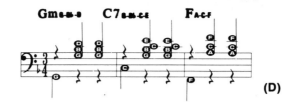

(D)

From the Columbia Pictures Release "YOU LIGHT UP MY LIFE"

YOU LIGHT UP MY LIFE THE ARRANGER

Words and Music by
JOE BROOKS

FOX TROT + WALTZ
TEMPO 3½/ The Conductor 105

(KEY SELECTOR C)

185

186

FEELINGS

(¿Dime?)

English Words and Music by
MORRIS ALBERT

Spanish Lyrics by
THOMAS FUNDORA

UPPER: Violin
OVERTURE 170:
+ Cello, Sustain
LOWER: Flute 8'
PEDALS: Flute 8'
MOTION: Tremolo, Vibrato, String Chorus

JAZZ ROCK
TEMPO 3/ The Conductor 95

(KEY SELECTOR G)

AFTER THE LOVIN'

Words and Music by
ALAN BERNSTEIN and
RITCHIE ADAMS

UPPER: Flute 16', 8', 4', 2', 1'
LOWER: Flute 8', Cello 8',
       Piano
PEDALS: Flute 16', String Bass
MOTION: Tremolo

BALLAD ROCK
TEMPO 3/ The Conductor 90

(KEY SELECTOR C)

BREAKING UP IS HARD TO DO

UPPER: Flute 16', 8', 4'
        Violin, Cello
LOWER: Flute 8', Cello 8',
        Guitar, Piano
PEDALS: Flute 16', 8',
        String Bass
MOTION: Tremolo, Vibrato, String Chorus

JAZZ ROCK
TEMPO 3½/ The Conductor 100

(KEY SELECTOR Ø)

Words and Music by
NEIL SEDAKA and
HOWARD GREENFIELD

194

YOU ARE THE SUNSHINE OF MY LIFE

THE ARRANGER

JAZZ ROCK + BOSSA NOVA
TEMPO 5/ The Conductor 150

Words and Music by
STEVIE WONDER

(KEY SELECTOR Ø)

197

From the "BALLET FOR A GIRL IN BUCHANNON" From the Columbia L.P. "CHICAGO"®

COLOUR MY WORLD

UPPER: Flute 16', 8',
Violin, Cello
LOWER: Flute 8', String Bass
PEDALS: Flute 8', String Bass
MOTION: Tremolo, Vibrato

BALLAD ROCK
TEMPO 2/ The Conductor 70

By
JAMES PANKOW

(KEY SELECTOR Ø)

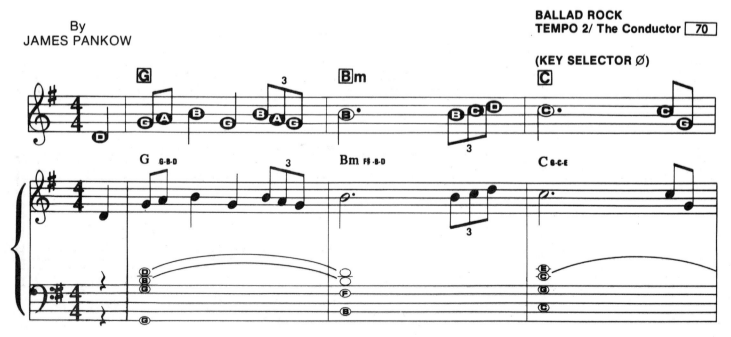

GAMES PEOPLE PLAY

UPPER: Flute 8′, Violin, Piano
LOWER: Flute 8′, Guitar, Piano
PEDALS: String Bass
MOTION: Tremolo

DIXIE (SWING)
TEMPO 4/ The Conductor 145

(KEY SELECTOR F)

Words and Music by
JOE SOUTH

WONDERLAND BY NIGHT
(Wunderland Bei Nacht)

Music by
KLAUS GUNTER-NEUMANN

UPPER: Trumpet
LOWER: Guitar
PEDALS: String Bass
MOTION: Vibrato

FOX TROT
TEMPO 2/ The Conductor 70

(KEY SELECTOR F)

203

IT WAS ALMOST LIKE A SONG

Music by
ARCHIE JORDAN

THE ARRANGER

JAZZ ROCK
TEMPO 3½/ The Conductor 100

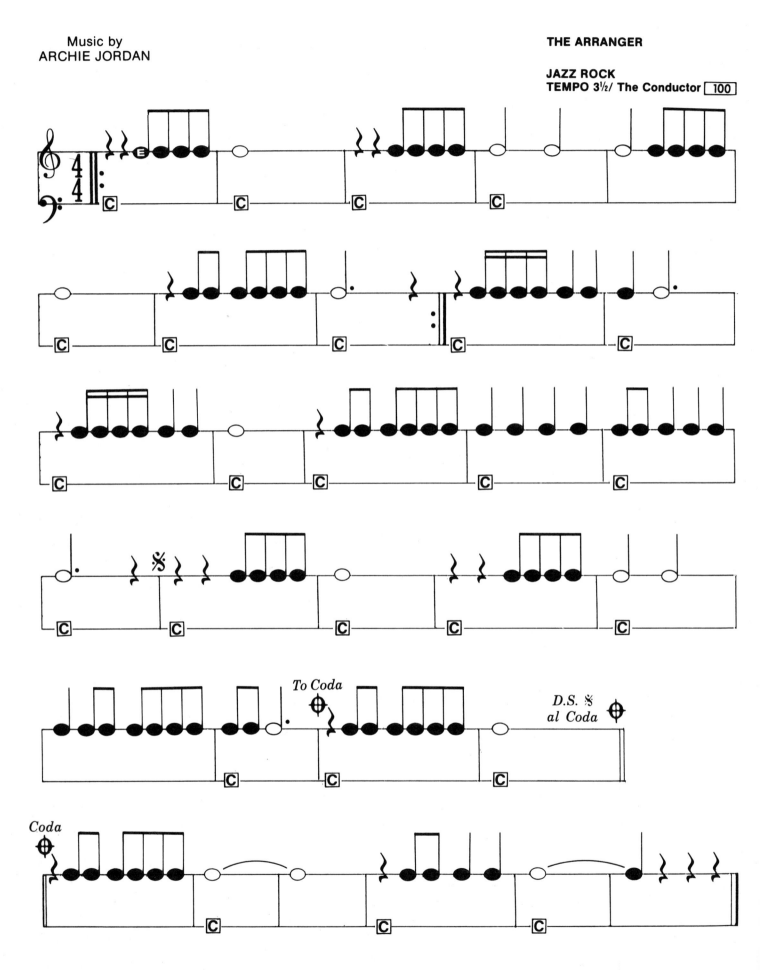

IT WAS ALMOST LIKE A SONG

Music by
ARCHIE JORDAN

UPPER: Clarinet (Trumpet)
LOWER: Flute 8', Guitar
PEDALS: String Bass
MOTION: Tremolo, Vibrato

JAZZ ROCK
TEMPO 3½/ The Conductor [100]

(KEY SELECTOR C)

206

DISCO OR BLUES

UPPER: Flute 16', 8', 4', 1'
LOWER: Flute 8', Piano
PEDALS: Flute 8', String Bass
MOTION: ∅

SWING/JAZZ ROCK
TEMPO 5½/ The Conductor 160

DISCO
TEMPO 8/ The Conductor 240

SONGS FOR YOUR ENJOYMENT

CANCIONES PARA SU DIVERSION

CHANSONS POUR VOTRE PLAISIR

LIEDER DIE SIE GERNE MÖGEN

LIEDJES VOOR UW PLEZIER

ENGLISH

The songs in this book are designed to be played on your Baldwin MCO instrument. To make each song sound best, use the suggested registration at the beginning of each song. As an aid to your playing, follow the hints below.

1. If you are playing on a Model 145, the translation for the registrations is:

   UPPER = SOLO
   LOWER = ACCOMPANIMENT
   PEDAL = BASS

2. When two rhythms are listed, press the buttons in left-to-right order.

3. The songs are designed to be played on all the Baldwin MCO instruments; therefore, ignore any listed controls and voices not on your instrument.

Sharps and Flats

A sharp sign (♯) preceding a note indicates to play the next black key to the right.

A flat sign (♭) preceding a note indicates to play the next black key to the left.

Sharps and flats preceding notes affect all the identical notes that follow in that measure.

Sharps or flats appearing in the beginning of a song indicate which black keys to play throughout the song.

Natural signs (♮) cancel sharps or flats.

ESPAÑOL

Las canciones en este libro han sido diseñadas para ser tocadas en su instrumento Baldwin MCO. Use los sugeridos registros que encuentre al comienzo de cada canción, y les dara un mejor sonido. Para su ayuda a tocar, siga las siguientes ideas:

1. Si esta tocando en un Modelo 145, la traducción para sus registros es:

   SUPERIOR = SOLO
   INFERIOR = ACOMPAÑAMIENTO
   PEDAL   = BAJO

2. Cuando encuentre numerados dos ritmos, presione los botones en orden de izquierda a derecha.

3. Las canciones han sido diseñadas para ser ejecutadas en todo instrumento Baldwin MCO; por lo tanto, ignore cualquier control numerado o listado y voces que no existan en su instrumento.

4. En los registros se incluyen las palabras "off" y "optional". Estas palabras no traducidas significan "APAGAR" (off) — "OPCIONAL" (optional).

Sostenidos y Bemoles

Un signo de Sostenido (♯) precidiendo una nota, indica que la próxima tecla negra a la derecha debe ser tocada.

Un signo de Bemol (♭) precidiendo una nota, indica que la próxima tecla negra a la izquierda debe ser tocada.

Cuando un signo de Sostenido a un signo de Bemol aparecen antes de una nota en un compás indicado, afecta todos los notas que son idénticas y que siguen al compás.

Signos de Sostenidos y signos de Bemoles al principio de una canción, indican que se deben tocar las correspondientes teclas negras en toda la canción.

Los signos Becuadro (♮) cancelan los Sostenidos o los Bemoles.

FRANÇAIS

Les morceaux selectionnés dans cette brochure sont spécialement arrangés pour votre orgue Baldwin MCO. Si vous voulez interpreter chaque morçeau avec les sonorités les plus seduisantes, utilisez la régistration suggerée au début de chaque partition. Pour vous aider dans votre interprétation, suivez les indications ci dessous:

1. Si vous jouez sur un modèle 145, la traduction pour la régistration est:

   CLAVIER DU HAUT = SOLO
   CLAVIER DU BAS = ACCOMPAGNEMENT
   PÉDALIER   = BASSES

2. Lorsque deux rythmes sont indiqués, appuyez sur les boutons correspondants dans l'ordre, de gauche a droite.

3. Les morceaux sont arrangés pour être joués sur tous les orgues Baldwin: par conséquent, faites abstraction de tous les contrôles et voix qui ne sont pas sur votre instrument.

4. Les régistrations comportent les mots anglais "off" et "optional" ces mots non traduits signifient "sans" ou "coupé" et "optionnel".

Dièses et Bémols

Un dièse (♯) devant une note indique que l'on doit jouer la première touche noire à droite.

Un bémol (♭) devant une note indique que l'on doit jouer la première touche noire à gauche.

Les dièses et les bémols devant les notes affectent toutes les notes identiques qui suivent dans cette mesure.

Les dièses et les bémols qui apparaissent au début d'une chanson indiquent que l'on doit jouer les touches noires correspondantes dans toute la chanson.

Les bécarres (♮) suppriment les dièses ou les bémols.

DEUTSCH

Die Lieder in diesem Heft sind so geplant, daß Sie sie auf Ihrem Baldwin MCO Instrument spielen können. Damit jedes Lied am besten klingt, benutzen Sie die vorgeschlagenen Registrierungen am Anfang jedes Liedes. Als eine Hilfe für Ihr Spielen beachten Sie folgenden Hinweise:

1. Wenn Sie auf einem Modell 145 spielen, dann ist die Übersetzung der Registrierung wie folgend:

   OBEN   = SOLO
   UNTEN = BEGLEITUNG
   PEDALE = BASS

2. Wenn zwei Rhythmen angegeben sind, drücke die Knöpfe von Inks nach rechts.

3. Die Lieder sind so geplant, daß sie auf allen Baldwin MCO Instrumenten gespielt werden können; deshalb beachten Sie nicht die angegebenen Kontrollen und Stimmen, welche nicht auf Ihrem Instrument zu finden sind.

4. Die Registrierungen sind mit den englischen Worten "off" und "optional" versehen. In der Übersetzung heißen diese Worte "aus" und "wahlweise".

Kreuze und B's

Ein Kreuz (♯), das vor einer Note steht, weist darauf hin, die schwarze Taste rechts daneben zu spielen.

Ein B (♭) vor einer Note bedeutet, daß man die schwarze Taste links daneben spielt.

Kreuze und B's vor einer Note zeigen zuch an, daß alle anderen gleichen Noten im Takt erhöht oder erniedrigt werden.

Kreuze und B's die am Anfang eines Liedes stehen, besagen, daß alle diese Noten im ganzen Lied erhöht oder erniedrigt werden.

Auflösungszeichen (♮) lösen den Wert des Kreuzes oder des B's auf.

NEDERLANDS

De melodieën in dit boek zijn speciaal voor uw Baldwin MCO geschreven. Gebruik,om ze het best tot hun recht te laten komen, de registratie aanwijzingen aan het begin van elk muziekstuk. De volgende hints kunnen u bij het spelen van dienst zijn:

1. Als u op een model 145 speelt, kunt u de registratie aanduidingen het beste zo lezen:

   BOVENKLAVIER = SOLO
   ONDERKLAVIER = BEGELEIDING
   PEDAAL   = BASS

2. Als er twee ritmes worden genoemd, druk dan de knopjes in te beginnen bij de meest linkse knop.

3. De melodieën zijn speciaal voor alle Baldwin MCO instrumenten geschreven. Negeer daarom eventuele andere registres of speelhulpen als die worden genoemd en uw orgelmodel ze niet heeft.

4. Bij de registraties worden vaak de engelse woorden "OFF" en "OPTIONAL" gebruikt. De betekenis hiervan is respectievelijk "UIT" en "NAAR KEUZE".

Kruisen en Mollen

♯ EEN KRUIS betekent, dat de noot een halve toon hoger gespeeld moet worden.

♭ EEN MOL betekent, dat de noot een halve toon lager gespeeld moet worden.

Wanneer er voor een noot een kruis of een mol staat, geldt dit teken voor alle gelijke noten die in diezelfde maat voorkomen.

Een kruis of een mol aan het begin van een melodie geeft aan welke noot u verhoogd of verlaagd. Voor alle noten in de melodie.

Herstellingstekens (♮) heffen een kruis of mol op.

ALOHA OE

UPPER: Hawaiian Guitar
(Clarinet, Sustain, Vibrato)
LOWER: Flute 8', Guitar
PEDALS: Flute 8', String Bass
MOTION: Tremolo

FOX TROT
TEMPO 3½/ The Conductor ⟨105⟩
EASY PLAYERS: (Plain) FunBass
PRO

212

Columbia Pictures and Carl Foreman Present

BORN FREE

Music by
JOHN BARRY

THE ARRANGER

FOX TROT + RHUMBA (BOSSA NOVA)
TEMPO 3½/ The Conductor [105]
EASY PLAYERS: (Fancy) FunBass
PRO

(KEY SELECTOR C)

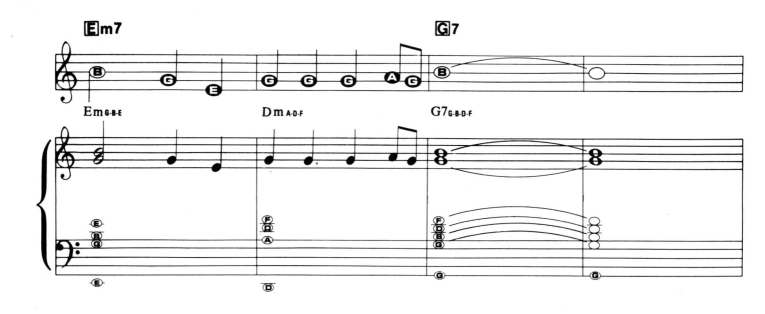

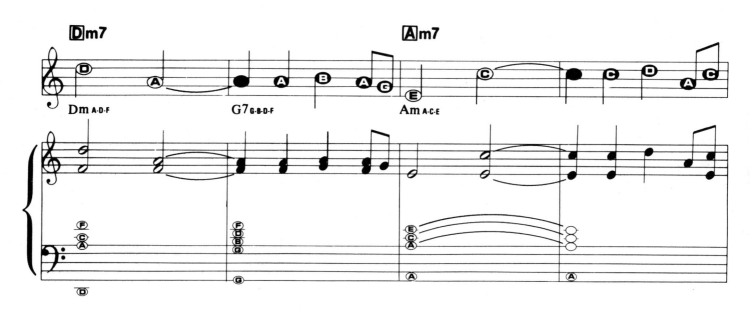

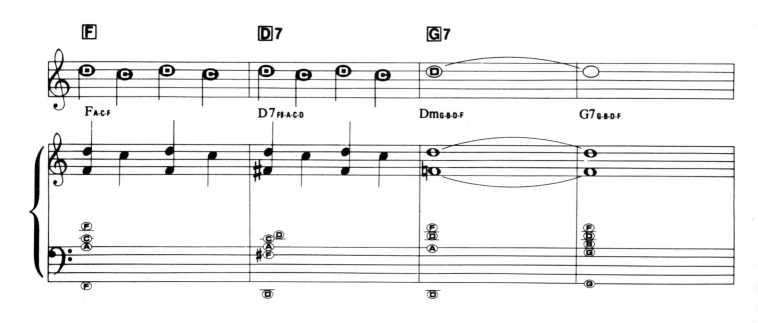

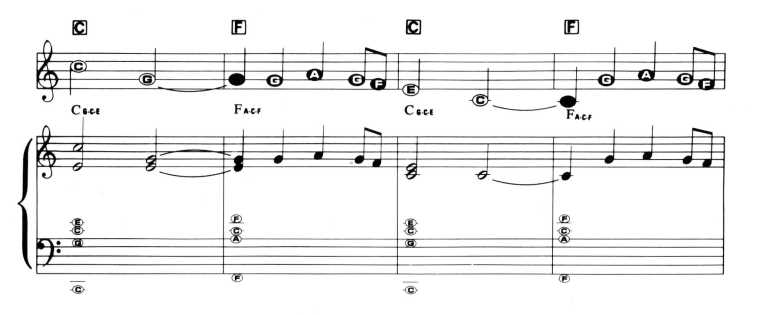

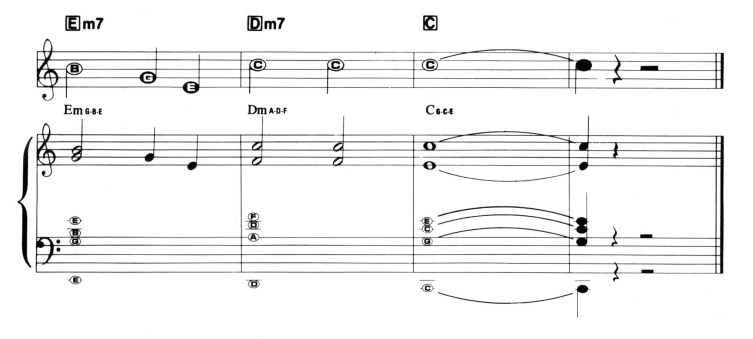

(From The Broadway Musical "THE WIZ")

EASE ON DOWN THE ROAD

Words and Music by
CHARLIE SMALLS

THE ARRANGER

JAZZ ROCK + DISCO
TEMPO 7½/ The Conductor 240
EASY PLAYERS: (Fancy) FunBass
PRO

(KEY SELECTOR B♭)

FOR ONCE IN MY LIFE

Music by
ORLANDO MURDEN

THE ARRANGER

SWING
TEMPO 7½/ The Conductor 240
EASY PLAYERS: (Fancy) FunBass
PRO

(KEY SELECTOR C)

GEORGIA ON MY MIND

Music by
HOAGY CARMICHAEL

UPPER: Clarinet (Trombone)
LOWER: Flute 8', Guitar, Banjo
PEDALS: String Bass
MOTION: Ø (Vibrato)

DIXIE (SWING)
TEMPO 4/ The Conductor [115]
EASY PLAYERS: (Fancy) FunBass

(KEY SELECTOR F)

224

225

I BELIEVE IN MUSIC

Words and Music by
MAC DAVIS

THE ARRANGER

BALLAD ROCK
TEMPO 5/ The Conductor 145
EASY PLAYERS: (Fancy) FunBass
PRO

(KEY SELECTOR C)

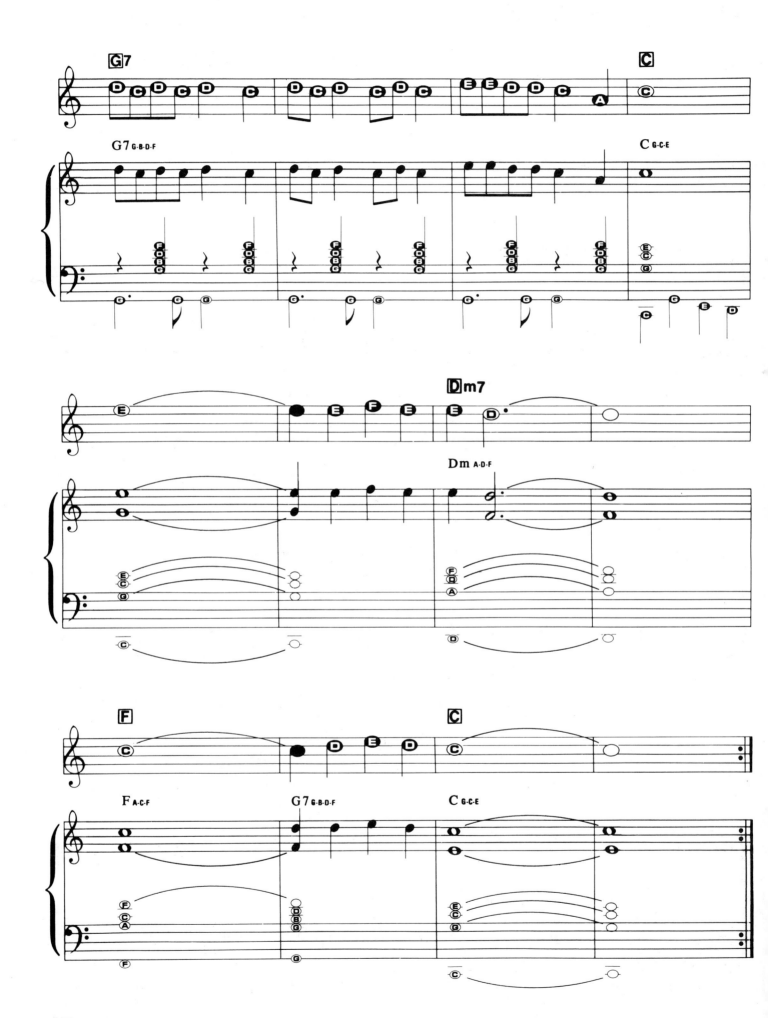

LOVE ME WITH ALL YOUR HEART
(Cuando Calienta El Sol)

Music by
CARLOS RIGUAL &
CARLOS A. MARTINOLI

THE ARRANGER

BALLAD ROCK
TEMPO 2/ The Conductor [70]
EASY PLAYERS: (Fancy) FunBass
PRO

(KEY SELECTOR C)

230

MAS QUE NADA
(Pow, Pow, Pow)

Portuguese Words & Music by
JORGE BEN

THE ARRANGER

BOSSA NOVA
TEMPO 7/ The Conductor 200
EASY PLAYERS: (Fancy) FunBass
PRO

(KEY SELECTOR C + A)

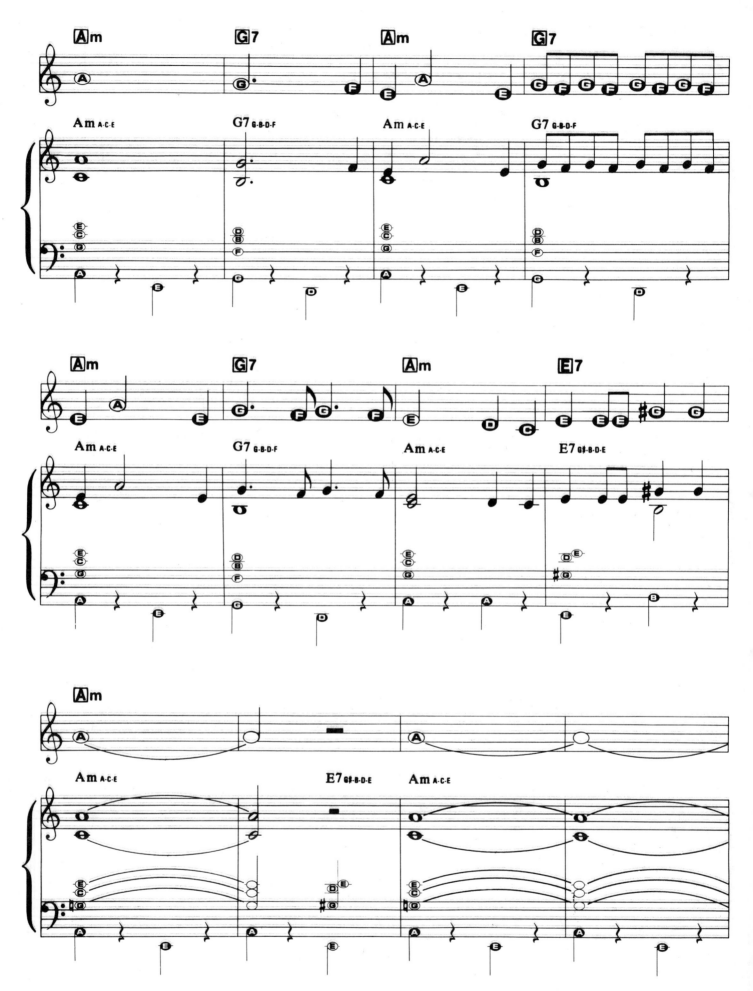

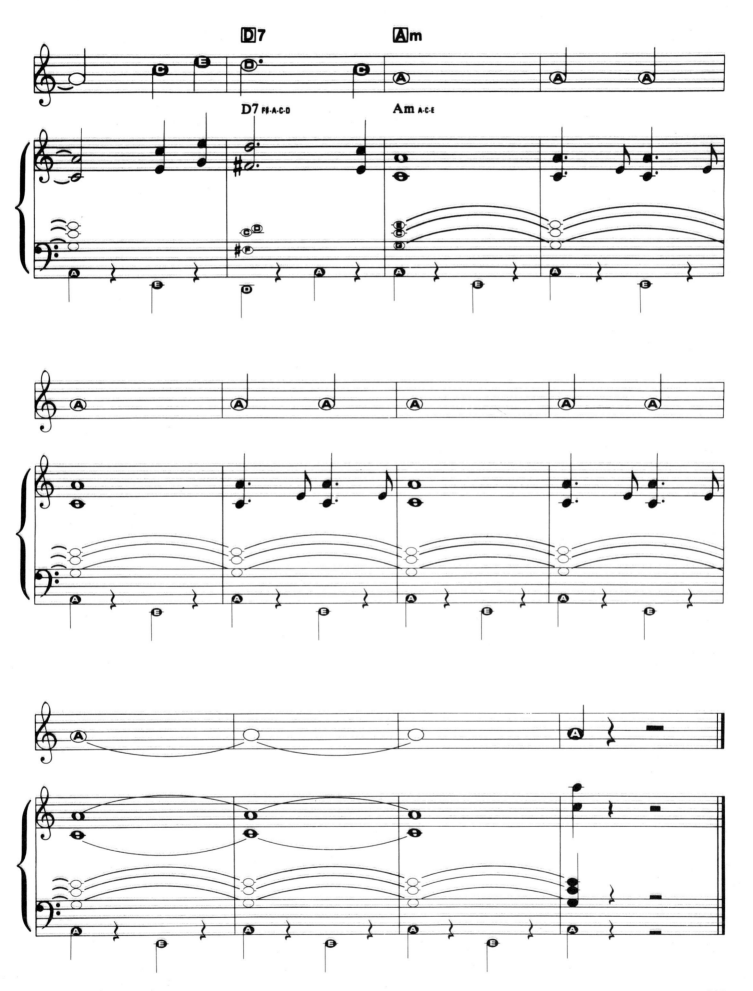

IF

Words and Music by
DAVID GATES

UPPER: Flute 16', 4', 1'
    (Flute, Trombone)
    Sustain
LOWER: Flute 8', Cello 8'
PEDALS: Flute 16', 8', String Bass
MOTION: String Chorus

JAZZ ROCK
TEMPO 3½/ The Conductor [105]
EASY PLAYERS: (Plain) FunBass

(KEY SELECTOR F)

237

238

ROCKY TOP

By
BOUDLEAUX BRYANT
and FELICE BRYANT

UPPER: Cello, Violin, Accordion
(Banjo)
LOWER: Cello 8′, Banjo (Guitar)
PEDALS: String Bass
MOTION: (Vibrato)

POLKA/MARCH
TEMPO 8/ The Conductor 280
EASY PLAYERS: (Plain) FunBass
PRO

(KEY SELECTOR Ø)

239

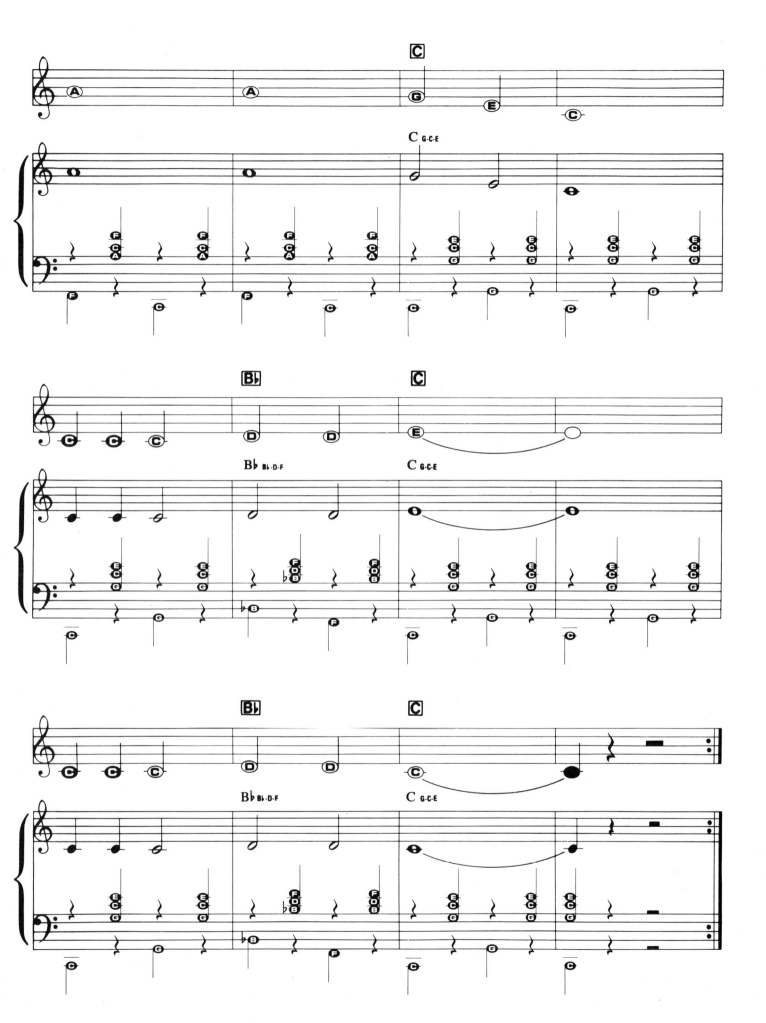

MY CHERIE AMOUR

Words and Music by
STEVIE WONDER, HENRY COSBY
and SYLVIA MOY

THE ARRANGER

JAZZ ROCK
TEMPO 5/ The Conductor [145]
EASY PLAYERS: (Fancy) FunBass
PRO

(KEY SELECTOR Ø)

242

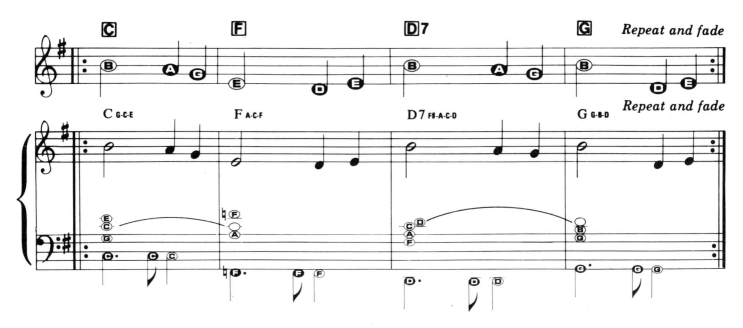

YOU BELONG TO MY HEART
(Solamente Una Vez)

Music by
AGUSTIN LARA

(THE ARRANGER)

UPPER: Marimba (Piano)
LOWER: Flute 8', Guitar
PEDALS: Flute 8', String Bass
MOTION: Ø

TANGO
TEMPO 3½/ The Conductro 105
EASY PLAYERS: (Fancy) FunBass
PRO

(KEY SELECTOR C)

244

UPPER: Flute 8', Accordion (Piano)
LOWER: Flute 8', Cello 8', Piano
PEDALS: Flute 8', String Bass
MOTION: Tremolo, Vibrato, String Chorus

WALTZ
TEMPO 3½/ The Conductor 100
EASY PLAYERS: (Plain) FunBass
(PRO)

From the Motion Picture "MOULIN ROUGE"

SONG FROM MOULIN ROUGE

(Where Is Your Heart)

Music by
GEORGES AURICK

(KEY SELECTOR C)

From the Twentieth Century-Fox Motion Picture "STAR WARS"

STAR WARS
(Main Title)

Music by
JOHN WILLIAMS

THE ARRANGER

DISCO
TEMPO 7½/ The Conductor 240
EASY PLAYERS: (Fancy) FunBass
PRO

(KEY SELECTOR G)

THIS MASQUERADE

Words and Music by
LEON RUSSELL

THE ARRANGER

BOSSA NOVA
TEMPO 4/ The Conductor [115]
EASY PLAYERS: (Fancy) FunBass

(KEY SELECTOR Ø)

From the Columbia Picture, Raster Production "THE WAY WE WERE"

THE WAY WE WERE

Music by
MARVIN HAMLISCH

UPPER: Flute 16', 8', 4', 1'
(Flute, Violin)
LOWER: Flute 8', Cello 8', Guitar
PEDALS: Flute 16', 8', String Bass
MOTION: Tremolo, String Chorus
(Vibrato)

JAZZ ROCK
TEMPO 3½/ The Conductor 100
EASY PLAYERS: (Plain) FunBass
PRO

(KEY SELECTOR C)

254

Copyright Copyright 1973 by Colgems—EMI Music Inc., Hollywood, Calif.
This arrangement Copyright 1980 by Colgems—EMI Music Inc.   Used by Permission
International Copyright Secured   Made in U.S.A.   All Rights Reserved

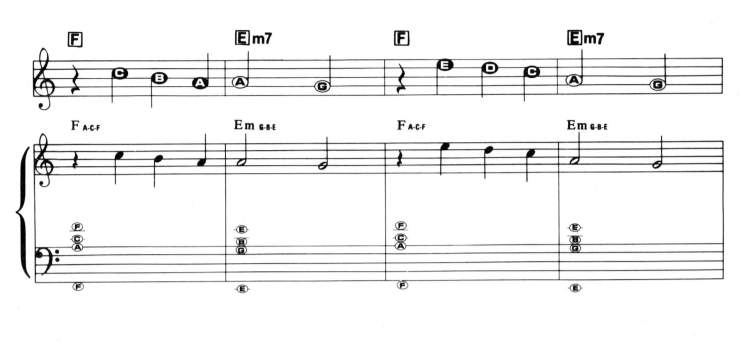

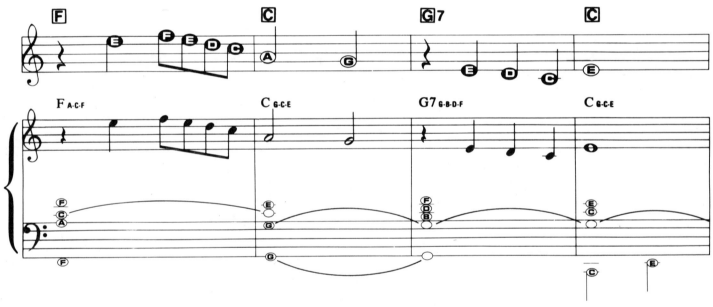

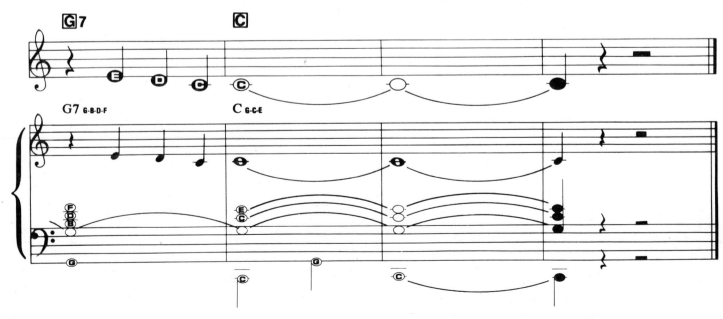